LLOYD FRANKENBERG

Invitation to poetry

A ROUND OF POEMS FROM
JOHN SKELTON TO DYLAN THOMAS
ARRANGED WITH COMMENTS

GREENWOOD PRESS, PUBLISHERS
WESTPORT, CONNECTICUT

Originally published in 1956 by Doubleday & Company, Inc.

Reprinted with the permission of Doubleday & Company, Inc.

Reprinted in 1968 by Greenwood Press
A division of Congressional Information Service, Inc.
88 Post Road West, Westport, Connecticut 06881

Library of Congress Catalog Card Number 68-8061

ISBN 0-8371-0077-1
Printed in the United States of America

10 9 8 7 6 5 4 3

FOR LOREN

Three words of thanks

to Cecil Scott, who goaded me into it,

to Donald Elder, who guided it to Doubleday,

to Timothy Seldes, who got it through, with a tact that entitles him to hang out the shingle: "EDITOR: Painless Extraction."

ACKNOWLEDGMENTS

"Edward Lear" from *The Collected Poetry of W. H. Auden*, by W. H. Auden. Copyright 1945 by W. H. Auden, reprinted by permission of Random House, Inc. Also from *Collected Shorter Poems*, by W. H. Auden, reprinted by permission of Faber and Faber, Ltd.

"Dear, though the night is gone" and "Look, stranger, on this island now" from *On This Island*, by W. H. Auden. Copyright 1937 by Random House, Inc., reprinted by permission of Random House, Inc. Also from *Collected Shorter Poems*, by W. H. Auden, reprinted by permission of Faber and Faber, Ltd.

"The arrest of Oscar Wilde" from *Selected Poems*, by John Betjeman, and *Slick, But Not Streamlined*, by John Betjeman. Copyright 1947 by John Betjeman, reprinted by permission of John Murray (Publisher) Ltd. and Doubleday & Company, Inc.

"The prodigal" from *Poems*, by Elizabeth Bishop, reprinted by permission of Houghton Mifflin Company.

"She moved through the fair" from *Collected Poems*, by Padriac Colum, reprinted by permission of the author.

"what a proud dreamhorse" from *Poems 1923–1954*, by E. E. Cummings; Harcourt, Brace & Company, Inc. Copyright 1935 by E. E. Cummings, reprinted by permission of Brandt & Brandt.

"no man,if men are gods" and "darling!because my blood . . ." from *Poems 1923–1954*, by E. E. Cummings; Harcourt, Brace & Company, Inc. Copyright 1944 by E. E. Cummings, reprinted by permission of Brandt & Brandt.

"The listeners" from *Collected Poems*, by Walter de la Mare. Copyright 1920 by Henry Holt & Company, Inc. Copyright 1948 by Walter de la Mare, reprinted by permission of the author, Henry Holt & Company, Inc., and Faber and Faber, Ltd.

"A bird came down the walk" and "To know just how he suffered" by Emily Dickinson, reprinted by permission of Little, Brown & Company.

"Sweeney among the nightingales" from *Collected Poems 1909–1935*, by T. S. Eliot. Copyright 1936 by Harcourt, Brace & Company, Inc., used with their permission and by permission of Faber and Faber, Ltd.

"Arachne" from *Collected Poems of William Empson*, by William Empson. Copyright 1935, 1940, 1949 by William Empson, reprinted by permission of Harcourt, Brace & Company, Inc., and Chatto and Windus, Ltd.

"Cobb would have caught it" from *A Wreath for the Sea*, by Robert Fitzgerald. Copyright 1943 by Robert Fitzgerald, reprinted by permission of the publisher, New Directions.

"The bonfire" from *Complete Poems of Robert Frost*, by Robert Frost. Copyright 1930, 1949 by Henry Holt & Company, Inc., reprinted with their permission and that of Jonathan Cape, Ltd.

"The windhover," "Hurrahing in harvest," and "Pied beauty" from *The Poems of G. M. Hopkins*, by Gerard Manley Hopkins, reprinted by permission of Oxford University Press, London.

"A sick child" from *The Seven-League Crutches*, by Randall Jarrell. Copyright 1951 by Randall Jarrell, reprinted by permission of Harcourt, Brace & Company, Inc. Also from *Selected Poems*, by Randall Jarrell, reprinted by permission of Faber and Faber, Ltd.

"Alone" and "A memory of the players in a mirror at midnight" from "Pomes Penyeach" in *Collected Poems*, by James Joyce. Copyright 1927 by James Joyce, Reprinted by permission of The Viking Press, Inc., New York, and Faber and Faber, Ltd.

"Piano" from *Collected Poems of D. H. Lawrence*. Copyright 1929 by Jonathan Cape and Harrison Smith, Inc., reprinted by permission of The Viking Press, Inc., New York, Mrs. Frieda Lawrence, and Messrs. William Heinemann, Ltd.

"The holy innocents" from *Poems 1938–1949* by Robert Lowell, and from *Lord Weary's Castle*. Copyright 1944, 1946 by Robert Lowell, reprinted by permission of Harcourt, Brace & Company, Inc., and Faber and Faber, Ltd.

"ballade of the underside" from *archy's life of mehitabel*, by Don Marquis. Copyright 1928, 1932, 1933 by Don Marquis, reprinted by permission of Doubleday & Company, Inc.

"Modern love" (Sonnet XVIII) by George Meredith, reprinted by permission of the author's estate and Charles Scribner's Sons.

"The frigate pelican" and "The mind is an enchanting thing" from *Collected Poems*, by Marianne Moore, reprinted by permission of The Macmillan Company.

"Dulce et decorum est" from *Poems*, by Wilfred Owen. All rights reserved, reprinted by permission of the publisher, New Directions, and Chatto and Windus, Ltd.

"Well pleaseth me the sweet time of Easter" from *The Spirit of Romance*, by Ezra Pound. All rights reserved, reprinted by permission of the publisher, New Directions, and Arthur V. Moore.

"Me happy, night, night full of brightness" from "Propertius" in *Personae*, translated by Ezra Pound. Copyright 1926, 1952 by Ezra Pound, reprinted by permission of the publisher, New Directions, and Arthur V. Moore.

"Here lies a lady" from *Selected Poems*, by John Crowe Ransom. Copyright 1924, 1945 by Alfred A. Knopf, Inc., reprinted by permission of the publishers.

"For a dead lady" from *The Town Down the River*, by Edwin Arlington Robinson. Copyright 1910 by Charles Scribner's Sons, 1938 by Ruth Nivison, reprinted by permission of the publishers.

"Big wind" from *The Lost Son and Other Poems*, by Theodore Roethke. Copyright 1947 by The United Chapters of Phi Beta Kappa, reprinted by permission of MacDonald & Company (Publishers) Ltd., and Doubleday & Company, Inc., and published by John Lehmann, Ltd., London.

"Everyone sang" from *Collected Poems*, by Siegfried Sassoon. Copyright 1920 by E. P. Dutton & Company, 1920, 1936 by Siegfried Sassoon, reprinted by permission of The Viking Press, Inc., New York, and the author.

"The rivals" from *Collected Poems*, by James Stephens, reprinted by permission of St. Martin's Press, Mrs. James Stephens, and The Macmillan Company.

"Of modern poetry" from *The Collected Poems of Wallace Stevens*. Copyright 1942, 1954 by Wallace Stevens, reprinted by permission of Alfred A. Knopf, Inc., and Faber and Faber, Ltd.

"John Webster" from *Swinburne's Collected Poetical Works*, by A. C. Swinburne, reprinted by permission of William Heinemann, Ltd.

"In my craft or sullen art" from *Collected Poems of Dylan Thomas*, by Dylan Thomas. Copyright 1953 by Dylan Thomas and reprinted by permission of the publisher, New Directions, and J. M. Dent & Sons, Ltd.

"The son" by Ridgely Torrence, reprinted by permission of Miss Dunbar, executrix of the Estate of Olivia H. D. Torrence.

"Dr. Bill Williams" from *Poets and Sonnets*, by Ernest Walsh. Copyright 1934 by Harcourt, Brace & Company, Inc., and reprinted with their permission.

"The term" and "Poem" from *Selected Poems*, by William Carlos Williams. Copyright 1949 by William Carlos Williams, reprinted by permission of the author and of the publisher, New Directions.

"When you are old" and "Sailing to Byzantium" from *Collected Poems*, by W. B. Yeats, reprinted by permission of St. Martin's Press, Inc., Messrs. A. P. Watt & Son, and The Macmillan Company.

CONTENTS

INTRODUCTORY

The very idea

The Victorian idea of the anthology is the treasury: a repository of "gems of taste." Francis Turner Palgrave, selecting and arranging the two hundred and eighty-eight songs and lyrical poems he considered "the best," created the model. *The Golden Treasury*, first published in 1861, served to introduce generations of readers to English poetry.

It also served to stop many of these readers in their tracks. If this was, as it said, a collection of the best, why look farther? Why look, for instance, to the collected works of the poets themselves? Palgrave, guided as he acknowledged by Alfred Lord Tennyson, had undoubtedly read them all and skimmed the cream. For his readers a poet like John Donne, who did not fall within the scope of his taste, did not exist. ("Absence, hear thou my protestation," now sometimes attributed to Donne, was anonymous to Palgrave.) A poet like Henry Carey, on the strength of one pleasant jingle, "Sally in our alley," did. The method set a precedent for comparative ratings. Poets were to be scored by the number of their appearances in *The Golden Treasury*.

For readers to look farther, the only recourse was a different selection, another anthology. T. H. Ward, in the four volumes of his *The English Poets* (1883), and Sir Arthur Quiller-Couch, in *The Oxford Book of English Verse* (1900), did look farther, and further back. The rivalry of these and other anthologies denied any one of them an overweening authority. If the experts could disagree, there was more of a chance for the reader to disagree with them all, to stray off to the poetry itself and make his own choices.

But the motive was much the same: the competitive search for "which is best?" Like the anthologist, the reader on his own was apt to think of himself as a kind of arbitrator between conflicting claims. Poems were precious, semi-precious or common objects, to be scrutinized, compared and evaluated, rather than activities in which the reader participates.

The numerous and valuable collections of contemporary poetry tend to apply much the same principle to a comparatively non-Victorian present. There are perhaps sharper divergences of taste, and each anthology in its new editions will drop old names and poems and add new, very much in the manner of the *Social Register*. They are fascinating to compare, to see if the anthologist favors, say, the earlier or later styles of Wallace Stevens, and how well such-and-such a movement or "school" is represented. All this engenders enough activity so that, compared with the relative calm, as it seems to us now, of *The Golden Treasury*, the present is seen to be a very turbulent period. According to whether we remember our Palgrave with boredom or with nostalgia, we are apt to be violently partisan for or against "the new poetry," as it is still sometimes called; to deride or invoke "tradition"; to think of poetry as a steady progression or a sudden deterioration; to believe that vitality came into it only in the twentieth century, or to mourn the loss of "standards."

It is possibly true that more individual styles of poetry have developed in the last fifty years or so than in any comparable span of time. But the apparent serenity of the past is an oil spread by time. The standards we think we see there have for the most part been imposed by the editors of anthologies. Anyone reading the attacks on Keats and "the Cockney school," on Swinburne and "the Sensual school," on Dante Gabriel Rossetti for daring to celebrate conjugal love, on the style and morals of Alexander Pope, or on the style and personal habits of his detractors will find much to make the Ezra Pound controversy, for instance, seem like a ripple. Not visible on the smooth surface of anthologies, the struggle over "what standards?" has been going on since poetry first accompanied the lyre or the dance.

Besides the criterion of "the best," there is the division of poetry into periods or schools, or by theme. Invaluable to the student, these divisions raise further hazards. On the personal taste of the compiler is laid the additional burden of being "representative." This may lead him to include poems that by consensus are regarded as of historical importance, although they may be of dubious interest. Or he may feel obliged to include too many poems in the same vein or style.

Of "theme" anthologies there is literally no end. Poems can, and have been, collected around anything: love, war, friendship, flowers, food, animals, childhood, dreams. Walter de la Mare's *Behold, This Dreamer!* is one of the most delightful of these, and since he picks and packs his category poetically, it is less restrictive and monotonous than most. There is even *The Stuffed Owl: An Anthology of Bad Verse*, the bright idea of D. B. Wyndham Lewis and Charles Lee. This is, it should be said, the bad verse of good poets, although it does not include my own favorite worst opening line, Keats's "Young Calidore is paddling o'er the lake."

But there will be lines to vie with it here, in poems that I like. Perfection is not any longer a goal. As Wanda Landowska is said to have said, "Perfection is death." Even if we knew what it was; which, with changing tastes, with changing or quarreling standards, we never will. Yet the attitude *toward* perfection, the Victorian attitude (not that it is by any means exclusive to that era), persists.

How, I wonder, may an anthology be composed that will stimulate rather than deaden; that will open out toward poetry instead of cocooning it in? What categories may be discovered to expand rather than restrict the conception of poetry?

For categories, although unreal, are necessary. Poems that in the mind are free-floating, disembodied and undefinable, are in print physical entities; they must appear on this page or that, in one connection or another. How to connect them and yet leave them disengaged? The categories should be clear but self-dispelling. The anthologist's taste should be definite without imposing itself on the reader.

Not that the anthology that does try to impose its taste is uninteresting. If you think so, look at the inspired introduction and awesomely personal inclusions and exclusions of *The Oxford Book of Modern Verse*, edited by William Butler Yeats. Its chief interest lies, I think, in what it tells us about William Butler Yeats. The anthology itself is part of the breakup of the Victorian idea of the anthology; just as James Stephens, in his introduction to *English Romantic Poets* (1935), puts a term to "the official Classical and Romantic modes of poetry." "Our day," he says, "warrants the assumption that new values must be identified, and that a new method must be evolved for dealing with them."

He is speaking of poetry, but what he says applies equally to the anthology. What would such a "new method" be? It has seemed to me at times almost like the attempt to square the circle: to be authoritative while denying the pretensions of authority; to set up categories that disclaim themselves, criteria that admit to fallibility.

That, it seems to me, is the crux of the problem. One of the distinguishing features of this century is its conscious acceptance of fallibility: the "margin of error." We not only concede this; in a sense we put it to use, in theories of probability, in technological research, in the building of machinery, in sampling public opinion (where it is often much wider than we thought). The attempt is to narrow the margin down, to whittle it away to the vanishing point; but it is always there and to be allowed for.

In literary criticism it asserts itself in the detailed study of semantics, an attempt to isolate and control the margin of error in the area of meaning, and in the "objective correlative" and other formidable-sounding tools of "the critical apparatus." As these techniques multiply and ramify, it would appear that, rather than a margin of error, there is a margin of meaning, a slim segment that can be effectively, immediately and completely communicated.

This is a theme for specialists alone. And while we are accustomed to having specialists locate margins of error for us in everything from the figuring of our income tax to the beat of our hearts, we resent it in literature. Perhaps we don't want our meanings too clear; or rather, we don't want to realize how unclear they can be.

The man who drives an automobile does not have to know the workings of its internal-combustion engine. That might add to his pleasure in the mechanism but it is not necessary to his driving. The reader of a poem does not have to know semantics, although that might add even more to his enjoyment. To make an anthology for such a reader is more a matter of presentation than of technical criticism.

An approach to the new method, it seems to me, is to begin by allowing for the widest possible margin of error. Taste, as a continuing activity, does not congeal into absolute standards. Every time we read a poem we feel slightly different about it. It tends to go up or down in our estimation; to expand or contract; often to take on new and unsuspected meaning.

The critic is presumably a reader who exercises his taste more consciously and continuously. At least he exercises it in public. There would seem to be all the more reason for him to avoid final judgment. So much has been written about Shakespeare, for example, that by now we know we cannot exhaust either his meaning or our ways of responding. What we have are not final critical estimates but a series of opinions and insights.

In this anthology I should like to preserve as lively a sense of fluctuation as possible. I should like to think of its arrangement as corresponding in some degree with the motion of the mind thinking about poetry. I should like to look at these poems with a minimum of preconception, as if we were reading them for the first time.

That is, in effect, what I have found to be true for most of the poems I enjoy. Re-reading them is not so much a recalling of what I have already found in them as it is, in Gertrude Stein's phrase, "a beginning again." Naturally there is much that is cumulative; and from time to time, in reading particular poems, an equilibrium is reached; what psychologists call a "plateau." But the next reading may startle us into a new awareness.

Ideally poems would float about the book the way they do in the mind. A great deal depends on the sequence in which they are read, the similarities or contrasts brought out by varying juxtapositions. To repeat whole poems is obviously unfeasible. But I do hope to provide enough cross reference to prevail upon the reader to look at them in different lights.

The arrangement of the book is intended to explore poetry on its own terms. Part One asks what poetry is; poetry as defined by poets, in a group of poems in which they say or imply what they think it is. Part Two asks what poets think of themselves and each other, in poems defining or characterizing the nature of the poet. Parts Three to Twelve consider what poetry does, the different ways it has of intensifying different kinds of experiences—sensations, emotions, ideas—and how it relates these to make symbols of complete experience, the whole man.

Within these larger groups the poems are gathered in clusters of association. Occasionally the influence of one poet on another may be suggested, or variations on a theme compared. But the intention is less methodical than playful, in the sense of a free play of ideas. Rather than starting with preconceived notions, the hope is to begin with the poems and see where they lead.

In this way the nature of poetry may gradually unfold; how it is distinct from and yet approaches the other arts: prose, music, the dance, painting, sculpture. While the poems are grouped loosely as they go in these several directions, this is not to classify them as primarily pictorial, musical, amorous, witty, or intellectual. Categories are convenient but not imperative; they do not define. Most poems would fit quite as well into several. As this becomes more and more apparent, the dividing lines shimmer, grow translucent, and disappear.

The mixed chronology may help to break down the distinction between "modern" and "traditional" poetry. While the poetry of any age has its appropriateness to its time and place, it has also a timeless quality where all competition between the centuries ceases. The arrangement and comments hope to strike a balance between these qualities.

I have chosen poems I like, without considering whether they are the best, or their poets' best, or whether all types and periods have been proportionately represented. The object is to suggest, rather than to limit, variety.

The poems are relatively short, English and American, early and late. The long poem is a book in itself. Occasional translations are included when they seem to be poems in their own right. Except for quotations in the comments, songs from plays and lyric interludes from narrative poetry, the poems are complete.

The idea of the anthology, then, is that it is to be based on a personal taste evolving as the book evolves. Its wish is to reproduce the action of taste discovering itself. Its hope is to serve as example and inducement to the reader to explore his own.

A word about the style

The contemporary poems in this collection follow the usage of their authors. Earlier poems, except those in dialect like some of the ballads and the poems of Robert Burns, follow present-day spelling unless this would alter meaning or metre.

For example, the terminal e, as in George Herbert's "A true hymne," is part of a written, and not always consistent, convention. Its presence would be no more noticeable to the readers of its day than its absence is to us.

"The finenesse which a hymne or psalme affords" does have for us a period charm, a sensation of time, that it cannot have had for the contemporaries of George Herbert. At once it makes us *look back*. Has this sense of antiquity become an integral part of the poem; a patina? Or is it extraneous, like accumulated layers of varnish on old paintings?

Fortunately the question does not have to be resolved. In the case of poetry we can eat our cake and have it. Frequently we can have several cakes, if we follow a particular poem through its various editions. Time, which is or is not part of the poem, includes revisions and alternative versions by the poet, his poor handwriting or that of a copyist, the vagaries of friends, editors and printers, inspired or uninspired guesses of scholars filling in obliterated words or disputed passages, and sheer perversity. To cite a comparatively recent instance, Robert Bridges changes the word "combs" to "moulds" in a sonnet dedicated to him by Gerard Manley Hopkins, "having no doubt that G.M.H. would have made some such alteration."

Only a scholar of scholars could resolve the conflicting claims of scholarship. I have taken the liberty, where different versions exist, of choosing the one that appeals to me. Since the present collection is a revolving one, with past and present intermingling, it has seemed appropriate to present the poems as contemporaneously as possible, short of translation.

Since, too, it is not a last resting place, but hopes to whirl the reader off to the poets themselves, he can look forward to added pleasures and fresh discoveries when he reads them in different settings.

Prose windows on poetry

Through the centuries prose writers, including poets when they are writing prose, have given us many definitions of poetry. Why have there been so many? Is it because, usually, they apply to one or another *kind* of poetry?

There is Wordsworth's "emotion recollected in tranquillity," which seems admirably to describe the generally calm, reflective, rather philosophic poems of Wordsworth.

For Aristotle, poetry is an imitation of the facts of nature, especially human action. Aristotle is speaking of epic and dramatic poetry; today his definition applies equally well to the novel and the prose drama.

Prose has gradually taken over many functions once considered the exclusive property of verse. Increasingly the difficulty has been to frame a definition of poetry that will exclude prose. This has led to skirmishes and jealousies between the two branches of writing that are not found, in quite the same form, in any other art.

"Prose is written speech; lyric poetry is written song," says Ernest Rhys in his introduction to *The Prelude of Poetry*; "that is the beginning of the whole matter, the radical definition which we may elaborate but can hardly make clearer."

Far from making matters clearer, this fails to account for the presence of colloquial speech rhythms in much lyric poetry, and their absence in much prose. Apart from dialogue, how much prose *is* "written speech"?

Coleridge puts it just as summarily in his *Table Talk:* "I wish our clever young poets would remember my homely definitions of prose and poetry; that is, prose,—words in their best order; poetry,—the best words in their best order."

This sounds a little like getting dressed up for church and leads to an apprehension of sermons. Besides the implied slur on prose—any old words will do—it leaves a great deal to the imagination. What are the "best" words? Are some intrinsically better or worse than others? Can a perfect order be established for all time and for every purpose? The statement can be, and has been, used to justify stilted "poetic diction" and conventional form.

This could not be Coleridge's intention. He dabbles in philosophical distinctions; rather too much for his literary criticism, and certainly for his poetry. One of his other definitions is a case in point. "A poem," he says in *Biographia Literaria*, "is that species of composition, which is opposed to works of science, by proposing for its *immediate* object pleasure; and from all other species (having *this* in common with it) it is discriminated by proposing to itself such delight from the *whole* as is compatible with a distinct gratification from each component *part*."

How this distinguishes a poem from *any* other species of literary composition is beyond me. However, in his remark about "the best words" he is undoubtedly trying to climb out of the pit he feels has been dug for both of them in Wordsworth's preface to their *Lyrical Ballads*.

Rather inadvisedly, he feels, Wordsworth introduced this joint collection of their poems with the remark that poetry was to be written in the language "of real life." It was a literary quarrel rather slow in the making. For years Coleridge contented himself by complaining, in private letters, that Wordsworth associated him with a sentiment to which he did not wholly subscribe. At the end, I think, Coleridge was rather piqued by the fact that Wordsworth's poetry, and the ill-advised remark, had aroused tremendous controversy.

Wordsworth succeeded in deflating the rather pompous "poetic diction" prevalent when he and Coleridge first brought out their poems. Coleridge was torn between a genuine admiration—even after their personal coolness—for many of Wordsworth's poems, and a somewhat jealous awareness of the critical inexactness of Wordsworth's pronouncement. As he quite justly points out, very little—and usually the poorest—of Wordsworth's poetry is written in a language even loosely approximating "real life"—whatever that is; the "written speech" of Ernest Rhys? I think Coleridge was trying for an equally challenging but more valid pronouncement.

More than a hundred and fifty years earlier, John Milton says of poetry that, compared to the "ornate rhetorick taught out of the rule of Plato," it is "less suttle and fine, but more simple, sensuous and passionate." This, especially the word "simple," is often cited by those who object to what they consider "difficult" poems. Let us get back to simplicity à la Milton, they counsel, forgetting that, of the triad, this is the least applicable word to *Paradise Lost*. Sensuous and passionate, yes, but is it simple? Unless we mean by simplicity the kind of unity in diversity Milton may have in mind.

Milton, however, is speaking comparatively. Poetry is not simple; it is simpler than the prose rhetoric of his day, its balanced periods, variously weighted phrases, and a whole repertoire of devices far more cumbersome than the conventions of prosody. "Written speech" indeed; the most elaborate verse forms are closer to common speech.

A writer of the early nineteenth century, William Lisle Bowles, whose early sonnets had an influence on Coleridge, enunciates a set of "invariable principles." In his "Concluding Observations on the Poetic Character of Pope" (whom he relegates to the second rank, but for the wrong reasons) he proposes certain "principles of Criticism which I imagine will be acknowledged by all." The first of these goes as follows: "I presume it will be readily granted, that 'all images drawn from what is beautiful or sublime in the works of NATURE, are more beautiful and sublime than any image drawn from ART, and that they are therefore, *per se*, more poetical.' "

How the Reverend Bowles comes to issue so confident a fiat is perhaps better understood if we recall Aristotle's precedent. To excite "pity and terror," which for Aristotle are the prime emotions of tragedy, the chief protagonists, he says, must be of heroic stature: kings, queens and the members of royal families. What he has to say about comedy and lyric poetry has not come down to us; but obviously, scholars reason, if he places tragedy first he must consider it supreme.

The schoolmen's great dream is to discover a similar hierarchy of principles for other kinds of poetry. It's a heady notion, this laying down of laws that subsequent poets will have to follow, whether they like or not. Of course Aristotle's principles are derived from existing Greek drama, not the other way around; there is no record of important Greek drama following his *Poetics*.

In his search for absolutes, Bowles goes on: "In like manner, those *Passions* of the human heart, which belong to Nature in general, are, *per se*, more adapted to *the higher species* of Poetry, than those which are derived from *incidental* and *transient* MANNERS. A description of a Forest is more *poetical*, than a description of a cultivated Garden: and the *Passions* which are portrayed in the Epistle of an Eloise, render such a Poem more *poetical* (whatever might be the difference of merit in point of execution), *intrinsically* more *poetical*, than a Poem founded on the characters, incidents and modes of *artificial life*; for instance, the Rape of the Lock."

This is all part of Bowles' scheme for putting Alexander Pope in his place, while leaving John Dryden wherever he is. The controversy it touched off raised a fine dust of extraneous issues. Pope's morals were attacked and defended, Bowles alleging that "Martha Blount did leave her friends and domesticate with him." This she would scarcely have done, he goes on to suggest, without some prior encouragement on the part of Pope. There is also the matter of certain ungentlemanly aspersions cast by Pope on the character of Lady Mary Wortley Montagu.

The countercharges include one pertinent remark by Byron in a letter to his publisher, John Murray: "So far are principles of poetry from being invariable that they never were nor ever will be settled. These principles mean nothing more than the predilections of a particular age, and every age has its own and a different from its predecessor."

In his "English Bards and Scotch Reviewers," Byron pillories poor Bowles quite unmercifully. Referring to him as "the maudlin prince of mournful sonnetteers," he elaborates on the penchant of "harmonious Bowles" for writing about bells:

Whether thou singest with equal ease, and grief,
The fall of empires, or a yellow leaf;
Whether thy muse most lamentably tells
What merry sounds proceed from Oxford bells,
Or, still in bells delighting, finds a friend
In every chime that jingled to Ostend;
Ah! how much juster were thy Muse's hap,
If to thy bells thou wouldst but add a cap!

The coup de grâce is unwittingly administered by a Reverend Gilfillian, editing a posthumous edition of Bowles' poems. In the preface he writes: "His particular theory about the superiority of the works of nature as poetical subjects perhaps led him to a too uniform selection of its grander features, while undoubtedly his genius fitted him better for depicting its softer and smaller objects."

Not all definitions are neo-Aristotelian. Plato comes closer to the romantic conception of poetry when he calls it an imitation of the thoughts and dreams of man. Or, as Wordsworth beautifully expresses it: "That which comes from the heart goes to the heart." Where Aristotle stresses the external in subject matter and the structural in a poem, Plato is more concerned with its inner connections. His theory of Ideas may be taken as an account of the workings of the imagination. This has the value of not pinning poetry down to a set of rules.

The muddy quarrel between "Classicism" and "Romanticism" would seem to go back to the classics themselves, and to be largely a clash of temperaments. Those who exalt discipline range themselves on the side of Apollonian "order." Those who exalt inspiration or vision take more favorably to the Dionysian "frenzy." In his cool way Aristotle himself states the mean position: "It is not enough to know what to say, but it is necessary also to say it in the right way."

"Men have asked," says Horace, "whether verse wins renown through nature or through art." From his own remarks in *Ars Poetica*, he would seem to favor the Apollonian: "Democritus believes that genius is more successful than wretched art, and would fain exclude from Helicon all sane poets. Therefore a large number of would-be poets refuse to pare their nails and trim their beards, seek solitude and shun the baths."

"Poetry," says Leigh Hunt expansively, "is the utterance of a passion for truth, beauty and power. . . Its means are whatever the universe contains; and its ends, pleasure and exaltation."

Rather more soberly Poe defines "the Poetry of words as the Rhythmical Creation of Beauty. Its sole arbiter is Taste."

"Poetry lifts the veil from the hidden beauty of the world," says Shelley, "and makes familiar objects to be as if they were not familiar."

"It begins in delight and ends in wisdom," says Robert Frost in "The Figure a Poem Makes," introducing his *Complete Poems*. "The figure is the same as for love."

The variety of definitions lends force to Arthur Quiller-Couch's temperate observation in his preface to *The Oxford Book of English Verse*: "But the lyrical spirit is volatile and notoriously hard to bind with definitions; and seems to grow wilder with the years."

One of my favorite definitions is from the double essay, *On Prose and Verse*, by the late Irish poet and novelist, James Stephens. He begins by saying that poetry, like reality, is incapable of definition. Not that we don't know what reality is. We don't know anything else.

"We cannot say what poetry is," says Stephens, "but we may adventure a speculation as to what it is not; and, by a negative definition, approach to something that has the appearance of the impossibly positive statement.

"Poetry is not action, nor passion, nor thought. It contains all of these, carelessly, as it were; but, in a true instance, when these qualities have been eliminated, there remains yet a quality, and that residue is poetry. Nor is it correct to say that a 'residue' remains—an excess remains, and that excess is poetry."

To speak of poetry in its absence is persuasion in a vacuum. We should expect something suggestive from poets. Apart from them, how remote, abstract, and unreal most definitions seem, with their endless distinctions and qualifications, their air of providing for every contingency. The obligation lies heavy on them to take into account not only every poem that has been, but every poem that conceivably might be, written. This enormous actual and potential aggregate must then be so thoroughly removed from a similar prose aggregate that neither of these billipedes can tread on a single toe of the other.

One object of such painstaking endeavor is to see the "thing-in-itself," absolutely separate from everything else; a truly mythical wish, for nothing exists in isolation. A poem on the page has no significant existence until it resumes its life in relation to a reader.

Another object is to form the ideal conception of a poem; just as mythical a wish. The most such a conception can accomplish is to interpose between the reader and the page, so that he does not see the poem that is there for the poem he imagines should be there.

It is from the poets themselves, in their poems—the "true instances" of which James Stephens speaks—that we get living definitions. Beyond what they may say or imply, the very action of the poems enters in, to alter or to enforce; always to illuminate.

PART ONE

"To hear with eyes"

1. *Kubla Khan*

SAMUEL TAYLOR COLERIDGE

In Xanadu did Kubla Khan
A stately pleasure-dome decree:
Where Alph, the sacred river, ran
Through caverns measureless to man
  Down to a sunless sea.
So twice five miles of fertile ground
With walls and towers were girdled round:
And here were gardens bright with sinuous rills
Where blossomed many an incense-bearing tree;
And here were forests ancient as the hills,
And folding sunny spots of greenery.

But oh that deep romantic chasm which slanted
Down the green hill athwart a cedarn cover!
A savage place! as holy and enchanted
As e'er beneath a waning moon was haunted
By woman wailing for her demon-lover!
And from this chasm, with ceaseless turmoil seething,
As if this earth in fast thick pants were breathing,
A mighty fountain momently was forced;
Amid whose swift half-intermitted burst
Huge fragments vaulted like rebounding hail,
Or chaffy grain beneath the thresher's flail:
And 'mid these dancing rocks at once and ever
It flung up momently the sacred river.

Five miles meandering with a mazy motion
Through wood and dale the sacred river ran,
Then reached the caverns measureless to man,
And sank in tumult to a lifeless ocean:
And 'mid this tumult Kubla heard from far
Ancestral voices prophesying war!

The shadow of the dome of pleasure
Floated midway on the waves;
Where was heard the mingled measure
From the fountain and the caves.
It was a miracle of rare device,
A sunny pleasure-dome with caves of ice!

A damsel with a dulcimer
In a vision once I saw:
It was an Abyssinian maid,
And on her dulcimer she played,
Singing of Mount Abora.
Could I revive within me
Her symphony and song,
To such a deep delight 'twould win me,
That with music loud and long,
I would build that dome in air,
That sunny dome! those caves of ice!
And all who heard should see them there,
And all should cry, Beware! Beware!
His flashing eyes, his floating hair!
Weave a circle round him thrice,
And close your eyes with holy dread,
For he on honey-dew hath fed,
And drunk the milk of Paradise.

"In the summer of 1797," writes Samuel Taylor Coleridge—he had no head for dates; it may have been a year later—"the Author, then in ill health, had retired to a lonely farm-house between Porlock and Linton, on the Exmoor confines of Somerset and Devonshire. In consequence of a slight indisposition, an anodyne had been prescribed, from the effects of which he fell asleep in his chair at the moment that he was reading the following sentences, or words of the same substance, in 'Purchas's Pilgrimage': 'Here the Khan Kubla commanded a palace to be built, and a stately garden thereunto. And thus ten miles of fertile ground were inclosed with a wall.' "

Coleridge slept for about three hours. During this time he dreamed a complete poem, some two to three hundred lines. "All the images," he says, "rose up before him as *things*, with a parallel production of the correspondent expressions, without any sensation or consciousness of effort."

On waking up he wrote out as much as he could remember of the poem "Kubla Khan." He was perhaps a quarter of the way through when he was interrupted by one of the most unfortunate calls in literary history. The intruder is nameless but does not go unscathed: "a person on business from Porlock," says Coleridge, who "detained" him for over an hour. On returning to his manuscript, he writes, "with the exception of some eight or ten scattered lines and images, all the rest had passed away like the images on the surface of a stream into which a stone has been cast, but alas! without the after restoration of the latter."

Doesn't "Kubla Khan" seem, however, complete? At once clear and mysterious, like blue sky seen through a fine golden haze, it seems all the more dreamlike for ending abruptly. Most dreams that we remember *are* interrupted. At the moment of interruption the waking mind tries to catch hold of the dream and complete it.

What gives these fifty-four lines their magical dreamlike quality? Part of it, I think, is the total absence of a sense of humor. We seldom make jokes in our sleep. What would seem absurd to the waking mind is perfectly acceptable in a dream; even the earth breathing "in fast thick pants."

Sartorial implications aside, this is pretty funny. Yet in the dream it blends with the shifting panorama and the prevailing sense of beauty. In the dream too, "His flashing eyes, his floating hair!" is eerie and credible. This is negative testimony to the poem's dreamlike compulsion. What is it that actively enforces its hypnotic power? Is it the music?

"Kubla Khan" has sometimes been called "pure poetry," a way of insinuating, I think, that it is largely verbal music with very little meaning. How far can we push the analogy with music? Usually the "music" of poetry and the "music" of music are very different things.

I tried an experiment with "Kubla Khan" on the piano. Taking the F above middle C as the lowest note to represent long oo, I worked out a scale of vowel sounds. It rises more or less as the mouth opens and widens, through F-sharp (short oo), G (long o), G-sharp (aw), and so on up to E, which happens to coincide with that vowel.

Then I translated the vowels of "Kubla Khan" to the corresponding notes. With a rhythm following the spoken beat the tune that results is quite melodic and Eastern; rather naturally the latter, since it employs the twelve-tone scale.

I don't suggest it as a musical equivalent of "Kubla Khan" or a new way of testing poetry. Some of Shakespeare's sonnets, similarly translated, sound musically quite meaningless. It does indicate, I think, by exaggeration, the particular structure of the vowel sounds in "Kubla Khan." The structure is very close to that of musical themes.

In the opening lines the vowels repeat, reverse, recur, and intertwine as they would in a melody. This circularity suggests the roundness of the "dome." The dome arrives as if the sounds had described or decreed it, its lone o set apart from everything that surrounds it. It seems to float there with visible elegance.

Then the river theme begins: "Where Alph, the sacred river, ran . . ." It is announced; then disappears, to return later. A new theme is introduced by the first *i* sounds, three in a row: "So twice five miles of fertile ground with walls and towers were girdled round." With them the rhythm of the poem alters and broadens. With the persuasiveness of a dream it leads us through passages of pure happiness to moments of abrupt terror. These, as in dream sequences, almost at once dissolve, possibly to have recurred later had the whole dream been remembered.

What about the meaning? Does the poem have one? We are talking about something going on outside waking awareness, and that, nowadays, is apt to bring on psychological speculation. Let's leave the dome, the river, the chasm and caverns to the Freudians. The analyst may find anxiety symptoms in the sudden menace of "Ancestral voices prophesying war." And why did Coleridge, a devout if extremely freethinking Christian, have such hankerings for the paradise of Mahomet?

These may be fascinating bypaths, but they lead away from "Kubla Khan." What is the poem saying? Isn't Coleridge giving us one of his motives for writing?

That with music loud and long,
I would build that dome in air . . .

He wants a music so powerful that it will make his visions real. The impulse is common to poetry. Here it has been expressed, it is true, in sleep. But how asleep *is* asleep?

In a remarkable piece of literary detection, *The Road to Xanadu,* John Livingston Lowes traces the connections between "Kubla Khan" and Coleridge's waking mind. The images, and much of the language, come from his reading. The musical vowel pattern is something worked on, consciously and intensively, in other poems: among them, "Christabel" and "The rime of the Ancient Mariner."

Poets when awake are noted for being dreamy. They reach into reverie. They articulate sensations and emotions that are ordinarily fleeting. Here, by an interesting reversal, part of Coleridge's waking mind seems to enter into the dream. As though without effort it shapes the dream, puts words to the shapes, and gives the words evocative rhythm.

There are other curious reversals. Not only do the vowel sounds often echo each other in a mirrorlike way. The Khan Kubla of the prose passage becomes, in the poem, Kubla Khan. The palace with its "stately garden" becomes a "stately pleasure-dome" with its garden.

The most significant reversal of all, it seems to me, is the change of attitude at the close of the poem. As the vision seems to be drifting away, the waking mind begins to assert itself. For the first time "I" comes into the poem:

> *Could I revive within me*
> *Her symphony and song,*
> *To such a deep delight 'twould win me,*
> *That with music loud and long,*
> *I would build that dome in air,*
> *That sunny dome! those caves of ice!*
> *And all who heard should see them there . . .*

Isn't this what the opening lines of "Kubla Khan" do? The pictures are all contained within the sounds. The dream is, as Coleridge says, a parallel production of image and expression; like the mythical birth of Athena fully armed from the head of Zeus, truly "a miracle of rare device."

"Kubla Khan" begins with fulfillment and ends by wishing for it. Doesn't this tell us more about the impulse of poetry than "words in their best order"? The poet's urgency, as James Stephens might say, is excessive. No matter how fully he may seem to have realized his vision, he wants more. He wants to "build that dome in air." He wants transitory experiences to become so permanent, and of such intensity, that "all who heard should see them there."

2. *To live merrily and to trust to good verses*
ROBERT HERRICK

Now is the time for mirth;
  Nor cheek or tongue be dumb;
For with the flowery earth
  The golden pomp is come.

The golden pomp is come;
  For now each tree does wear,
Made of her pap and gum,
  Rich beads of amber here.

Now reigns the rose, and now
  The Arabian dew besmears
My uncontrollèd brow
  And my retorted hairs.

Homer, this health to thee,
  In sack of such a kind
That it would make thee see
  Though thou wert ne'er so blind.

Next, Virgil I'll call forth,
  To pledge this second health
In wine whose each cup's worth
  An Indian commonwealth.

A goblet next I'll drink
  To Ovid; and suppose,
Made he the pledge, he'd think
  The world had all one nose.

Then this immensive cup
  Of aromatic wine,
Catullus, I quaff up
  To that terse Muse of thine.

Wild I am now with heat;
  O Bacchus! cool thy rays!
Or, frantic, I shall eat
  Thy thyrse, and bite the bays.

Round, round, the roof does run;
  And, being ravished thus,
Come, I will drink a tun
  To my Propertius.

Now, to Tibullus next,
  This flood I drink to thee.
But stay; I see a text
  That this presents to me:

Behold, Tibullus lies
  Here burnt, whose small return
Of ashes scarce suffice
  To fill a little urn.

Trust to good verses, then;
  They only will aspire,
When pyramids, as men,
  Are lost i' the funeral fire.

And when all bodies meet,
  In Lethe to be drowned,
Then only numbers sweet
  With endless life are crowned.

A sermon might be expected of the seventeenth-century clergyman poet, Robert Herrick. At nineteen his "wild, unbaptisèd rhymes," as he calls them, won him "adoption" by Ben Jonson. Somewhat dismayed at leaving London for the vicarage of Dean Prior in Devonshire, Herrick seems to have made the best of it. It is said that he was "florid and witty" in the pulpit and threw one of his sermons at an inattentive congregation.

This poem has resemblances to a sermon in its structure and its air of logical discourse. But, subject apart, what about the logic? Does the "text" follow from the premises? Doesn't it seem a muzzy afterthought?

I believe Herrick intends it so. The poem settles down at once to some serious drinking. Taking its cue and excuse from the intoxicated season, it begins in that glow of anticipatory geniality that often precedes the first glass. From a modest toast or two it goes on to a "goblet," then to an "immensive cup"; each proportionate to Herrick's esteem for the poet whose health he is proposing.

At this point the poem has a spell of giddiness:

Wild I am now with heat,
O Bacchus! cool thy rays!
Or, frantic, I shall eat
Thy thyrse, and bite the bays.

Bacchus, the god of wine and revelry, is traditionally crowned with bay leaves and carries a thyrse, a rod tipped with a pine cone. The resemblance to *thirst* is noticeable.

Now the poem, still reeling ("Round, round, the roof does run"), proceeds to a "tun" and finally an uncontained and uncontainable "flood." The rhythm sways; almost lurches.

Just in time the poem recovers, pulls itself to its full height and lays a finger alongside its nose: "But stay; I see a text . . ." Like a man walking a straight line or saying, "I'm as sober as a judge," it must justify its condition by proving itself capable of sober thought.

The first thought that presents itself is almost *too* sobering. Here it has been drinking Tibullus' "health," forgetting that Tibullus would scarce "fill a little urn." For a moment the poem threatens a crying jag.

But merriment wins out. Something survives after all: the sustained elation of a poem, preserving the brief elation of wine. There is little more logic than there is in the juxtaposition in "Kubla Khan" of "sunless sea" and "sunny dome." But as that conjunction intensifies the quality of dream, so Herrick's bleary pronouncement caps the emotional logic, the action, of the poem. Poetry is that country where we dream with Coleridge and drink with Herrick.

3. *Shall I compare thee to a summer's day?*
WILLIAM SHAKESPEARE

Shall I compare thee to a summer's day?
Thou art more lovely and more temperate:
Rough winds do shake the darling buds of May,
And summer's lease hath all too short a date:
Sometime too hot the eye of heaven shines,
And often is his gold complexion dimmed:
And every fair from fair sometime declines,
By chance, or nature's changing course, untrimmed.
But thy eternal summer shall not fade,
Nor lose possession of that fair thou owest,
Nor shall death brag thou wanderest in his shade,
When in eternal lines to time thou growest;
   So long as men can breathe, or eyes can see,
   So long lives this, and this gives life to thee.

The immortality conferred by poetry is the theme of many of Shakespeare's sonnets besides this, usually numbered XVIII. The seventeenth ends:

But were some child of yours alive that time,
You should live twice;—in it, and in my rime.

And in the nineteenth—"Devouring Time, blunt thou the lion's paws" —the boast is even more explicit:

Yet do thy worst, old Time; despite thy wrong,
My love shall in my verse ever live young.

In Sonnet LV:

Not marble, nor the gilded monuments
Of princes, shall out-live this powerful rime.

And in LXXXI:

You still shall live—such virtue hath my pen—
Where breath most breathes—even in the mouths of men.

Shakespeare's method with a subject is like the oyster's with the egg of a worm, to surround it. In the various sonnets pitting eternity against time he takes varying, sometimes opposite, attitudes. There is the modest hope, in LXV, "That in black ink my love may still shine bright." Yet in the previous sonnet:

Ruin hath taught me thus to ruminate—
That time will come and take my love away.
  This thought is as a death, which cannot choose
  But weep to have that which it fears to lose.

"Shall I compare thee to a summer's day?" builds to its conclusion so quietly and with such serene assurance that we find ourselves agreeing before we quite realize how much we're agreeing to. It is only when it is read aloud that the full meaning of its conclusion emerges. Slurred over by the eye, "So long as men can breathe" may seem another way of saying so long as they exist. This is enough, but it ignores a specific shade of the meaning.

The whole poem lies within the range of a conversational tone. For all its modulation, the progression of emotion does not rely on obvious dramatic contrast. Rather it must be read smoothly, almost levelly, from start to finish, with very gradually increasing intensity.

So long as men have the proper breath to read it, its emotion is transferred. The poem, and Shakespeare's nameless friend, continue to live "even in the mouths of men"; not just in their "good report," but quite literally "Where breath most breathes." This is Shakespeare's very practical idea of immortality.

4. *Ingrateful beauty threatened*

THOMAS CAREW

Know, Celia, since thou art so proud,
  'Twas I that gave thee thy renown.
Thou hadst in the forgotten crowd
  Of common beauties lived unknown,
Had not my verse extolled thy name,
And with it imped the wings of fame.

That killing power is none of thine;
   I gave it to thy voice and eyes;
Thy sweets, thy graces, all are mine;
   Thou art my star, shin'st in my skies;
Then dart not from thy borrowed sphere
Lightnings on him that fixed thee there.

Tempt me with such affrights no more,
   Lest what I made I uncreate;
Let fools thy mystic form adore,
   I know thee in thy mortal state.
Wise poets, that wrapt truth in tales,
Knew her themselves through all her veils.

To this Cavalier poet, poetry not only immortalizes. It creates beauty in the very act of praising it.

This is a "conceit," a fiction told for the delight of invention. His verse, Carew says, has "imped the wings of fame." To imp, in falconry, is to repair a wing by grafting feathers to it. The poet's quill, with which he writes verses to his lady, causes her fame to fly abroad. And what he has made he can "uncreate."

"Conceit" derives from the same root that gives the philosopher his "concept," something conceived in the mind. Where the latter hopes to square with reality, the former squares only with the imagination. Usually it belongs to the repertoire of gallantry; hyperbole, either of compliment or of airy insult.

From its frequently self-congratulatory tone very likely comes the current meaning of conceited: liking oneself rather too well. In the poem this tone is so obviously a pose that nobody is deceived, least of all the poet, who can see truth "through all her veils."

This playfulness with "truth" is very close to the "concept" of many of the poems of Wallace Stevens, for whom poetry is "the supreme fiction," a fiction paralleling life.

5. *On the Countess Dowager of Pembroke*

WILLIAM BROWNE

Underneath this sable hearse
Lies the subject of all verse:
Sidney's sister, Pembroke's mother:
Death, ere thou hast slain another,
Fair, and learn'd, and good as she,
Time shall throw a dart at thee.

Marble piles let no man raise
To her name; in after-days,
Some kind woman born as she,
Reading this, like Niobe
Shall turn marble, and become
Both her mourner and her tomb.

A conceit is not necessarily light or humorous. Milton uses one quite soberly in his tribute to Shakespeare (poem 28), possibly because Shakespeare himself is such an adept.

Strikingly similar to Milton's is "Some kind woman . . . Shall turn marble," a conferring of immortality in reverse. The weight, the balanced phrases, the somber hue, and the stylized classical allusion all conspire to give this poem a curious headstone density, the quality of poetry freezing to sculpture. So thoroughly imbued is it with the Elizabethan and seventeenth-century preoccupation with death and monuments that it seems almost capable of carrying out its macabre intention.

6. *Can you paint a thought?*

JOHN FORD

Can you paint a thought? or number
Every fancy in a slumber?
Can you count soft minutes roving
From a dial's point by moving?
Can you grasp a sigh? or lastly,
Rob a virgin's honour chastly?

No, O no; yet you may
  Sooner do both that and this,
  This and that, and never miss,
Then by any praise display
  Beauty's beauty, such a glory
  As beyond all fate, all story,
    All arms, all arts,
    All loves, all hearts,
  Greater then those, or they,
  Do, shall, and must obey.

Then: than

This song from *The Broken Heart,* first acted about 1629 and printed in 1633, confesses to limitations. Absurdly lighthearted, it anticipates some of the gayer aspects of surrealism in its reaching beyond "that or this, / This or that." The whimsical questioning, too, is not unlike reputed techniques of Zen Buddhism, taxing the mind beyond its usual capacity in order to grasp an unseizable truth, "beauty's beauty," an insight by attrition.

Nowadays thoughts *are* painted. The "fancies in a slumber" are not only numbered but dissected. Time is a matter of split seconds; sighs are recorded on charts, and virgins robbed, if not chastely, without dishonor. Only "beauty's beauty" remains inviolable.

7. *As an unperfect actor on the stage*

WILLIAM SHAKESPEARE

As an unperfect actor on the stage,
Who with his fear is put besides his part,
Or some fierce thing replete with too much rage,
Whose strength's abundance weakens his own heart;
So I, for fear of trust, forget to say
The perfect ceremony of love's rite,
And in mine own love's strength seem to decay,
O'ercharged with burthen of mine own love's might.

Oh! let my books be then the eloquence
And dumb presagers of my speaking breast;
Who plead for love, and look for recompense,
More than that tongue that more hath more expressed.
  Oh! learn to read what silent love hath writ;
  To hear with eyes belongs to love's fine wit.

In Sonnet XXIII an alleged Shakespearean actor confesses to "going up in his lines." He becomes tongue-tied in the presence of his friend, he says, through excess of emotion.

Such a strong feeling can best be expressed in writing: "emotion recollected in tranquillity." But the written poem has its disadvantages. It is not as loud, as immediately persuasive, as a glib tongue. To hear his "speaking breast" the friend must be willing to interpret the silent book.

This is Coleridge's magic wish that "all who heard should see them there" with a difference. For Shakespeare the wish must be mutual. The reader, too, must be willing to read, to translate silent speech, "To hear with eyes."

"I hear with my eyes and see with my ears," says Gertrude Stein to Picasso. In much of her writing—*Tender Buttons*, for instance, and *Geography and Plays*—she is using words with the immediacy of objects, making poems as self-contained as a cloak or clock or apple.

A line from *Saintly Emily* is made into a seal and, later, a decoration for *The Autobiography of Alice B. Toklas:*

ROSE IS A ROSE IS A ROSE IS A ROSE.

In his introduction to *Selected Writings of Gertrude Stein,* Carl Van Vechten quotes her explanation: "When I said, a rose is a rose is a rose, and then later made that into a ring, I made poetry, and what did I do I caressed completely caressed and addressed a noun."

She seems, too, to be playing with the attention, directing it away from the "idea" side of language, its logical sequence and customary usage, toward the rhythm of an object, a person, a landscape. "Rose is a rose . . ." is the way the mind, left to itself, often behaves, an emotional mulling-over. As circular as the flower, it seems too, half humorously, to be a questioning of Juliet's

What's in a name? That which we call a rose
By any other name would smell as sweet.

8. *The rivals*

JAMES STEPHENS

I heard a bird at dawn
  Singing sweetly on a tree,
That the dew was on the lawn,
  And the wind was on the lea;
But I didn't listen to him,
  For he didn't sing to me.

I didn't listen to him,
  For he didn't sing to me
That the dew was on the lawn
  And the wind was on the lea;
I was singing at the time
  Just as prettily as he.

I was singing all the time,
  Just as prettily as he,
About the dew upon the lawn
  And the wind upon the lea;
So I didn't listen to him
  As he sang upon a tree.

Does poetry imitate nature or compete with it? The question is raised by this duel that turns into a duet.

In its form "The rivals" gives itself the lie. It says it isn't listening to the bird. But the way it says this is a steal from the reiterated phrases of bird song.

Repeating the last two lines of each stanza in the next, it recalls Herrick's repetition (poem 2) of "The golden pomp is come." There the repetition speeds up the rhythm, hurrying the poem along toward its increasingly dizzy spin.

Stephens, reaching back an additional line, not only accelerates the tempo but conveys, too, a note of irritation. The poem seems to be clapping its hands to its ears and trying to drown out the bird. Yet the refrain of both, in the middle pair of lines, is identical.

These inversions and recapitulations are reminiscent of rondeau and triolet. But Stephens has invented a new, if similar, form thoroughly expressing rivalry. Rather gallantly he gives his rival the last word: "As he sang upon a tree."

9. *A fit of rime against rime*

BEN JONSON

Rime, the rack of finest wits,
That expresseth but by fits,
True conceit,
Spoiling senses of their treasure,
Cozening judgment with a measure,
But false weight;
Wresting words, from their true calling;
Propping verse, for fear of falling
To the ground;
Jointing syllabes, drowning letters,
Fastening vowels, as with fetters
They were bound!
Soon as lazy thou wert known,
All good poetry hence was flown,
And art banished.

For a thousand years together,
All Parnassus' green did wither,
And wit vanished.
Pegasus did fly away,
At the wells no Muse did stay,
But bewailed
So to see the fountain dry,
And Apollo's music die,
All light failed!
Starveling rimes did fill the stage
Not a poet in an age,
Worth a crowning;
Not a work deserving bays,
Nor a line deserving praise,
Pallas frowning.
Greek was free from rime's infection,
Happy Greek, by this protection,
Was not spoiled;
Whilst the Latin, Queen of Tongues,
Is not yet free from rime's wrongs,
But rests foiled.
Scarce the hill again doth flourish,
Scarce the world a wit doth nourish,
To restore
Phoebus to his crown again;
And the Muses to their brain:
As before.
Vulgar languages that want
Words, and sweetness, and be scant
Of true measure,
Tyran rime hath so abused,
That they long since have refused
Other ceasure.
He that first invented thee,
May his joints tormented be,
Cramped forever;

Still may syllabes jar with time,
Still may reason war with rime,
Resting never.
May his sense, when it would meet
The cold tumor in his feet,
Grow unsounder;
And his title be long fool,
That in rearing such a school,
Was the founder.

syllabes: syllables; *ceasure:* caesura, rhythmic pause

Jonson's tirade may have its occasion in a literary controversy between Thomas Campion and Samuel Daniel.

Campion, whose exquisite songs and lyrics are nearly all rhymed, proclaims in his *Observations in the Art of English Poesie* (1602) the "altogether intollerable" faults of rhyme. He advocates a return to unrhymed Latin metres, examples of which he tosses off in Latin and in English.

Daniel, in his *Defence of Rime* a year later, asserts the practice to be so unquestionable as to seem "from a Graunt of Nature." He backs up his argument with copious Latin quotations, all unrhymed, and not a single example in English.

Jonson seems to be taking a mean position, perhaps in derision of both pamphlets, flaying the subject with knouts of barbed rhyme. It's true, this is "literary" humor. Its irony depends on a recognition of the discrepancy between what it is saying and the form in which it says it. Compared with the delicate irony of James Stephens' "The rivals" (poem 8), Jonson's "learnèd sock" does seem to clump.

In our day a similar tone—rather more, it seems to me, witty and urbane—is to be found in many of W. H. Auden's poems. "Under which lyre" (in *Nones*, page 64) is an apparent defense of Hermetic (or Dionysian) "frenzy" as opposed to Apollonian "order," written in a very strictly ordered verse form.

Irritation with poetry is not uncommon among poets. In our own century Ogden Nash takes it to task, in "Very like a whale" (*The Face Is Familiar*, page 104), for a different failing:

One thing that literature would be greatly the better for
Would be a more restricted employment by authors of simile and metaphor.

He documents his case by citing George Gordon Byron's Assyrian, coming down like a wolf on the fold, "with purple and gold cohorts." Nash's own rhythms, coming down like a gimpy nag heading for the collapsing barn of his rhyme, are themselves a parody of "the wingèd steed" when its rider's rapture is more careless than fine.

In "Poetry" (*Collected Poems*, page 40), Marianne Moore confesses: "I, too, dislike it: there are things that are important beyond all this fiddle." But its "raw material," as she demonstrates in a cascade of instances, is infinite. Everything is available, whether eccentric like an upside-down bat or common to all like the bat foraging. Even "business documents and school-books" may be put to poetic use.

She discovers in it, "after all, a place for the genuine." Genuine poets are "literalists of the imagination" and can present for inspection "imaginary gardens with real toads in them."

10. *The argument of his book*

ROBERT HERRICK

I sing of brooks, of blossoms, birds, and bowers,
Of April, May, of June and July flowers.
I sing of Maypoles, hock-carts, wassails, wakes,
Of bridegrooms, brides, and of their bridal-cakes.
I write of youth, of love, and have access
By these to sing of cleanly wantonness.
I sing of dews, of rains, and, piece by piece,
Of balm, of oil, of spice, and ambergris.
I sing of times trans-shifting, and I write
How roses first came red and lilies white.
I write of groves, of twilights, and I sing
The court of Mab and of the fairy king.
I write of hell; I sing (and ever shall)
Of heaven, and hope to have it after all.

The all-inclusiveness of which Marianne Moore speaks provides the theme of Herrick's introduction to *Hesperides* (1648). Characteristically he is more apt to sing of wassails than of wakes; of heaven than of hell and of blossoms than of either; and to celebrate what he calls "cleanly wantonness." His favorite pig, it is alleged, was taught to drink out of a tankard. His secular poems greatly outnumber his *Noble Numbers*. Even these are more often gay than grave (see poem 114). Perhaps his avoidance of the darker side of life—in this poem he gets through hell in a hurry—helps account for an occasional oversweetness. Too many of his poems at one sitting may become cloying.

11. *A true hymn*

GEORGE HERBERT

"My Joy, my Life, my Crown!"
My heart was meaning all the day.
Somewhat it fain would say,
And still it runneth muttering up and down
With only this, "My Joy, my Life, my Crown!"

Yet slight not these few words;
If truly said, they may take part
Among the best in art:
The fineness which a hymn or psalm affords
Is when the soul unto the lines accords.

He who craves all the mind,
And all the soul, and strength, and time,
If the words only rime,
Justly complains that somewhat is behind
To make his verse, or write a hymn in kind.

Whereas, if the heart be moved,
Although the verse be somewhat scant,
God doth supply the want;
As when the heart says, sighing to be approved,
"O could I love!" and stops, God writeth "Loved."

Not all seventeenth-century clergymen are exclusively merry. There is a rumor, probably unfounded, that George Herbert, who began by seeking preferment at the court of Charles I, destroyed all his love poems upon becoming, in his own words, "a Countrey Parson." But Herbert is no Puritan. "Stay at the third glasse," is his advice to drinkers; and we are told that "he had a very good hand on the lute, and sett his own lyrics or sacred poems," of which "A true hymn" is one.

Herbert's devotional poems are more often joyous than solemn. Sometimes, like Gertrude Stein's "seal," Dylan Thomas' "Vision and prayer," Guillaume Apollinaire's rain-poem trickling down the page, and E. E. Cummings' meaningful typographic arrangements, Herbert augments his effect by suiting the shape of the poem to its subject, as in "Easter-wings" and "The altar."

"A true hymn" poses a question that, in one form or another, is debated in every age. Which is more important to a poem, inspiration or execution; its content or its form? Neither, says Herbert. Form in itself is not self-sufficient: "If the words only rhyme . . . somewhat is behind." He is inclined to favor the content; in this case, his religious emotion: "My Joy, my Life, my Crown!" The urgency of this emotion compels him to make a poem of it.

The word "poetry" comes from the Greek verb "poiein," meaning "to make." Herbert's poem has both a religious and an aesthetic application. As faith without works is dead, so is emotion without expression; without "making." The two balance each other:

The fineness which a hymn or psalm affords
Is when the soul unto the lines accords.

12. *Piping down the valleys wild*

WILLIAM BLAKE

Piping down the valleys wild,
Piping songs of pleasant glee,
On a cloud I saw a child,
And he laughing said to me:

"Pipe a song about a lamb!"
So I piped with merry cheer.
"Piper, pipe that song again!"
So I piped: he wept to hear.

"Drop thy pipe, thy happy pipe.
Sing thy songs of happy cheer!"
So I sang the same again,
While he wept with joy to hear.

"Piper, sit thee down and write
In a book, that all may read."
So he vanished from my sight,
And I plucked a hollow reed,

And I made a rural pen,
And I stained the water clear,
And I wrote my happy songs
Every child may joy to hear.

In this introductory poem to *Songs of Innocence* (1789) William Blake seems to be for pure inspiration. He begins with the vision, such as the one he claims to have had in childhood, of God's face pressed against the windowpane; or that other, of angels roosting in a tree on Peckham Rye.

"When I am commanded by the Spirits," he tells a friend, "then I write, and the moment I have written, I see the words fly about the room in all directions. It is then published. The Spirits can read and my manuscript is of no further use. I have been tempted to burn my manuscript, but my wife won't let me."

The course of Blake's inspiration—from spirits to him, its writing, its publication in the air, its return to its source, an audience of spirits—parallels the course of his poem. First there is the piper, in solitude, piping for his own delight. The child—inspiration or vision—urges him to make a song; to give shape to his spontaneous access of joy. This melody can be repeated. Then the child commands him to put words to his wordless tune; finally to share them, to write them out. So written, they are free to return to their source, with one difference: every child.

The sequence of the poem has charted the route between inspiration and communication; from solitary to shared delight. Incidentally, it answers those criticisms of poetry—usually, in our time, leveled against "modern" poetry—that refer to it as "poets talking to each other." The answer is that that is precisely what poetry is. "Every *child* may joy to hear." The child is the poet in each of us; the part of us that responds to vision.

Some of Blake's later "Prophetic Books" seem literally written by spirits for spirits. To read them it is sometimes necessary to get up and "fly about the room in all directions" with them. As in his drawings, there is a great rush of wings, but the "Minute Particulars" he keeps summoning may give way to rather featureless generalities.

13. *To R.B.*

GERARD MANLEY HOPKINS

The fine delight that fathers thought; the strong
Spur, live and lancing like the blowpipe flame,
Breathes once and, quenchèd faster than it came,
Leaves yet the mind a mother of immortal song.
Nine months she then, nay years, nine years she long
Within her wears, bears, cares and combs the same:
The widow of an insight lost she lives, with aim
Now known and hand at work now never wrong.
   Sweet fire the sire of muse, my soul needs this;
I want the one rapture of an inspiration.
O then if in my lagging lines you miss
The roll, the rise, the carol, the creation,
My winter world, that scarcely breathes that bliss
Now, yields you, with some sighs, our explanation.

That action of the poem that will imprison the action of its subject inspires the Jesuit poet, Gerard Manley Hopkins, in this last despairing sonnet, sent in 1889 to his friend, later Poet Laureate of England, Robert Bridges.

During the last five years of his life Hopkins completed some fourteen poems. In 1884 he was appointed Professor of Classics in University College, Dublin. Always excessively conscientious—he once gave up writing for seven years because his ecclesiastical superiors might not approve—he seems to have been overtaxed by his new duties. He despairs of himself as a poet—"time's eunuch" he calls himself in another sonnet—and as a priest. "I have never wavered in my vocation," he writes to a friend, "but I have not lived up to it."

Yet this most despairing poem is an extraordinary example of affirmation in the very act of denial. What uninspired man could call inspiration "the fine delight that fathers thought"? His poet's nature seeks spontaneity: "the dearest freshness," as he says in "God's grandeur" (poem 96), that "lives . . . deep down things." His poet's craft demands premeditation: the "Nine months . . . nay years" of "wears, bears, cares and combs."

How magnificently the two come together in the very breath of saying that he has missed "The roll, the rise, the carol, the creation." This suggests, in compressed form, the action of the lark in Shakespeare's twenty-ninth sonnet (poem 105). There the preparatory motion, the sudden ascent, the high song, and the transfiguration are described with breath-taking accuracy. Description is enactment.

Hopkins' style is more compressed. It crystallizes the action of an emotion in a sequence that suggests any number of images: a lark, the playing of an organ, the sea, the creation of the world.

Such compression finds still farther dimension in some modern poems, like E. E. Cummings' "what a proud dreamhorse" (poem 121), where the poem itself becomes the complex action it is describing. In his "might these be thrushes climbing through almost(do they" (*Poems: 1923–1954*, page 414), the ineffable quality of their darting and singing so permeates the poem that "nothing but the impossible shall occur."

This is not to say that one style is "better" than another. Every good style expresses the temperament of the poet, and through him the temper of his time. The relaxed style of a great poet becomes, in the hands of his imitators, limp. The taut style goes rigid. Tradition lives, not by repetition, but reanimation; an urgency continually seeking unique means of expression.

14. *Of modern poetry*

WALLACE STEVENS

The poem of the mind in the act of finding
What will suffice. It has not always had
To find: the scene was set; it repeated what
Was in the script.
Then the theatre was changed
To something else. Its past was a souvenir.

It has to be living, to learn the speech of the place.
It has to face the men of the time and to meet
The women of the time. It has to think about war
And it has to find what will suffice. It has
To construct a new stage. It has to be on that stage
And, like an insatiable actor, slowly and
With meditation, speak words that in the ear,
In the delicatest ear of the mind, repeat,
Exactly, that which it wants to hear, at the sound
Of which, an invisible audience listens,
Not to the play, but to itself, expressed
In an emotion as of two people, as of two
Emotions becoming one. The actor is
A metaphysician in the dark, twanging
An instrument, twanging a wiry string that gives
Sounds passing through sudden rightnesses, wholly
Containing the mind, below which it cannot descend,
Beyond which it has no will to rise.
It must
Be the finding of a satisfaction, and may
Be of a man skating, a woman dancing, a woman
Combing. The poem of the act of the mind.

In his *Collected Poems*, published a year before his death in 1955, the American poet Wallace Stevens regards poetry in a multitude of shifting lights. Here many of his reflections fuse and focus.

Where James Stephens, in his essay, is talking about the effect of poetry—its excess of action, passion, thought—and Marianne Moore is speaking of its subject matter—anything is grist to its mill—Stevens approaches it by way of the poet's attitude today. How shall he find his theme?

In the past, or so it seems to us, the poet's themes were more easily recognized, by himself and by his audience. The poet had only, in a sense, "to repeat what was in the script."

Today every theme is available, but the recognition is dispersed. The poet must set his own stage, invent his own rules, and be his own audience, listening for those "sounds passing through sudden rightnesses" that are his only clues. Poetry is a condition of emotional rapport, but the rapport begins with himself: "An emotion as of two people, as of two / Emotions becoming one."

For Wallace Stevens poetry is primarily the search for poetry. Our definitions end where they begin, with the question, "What is poetry?"

Perhaps this is true in every age. At any time in history "its past is a souvenir." Definitions are based on these souvenirs; they cannot encompass the future. All we can say is that poetry is defined by poets. With each new poet, with each new poem, the definition somewhat changes.

With Coleridge it is a dream. With Herrick it is an elation, anything gay. With Shakespeare it is immortality, the great or slim hope of it, at the very least the transference of his "breath."

For each poet—and for many poets in their different poems—poetry is something different. But it is never alien. No definition of poetry by poets that I can think of rules out another. Poetry is at once individual and all-inclusive. It is written by poets. What do these poets think of themselves and each other?

PART TWO

"On wings of paper"

"Perhaps no person can be a poet, or even enjoy poetry, without a certain unsoundness of mind," says Thomas Babington, Lord Macaulay. He is writing toward the middle of the nineteenth century, a period that is perhaps the last stand of "soundness." "A sound mind in a sound body" is still thought not only desirable but possible.

The Greeks, with their predilection for order, proportion and harmony, do not always consider them appropriate to poetry.

"All good poets, epic as well as lyric," Plato has Socrates say in the dialogue *Ion*, "compose their beautiful poems, not by art, but because they are inspired and possessed. And as the Corybantian revelers when they dance are not in their right mind, so the lyric poets are not in their right mind when they are composing their beautiful strains; but when falling under the power of music and metre they are inspired and possessed; like Bacchic maidens who draw milk and honey from the rivers when they are under the influence of Dionysus, but not when they are in their right mind.

"And the soul of the lyric poet does the same, as they themselves say; for they tell us that they bring songs from the honeyed fountains, calling them out of the gardens and dells of the Muses; they, like the bees, winging their way from flower to flower.

"And this is true, for the poet is a light and wingèd and holy thing, and there is no invention in him until he has been inspired and is out of his senses, and the mind is no longer in him."

In *Phaedrus*, Plato again quotes Socrates: "There are several kinds of divine madness. That which proceeds from the Muses, taking possession of a tender and unoccupied soul, awakening and bacchically inspiring it toward songs and other poetry, adorning myriads of ancient deeds, instructs succeeding generations. But he who, without this madness from the Muses, approaches the poetical gates, having persuaded himself that by art alone he may become sufficiently a poet, will find in the end his own imperfection, and see the poetry of his cold prudence vanish into nothingness before the light of that which has sprung from divine insanity."

"Divine insanity" may have some correspondence with what, in our own time, T. S. Eliot calls, in his essay on Dante, "the *high dream.*" "The modern world," he writes, "seems capable only of the *low dream.*" Is this a distasteful side glance at the erotic content of Freudian symbolism?

Shakespeare seems unconcerned about "higher" or "lower" forms of imagination. Coleridge's distinction between "imagination" and "fancy" would leave him cold. He moves too freely from one to the other to care about it. But he does exercise the maker's privilege of seeing through them all. Being a poet, he can be playful about "the poet."

In *A Midsummer Night's Dream,* Theseus answers Hippolita's remark, " 'Tis strange, my Theseus, that these lovers speak of," with lines seldom quoted in full when the passage is excerpted among the "great speeches":

More strange than true: I never may believe
These antic fables, nor these fairy toys.
Lovers and madmen have such seething brains,
Such shaping fantasies, that apprehend
More than cool reason ever comprehends.
The lunatic, the lover and the poet
Are of imagination all compact:
One sees more devils than vast hell can hold,
That is, the madman: the lover, all as frantic,
Sees Helen's beauty in a brow of Egypt:
The poet's eye, in a fine frenzy rolling,
Doth glance from heaven to earth, from earth to heaven;
And as imagination bodies forth
The forms of things unknown, the poet's pen
Turns them to shapes, and gives to airy nothing
A local habitation and a name.
Such tricks hath strong imagination,
That, if it would but apprehend some joy,
It comprehends some bringer of that joy;
Or in the night, imagining some fear,
How easy is a bush supposed a bear!

In the speech all imagination is a form of deception. Perhaps the poet is set apart from the lunatic and the lover by being the deceiver rather than the deceived. In any event, Theseus distrusts them all. It is, of course, one of Shakespeare's characters speaking, not Shakespeare himself. But he seems to be smiling through the lines.

As Thomas Carew concludes "Ingrateful beauty threatened" (poem 4):

Wise poets, that wrapt truth in tales,
Knew her themselves through all her veils.

This conception of the imagination reappears, with inimitable modifications, in Wallace Stevens. He writes in "A high-toned old Christian woman" (*Collected Poems*, page 59): "Poetry is the supreme fiction, madame." And in "Notes toward a supreme fiction" (page 380) he elaborates his idea of myth and poetry as fictions paralleling "reality" in such lines as:

The poem goes from the poet's gibberish to
The gibberish of the vulgate and back again.

What opinions do these highly unrealistic people have of each other and themselves? Another contemporary poet, who has had more than a cursory glance at the past as well as at himself, expresses it roundly.

15. *no man,if men are gods*

E. E. CUMMINGS

no man,if men are gods;but if gods must
be men,the sometimes only man is this
(most common,for each anguish is his grief;
and,for his joy is more than joy,most rare)

a fiend,if fiends speak truth;if angels burn

by their own generous completely light,
an angel;or(as various worlds he'll spurn
rather than fail immeasurable fate)
coward,clown,traitor,idiot,dreamer,beast—

such was a poet and shall be and is

—who'll solve the depths of horror to defend
a sunbeam's architecture with his life:
and carve immortal jungles of despair
To hold a mountain's heartbeat in his hand

Shakespeare's "fine frenzy" is articulated by Cummings' poet, who is and is not man, god, fiend, angel, coward, clown, traitor, idiot, dreamer, beast.

An arc refracting opposites, the poem brings together Apollonian order—it is a sonnet—and Dionysian abandon—the sonnet form is dispersed and reassembled. So, too, is the order of the words: the angels that burn "by their own generous completely light." Their light is more than completely generous, it is also completely light.

Cummings' poet is everything except one: he is not man, "if men are gods." He is not, that is, the all-powerful male of technological "progress," the engineer moving mountains to extract uranium. The poet's exploration, with its own risks, is for equally fissionable material, "a mountain's heartbeat." His balancing of opposites, of heartbeats and "immortal jungles of despair," of "depths of horror" and "a sunbeam's architecture," yields little but loveliness.

16. *The story of Phoebus and Daphne applied, etc.*

EDMUND WALLER

Thyrsis, a youth of the inspired train,
Fair Sacharissa loved, but loved in vain;
Like Phoebus sung the no less amorous boy;
Like Daphne she, as lovely and as coy;
With numbers he the flying nymph pursues,
With numbers, such as Phoebus' self might use;
Such is the chase, when love and fancy leads
O'er craggy mountains, and through flowery meads;
Invoked to testify the lover's care,
Or form some image of his cruel fair:

Urged with his fury like a wounded deer
O'er these he fled, and now approaching near,
Had reached the nymph with his harmonious lay,
Whom all his charms could not incline to stay.
Yet what he sung in his immortal strain,
Though unsuccessful, was not sung in vain;
All but the nymph that should redress his wrong,
Attend his passion, and approve his song.
  Like Phoebus thus acquiring unsought praise,
  He catched at love, and filled his arm with bays.

One of the rôles Cummings assigns the poet is played by the hero of this seventeenth-century retelling of a Greek myth.

As the god Phoebus Apollo becomes man in his pursuit of Daphne, who eludes him by turning into a laurel bush, so Thyrsis becomes god-like, inspired by love. His "care" and the "image of his cruel fair" supply him with pastoral metaphors: "craggy mountains" and "flowery meads."

Waller's poet owes his triumph to his failure in courtship. His is a case of "compensation" or involuntary "sublimation." Poets often precede psychologists. In "Julian and Maddalo," Shelley says:

Most wretched men
Are cradled into poetry by wrong,
They learn in suffering what they teach in song.

And in the seventeenth-century Samuel Butler's "Fragments" are the lines:

And poets by their sufferings grow,—
As if there were no more to do,
To make a poet excellent,
But only want and discontent.

17. *The progress of poetry*

JONATHAN SWIFT

The farmer's goose, who in the stubble
Has fed without restraint or trouble,
Grown fat with corn and sitting still,
Can scarce get o'er the barndoor sill;
And hardly waddles forth to cool
Her belly in the neighboring pool:
Nor loudly cackles at the door;
For cackling shows the goose is poor.
  But, when she must be turned to graze,
And round the barren common strays,
Hard exercise and harder fare,
Soon make my dame grow lank and spare:
Her body light, she tries her wings,
And scorns the ground, and upward springs;
While all the parish, as she flies,
Hear sounds harmonious from the skies.
  Such is the poet fresh in pay,
The third night's profits of his play;
His morning draughts till noon can swill,
Among his brethren of the quill:
With good roast beef his belly full,
Grows lazy, foggy, fat, and dull.
Deep sunk in plenty and delight,
What poet e'er could take his flight?
Or, stuffed with phlegm up to the throat,
What poet e'er could sing a note?
Nor Pegasus could bear the load
Along the high celestial road;
The steed, oppressed, would break his girth,
To raise the lumber from the earth.
  But view him in another scene,
When all his drink is Hippocrene,
His money spent, his patrons fail,
His credit out for cheese and ale;

His two-years' coat so smooth and bare,
Through every thread it lets in air;
With hungry meals his body pined,
His guts and belly full of wind;
And like a jockey for a race,
His flesh brought down to flying case;
Now his exalted spirit loathes
Remembrances of food and clothes;
And up he rises, like a vapor,
Supported high on wings of paper;
He singing flies, and flying sings,
While from below all Grub Street rings.

Jonathan Swift is no respecter of people. His reputation as satirist rests chiefly on comparisons in *Gulliver's Travels* between humans and animals, not to the greater glory of the former.

Here he may seem to be taking literally Butler's ironic prescription. But his goose is no swan; she is a thoroughly domesticated fowl. Leanness permits her to fly over "all the parish." There is no question of the empyrean.

So his poet, "supported on wings of paper," making equally harmonious sounds, rises above London's Grub Street, described in the same century by Samuel Johnson as being "much inhabited by writers of small histories, dictionaries, and temporary poems, whence any mean production is called *grub-street*." The time is the first half of the eighteenth century, distinguished more for middle than for high flights of poetry.

The question Waller raises is still unanswered: What causes poetic talent? Waller begs it; his Thyrsis is already "of the inspired train." If irritation develops the pearl, it still does not account for the presence of nacre.

18. *The Mermaid Tavern*

JOHN KEATS

Souls of poets dead and gone,
What Elysium have ye known,
Happy field or mossy cavern,
Choicer than the Mermaid Tavern?
Have ye tippled drink more fine
Than mine host's Canary wine?
Or are fruits of paradise
Sweeter than those dainty pies
Of venison? O generous food!
Dressed as though bold Robin Hood
Would with his Maid Marian,
Sup and bowse from horn and can.

I have heard that on a day
Mine host's signboard flew away
Nobody knew whither, till
An astrologer's old quill
To a sheepskin gave the story:
Said he saw you in your glory
Underneath a new-old sign
Sipping beverage divine,
And pledging with contented smack
The Mermaid in the Zodiac.

Souls of poets dead and gone,
What Elysium have ye known,
Happy field or mossy cavern,
Choicer than the Mermaid Tavern?

Perhaps Grub Street, in poem 17, does not entirely represent its period, nor the flight of geese the level of late seventeenth- and early eighteenth-century poetry. But the more exalted trajectory of "mine host's signboard" does seem to fit the Elizabethan.

Surely not all the poets of that era are inspired by conviviality. There are plenty of literary hacks, second-rate dramatists, and third-rate sonneteers. But deprivation as the source of talent does not find widespread expression. It is natural for later poets to look back with affectionate nostalgia to a time that seems, at least, more exuberant and more propitious to the full flowering of poetry.

Nostalgia for past ages, golden or nonexistent, runs through much of Keats's poetry. Sometimes it can lead him to the brink of mawkishness, as in some lines of his beautiful "Ode to a Grecian urn." Here, in lighter vein, it is engagingly youthful and gay.

19. *To a skylark*

PERCY BYSSHE SHELLEY

Hail to thee, blithe spirit!
Bird thou never wert,
That from heaven or near it
Pourest thy full heart
In profuse strains of unpremeditated art.

Higher still and higher
From the earth thou springest
Like a cloud of fire;
The blue deep thou wingest,
And singing still dost soar, and soaring ever singest.

In the golden lightning
Of the sunken sun,
O'er which clouds are brightening,
Thou dost float and run
Like an unbodied joy whose race is just begun.

The pale purple even
Melts around thy flight;
Like a star of heaven
In the broad daylight.
Thou art unseen, but yet I hear thy shrill delight,

Keen as are the arrows
Of that silver sphere,
Whose intense lamp narrows
In the white dawn clear
Until we hardly see, we feel that it is there.

All the earth and air
With thy voice is loud,
As, when night is bare,
From one lonely cloud
The moon rains out her beams, and heaven is overflowed.

What thou art we know not;
What is most like thee?
From rainbow clouds there flow not
Drops so bright to see
As from thy presence showers a rain of melody.

Like a poet hidden
In the light of thought,
Singing hymns unbidden,
Till the world is wrought
To sympathy with hopes and fears it heeded not:

Like a high-born maiden
In a palace tower,
Soothing her love-laden
Soul in secret hour
With music sweet as love, which overflows her bower:

Like a glow-worm golden
In a dell of dew,
Scattering unbeholden
Its aërial hue
Among the flowers and grass which screen it from the view:

Like a rose embowered
In its own green leaves,
By warm winds deflowered,
Till the scent it gives
Makes faint with too much sweet those heavy-wingèd thieves:

Sound of vernal showers
On the twinkling grass,
Rain-awakened flowers,
All that ever was
Joyous and clear and fresh, thy music doth surpass:

Teach us, sprite or bird,
What sweet thoughts are thine:
I have never heard
Praise of love or wine
That panted forth a flood of rapture so divine.

Chorus hymeneal
Or triumphant chant,
Matched with thine would be all
But an empty vaunt,
A thing wherein we feel there is some hidden want.

What objects are the fountains
Of thy happy strain?
What fields, or waves, or mountains?
What shapes of sky or plain?
What love of thine own kind? what ignorance of pain?

With thy clear keen joyance
Languor cannot be:
Shadow of annoyance
Never came near thee:
Thou lovest, but ne'er knew love's sad satiety.

Waking or asleep,
Thou of death must deem
Things more true and deep
Than we mortals dream,
Or how could thy notes flow in such a crystal stream?

We look before and after,
And pine for what is not:
Our sincerest laughter
With some pain is fraught;
Our sweetest songs are those that tell of saddest thought.

Yet, if we could scorn
  Hate and pride and fear,
If we were things born
  Not to shed a tear,
I know not how thy joy we ever should come near.

Better than all measures
  Of delightful sound,
Better than all treasures
  That in books are found,
Thy skill to poet were, thou scorner of the ground!

Teach me half the gladness
  That thy brain must know,
Such harmonious madness
  From my lips would flow
The world should listen then, as I am listening now.

Poets, and not only poets, are continually harking back to the freedom of a golden age. As we follow them back in time, the age is pushed progressively earlier, until it recedes into prehistory.

The prehuman, or other than human, also abounds in symbols of liberation. Among the so-called lower animals birds, perhaps because of their flight, seem highest. They are frequently symbols for poets, for whom their "art"—as it does for Shelley—seems "unpremeditated."

Shelley's "To a skylark," written in 1820, tells us what he wishes the poet—himself—could be. Somewhat earlier William Blake says, "One power alone makes a poet. Imagination, the Divine Vision." And he goes on, countering Wordsworth's location of inspiration in nature, "Natural objects always weaken, deaden and obliterate inspiration in me."

Whether in direct answer or not, William Morris—possibly sitting, a good many years later, in one of the chairs that bear his name—retorts, "That talk of inspiration is sheer nonsense . . . there is no such thing; it is a mere matter of craftsmanship." Why, if craftsmanship is so all-important, does he call it "mere"? This might be called a non-Freudian slip.

Shelley certainly does not agree with Blake's aversion to nature.

But he would find abhorrent Morris' denial of inspiration. His wish is that his art should be *all* inspiration:

Like a poet hidden
In the light of thought,
Singing hymns unbidden,
Till the world is wrought
To sympathy with hopes and fears it heeded not . . .

Like the Blake of some of the "Prophetic Books," Shelley might seem to be demanding more of inspiration than inspiration can give:

Teach me half the gladness
That thy brain must know,
Such harmonious madness
From my lips would flow
The world should listen then, as I am listening now.

Yet though the poem *says* this, what does it *do*? It creates a form that circles, darts, and soars: "And singing still dost soar, and soaring ever singest." The sound of each stanza is shaped like a lark; each reels off and rolls out in spiraling flight and song, all the more glorious for being "premeditated."

This is William Morris' "mere craftsmanship," indeed, put to the service of "Imagination." Following an "impossible" ideal, the poet achieves it. The world that has ears does listen. What it hears, through Shelley's calculated cadences, is the spontaneous delight he experienced, the song of the skylark caged in the action of the poem.

20. *Chaucer*

HENRY WADSWORTH LONGFELLOW

An old man in a lodge within a park;
The chamber walls depicted all around
With portraitures of huntsman, hawk, and hound,
And the hurt deer. He listeneth to the lark,
Whose song comes with the sunshine through the dark
Of painted glass in leaden lattice bound;

He listeneth and he laugheth at the sound,
Then writeth in a book like any clerk.
He is the poet of the dawn, who wrote
The Canterbury Tales, and his old age
Made beautiful with song; and as I read
I hear the crowing cock, I hear the note
Of lark and linnet, and from every page
Rise odors of ploughed field or flowery mead.

It is customary to think of poets as young. Yet who can picture Whitman, Tennyson or Browning without a beard? Quite appropriately another elderly poet, Henry Wadsworth Longfellow, pays tribute to the grand old man of English poetry.

Perhaps we think of Geoffrey Chaucer as perennially on in years because both his person and his language are remote in time. Remote, yet not foreign; which makes attempts to do him into modern English so generally inept.

The more removed the language, the greater leeway there is for translation. It never can hope to reproduce, but it may achieve comparable feats in English.

Chaucer cannot be "translated." His language is the ancestor of our own, its syllables altered and lengthened; rather, ours have been altered and clipped. How could such apparently simple lines be rendered?

And smale foweles maken melodyë,
That slepen al the nyght with open eyë.

Yet the attempt has been made, at least twice:

And the small fowl are making melody
That sleep away the night with open eye.

And:

And many little birds make melody
That sleep through all the night with open eye.

The first "translation" destroys the cadence and mars the extraordinary consonance, in the original, between the sound and the sense. "Fowl," descended though it is from "foweles," suggests the screechings of the barnyard. And "sleep away the night" is obvious padding, in which Chaucer, for all the seeming ease of his style, never indulges. All the urgency, the lovely idea of impatient waiting, has gone out of "open eye." So, too, "many" and "through" in the second version are merely additional words filling out the meter.

As Longfellow writes, catching the flavor of Chaucer's verse, "He is the poet of the dawn." To read him we must get up early with his Early English. Then we can really hear "the crowing cock," smell the "ploughed field" and enjoy that savor of maturity "made beautiful with song" that Longfellow's portrait so beautifully conveys.

21. *John Webster*

ALGERNON CHARLES SWINBURNE

Thunder, the flesh quails, and the soul bows down.
  Night: east, west, south, and northward, very night.
  Star upon struggling star strives into sight,
Star after shuddering star the deep storms drown.
The very throne of night, her very crown,
  A man lays hand on, and usurps her right.
  Song from the highest of heaven's imperious height
Shoots, as a fire to smite some towering town.
Rage, anguish, harrowing fear, heart-crazing crime,
Make monstrous all the murderous face of time
  Shown in the spheral orbit of a glass.
Revolving earth cries out from all her graves.
Frail, on frail rafts, across wide-wallowing waves,
  Shapes here and there of child and mother pass.

What a different world is entered here. Rarely, I think, does one poet so vividly realize another poet's effect, without recourse to his style or special language.

Webster, in his plays, comes close to Cummings' "a fiend,if fiends speak truth" and Swinburne re-creates their nightmare intensity; their quality of vortex, "Shown in the spheral orbit of a glass."

Swinburne's tendency to excessive alliteration, which makes cloying some of his more mellifluous poems, is here so brought under control as to be scarcely noticeable even in "wide-wallowing waves" or "Star upon struggling star strives into sight."

It is interesting to compare this with T. S. Eliot's reference to Webster in "Whispers of immortality" (*Collected Poems*, page 53), with its opening understatement: "Webster was much possessed by death."

22. *An ode for Ben Jonson*

ROBERT HERRICK

Ah, Ben!
Say how, or when
Shall we, thy guests,
Meet at those lyric feasts
Made at the Sun,
The Dog, the Triple Tun?
Where we such clusters had,
As made us nobly wild, not mad;
And yet each verse of thine
Outdid the meat, outdid the frolic wine.

My Ben!
Or come again,
Or send to us
Thy wit's great overplus;
But teach us yet
Wisely to husband it,
Lest we that talent spend;
And having once brought to an end
That precious stock, the store
Of such a wit the world should have no more.

This testifies to far different coruscations. Part of its wit lies in the title and in the gradually lengthening lines leading to expectations of oratory; at least a poetic after-dinner speech.

But along with the sack he absorbed as divinity student and youngest of Jonson's cronies, Herrick took in as well his master's literary precepts. One of these may well have been (since Jonson claims no jealousy of "My Beloved, the Author Mr. William Shakespeare") long-winded Polonius' "Brevity is the soul of wit."

Herrick's poems seldom exceed their lyric point. As here, having been wisely husbanded, it spreads in the mind.

23. *On Donne's poetry*

SAMUEL TAYLOR COLERIDGE

With Donne, whose muse on dromedary trots,
Wreathe iron pokers into true-love knots;
Rhyme's sturdy cripple, fancy's maze and clue,
Wit's forge and fire-blast, meaning's press and screw.

Like Ezra Pound's characterization of Browning, "Old Hippety-Hop o' the accents" (from "Mesmerism," *Personae*, page 13), Coleridge's quatrain characterizes him as much as it does John Donne. Coleridge seems to appreciate and undervalue Donne in about equal proportions.

He is absolutely right on three counts: "fancy's maze and clue, Wit's forge and fire-blast, meaning's press and screw." His chief misinterpretation is due to a false equation between music and smoothness. Donne's exquisite lyricism seems to evade him. Since it includes irony, it trots "on dromedary." Since it is baritone rather than tenor, pokers are twisted into love-knots.

The latter is nonetheless a superb image for Donne's love poems, which are never merely graceful but do twist the iron of his feeling. To Coleridge's rather categorical mind, wit and feeling are thought inimical. He cannot conceive of them as existing together.

That Coleridge is at cross-purposes is evidenced by two remarks in his critical writing. In *Biographia Literaria* (1817), he speaks of the typical faults of "our older poets": ". . . from Donne to Cowley, we find the most fantastic out-of-the-way thoughts, but in the most pure and genuine mother English. . . Our faulty elder poets sacrificed the passion and passionate flow of poetry to the subtleties of intellect, and to the starts of wit. . ."

Yet in his *Miscellanies* he can say of Donne: "Wonder-exciting vigour, intenseness, and peculiarity of thought, using at will the almost boundless stores of a capacious memory and exercised on subjects where we have no right to expect it—this is the wit of Donne!"

24. *Edward Lear*

W. H. AUDEN

Left by his friend to breakfast alone on the white
Italian shore, his Terrible Demon arose
Over his shoulder; he wept to himself in the night,
A dirty landscape-painter who hated his nose.

The legions of cruel inquisitive They
Were so many and big like dogs: he was upset
By Germans and boats; affection was miles away:
But guided by tears he successfully reached his Regret.

How prodigious the welcome was. Flowers took his hat
And bore him off to introduce him to the tongs;
The demon's false nose made the table laugh; a cat
Soon had him waltzing madly, let him squeeze her hand;
Words pushed him to the piano to sing comic songs;

And children swarmed to him like settlers. He became a land.

One of the wittiest poets of our time pays tribute here to a poet whose wit is associated with childhood. Combining Cummings' "coward" and "clown," Lear plays on his own frights and despairs to win the affection of things and children.

25. *By way of preface*

EDWARD LEAR

"How pleasant to know Mr. Lear!"
Who has written such volumes of stuff!
Some think him ill-tempered and queer,
But a few think him pleasant enough.

His mind is concrete and fastidious,
His nose is remarkably big;
His visage is more or less hideous,
His beard it resembles a wig.

He has ears, and two eyes, and ten fingers,
Leastways if you reckon two thumbs;
Long ago he was one of the singers,
But now he is one of the dumbs.

He sits in a beautiful parlor,
With hundreds of books on the wall;
He drinks a great deal of Marsala,
But never gets tipsy at all.

He has many friends, laymen and clerical,
Old Foss is the name of his cat:
His body is perfectly spherical,
He weareth a runcible hat.

When he walks in a waterproof white,
The children run after him so!
Calling out, "He's come out in his night-
Gown, that crazy old Englishman, oh!"

He weeps by the side of the ocean,
He weeps on the top of the hill;
He purchases pancakes and lotion,
And chocolate shrimps from the mill.

He reads but he cannot speak Spanish,
He cannot abide ginger-beer;
Ere the days of his pilgrimage vanish,
How pleasant to know Mr. Lear!

In Lear's own preface to *A Book of Nonsense* (1846) he reaches a rapport with his nose. It is at least attention-getting. Even perfectly ordinary things, fingers and thumbs, can excite admiration, like a baby playing with its toes. Everything is regarded with affectionate astonishment; tears and timidity are the life of the party.

Reading Auden's sonnet, he looks up with delighted amazement: "Posterity too?"

26. *Doctor Bill Williams*

ERNEST WALSH

There was once upon a time a man who lost the
Dictionary and he kept saying ladies and gentlemen
I have nothing up my sleeves and the audience smiled
Since the children were present and after all the children
Were happy and the happiness of children is a serious matter
If one lives in Rutherford New Jersey and owns a car and
Can never be caught in the wrong church on Sunday I mean
That if you suddenly saw a field of sunflowers and
Remembered your wife telling the maid that your room
Must be cleaned this time as a room should be cleaned
And absolutely you cannot keep that appointment with
Mrs. MacFalley the woman with waved hair and slim
Everything and besides the taxes are due on the
Thirty-first and the mirrors forget everything they see.

Ernest Walsh's "Doctor Bill Williams" represents posterity in reverse. Walsh died of consumption in 1926.

His poems, first published in *This Quarter*, one of the livelier "little magazines" of the twenties, are full of gusto and delicacies. In some he adopts a pseudo-archaic style, which seems to free his tongue for racy description: "My duchess was the werst she laffed she bitte" (*Poems & Sonnets*, page 96).

His poem to William Carlos Williams is so much of the essence, it sounds like yesterday. The almost breathless pace, the passion, the passionate interest in detail, in American detail, the rambling route to a point, and the point made, are all caught, by a nice irony, in a form that is anathema to the poet of *Paterson:* the sonnet. It's an extraordinarily limber sonnet.

27. *London 1802*

WILLIAM WORDSWORTH

Milton! thou shouldst be living at this hour:
England hath need of thee: she is a fen
Of stagnant waters: altar, sword, and pen,
Fireside, the heroic wealth of hall and bower,
Have forfeited their ancient English dower
Of inward happiness. We are selfish men;
Oh! raise us up, return to us again;
And give us manners, virtue, freedom, power.
Thy soul was like a star, and dwelt apart;
Thou hadst a voice whose sound was like the sea:
Pure as the naked heavens, majestic, free,
So didst thou travel on life's common way,
In cheerful godliness; and yet thy heart
The lowliest duties on herself did lay.

Wordsworth's portrait of Milton as England's guiding star recalls Cummings' angel, "if angels burn / by their own generous completely light." There is such nobility and conviction in the sonnet that I could wish one word away.

Wordsworth, in other poems, can be embarrassingly unaware of implications. He has little of that quality vaguely called a sense of humor. Like his friend Coleridge, he can make inadvertent jokes, as when, in "The thorn," he gravely measures a puddle from side to side: " 'Tis three feet long, and two feet wide." One shares his affection for the little water-body, but it is difficult to restrain a smile.

"Godliness" is so all-inclusive a characterization that *any* qualification raises doubts. To call it "cheerful"—to *have* to call it "cheerful"—makes it seem bleak indeed.

As with the pond, Wordsworth's admiration is undisturbed. We realize how deeply he is moved by the patience, singleness of purpose and courage—if not always good cheer—of the author of *Samson Agonistes*.

28. *On Shakespeare*

JOHN MILTON

What needs my Shakespeare for his honored bones
The labor of an age in pilèd stones?
Or that his hallowed relics should be hid
Under a star-ypointing pyramid?
Dear son of memory, great heir of fame,
What need'st thou such weak witness of thy name?
Thou in our wonder and astonishment
Has built thyself a livelong monument.
For whilst, to the shame of slow-endeavoring art,
Thy easy numbers flow, and that each heart
Hath from the leaves of thy unvalued book
Those Delphic lines with deep impression took;
Then thou, our fancy of itself bereaving,
Dost make us marble with too much conceiving,
And so sepulchred in such pomp dost lie
That kings for such a tomb would wish to die.

unvalued: inestimable

This is in the marmoreal vein of William Browne's elegy (poem 5) written some twenty years earlier. Its "conceit" is almost identical: Shakespeare's readers become his monuments.

But there is a difference. This is a tribute from one of the monuments; from a young man's fancy that, for a time at least, the "easy numbers" of Shakespeare's art have, like a gorgon, turned to stone. What is there left, with "slow-endeavoring art," to write about?

29. *Shakespeare*

MATTHEW ARNOLD

Others abide our question. Thou art free.
We ask and ask: thou smilest and art still,
Out-topping knowledge. For the loftiest hill
That to the stars uncrowns his majesty,
Planting his steadfast footsteps in the sea,
Making the heaven of heavens his dwelling-place,
Spares but the cloudy border of his base
To the foiled searching of mortality;
And thou, who didst the stars and sunbeams know,
Self-schooled, self-scanned, self-honored, self-secure,
Didst walk on earth unguessed-at. Better so!
All pains the immortal spirit must endure,
  All weakness that impairs, all griefs that bow,
  Find their sole voice in that victorious brow.

Arnold's more affectionate tribute to Shakespeare discovers the "mountain's heartbeat" through "jungles of despair": "All pains the immortal spirit must endure."

Arnold's image, "Planting his steadfast footsteps in the sea," may to the literal eye appear incongruous. How can foot*steps* be steadfast? Like Cubist painting, the image includes action and time. The mountain is continuously taking the stride that maintains its steadfast base. This seems to anticipate, too, some of the translations in physics between matter and energy.

Another "frozen action" is in the last line: "Find their sole voice in that victorious brow." Like Shakespeare's own "speaking breast" (poem 7), this locates the silent speech that precedes the spoken word.

Shakespeare, "unguessed-at" in his lifetime, is mightily guessed at since. One of the chief reasons advanced for giving his plays more aristocratic authorship has been his dubious schooling. Yet Arnold, one of the most learned schoolmen of the nineteenth century, praises him as "self-schooled, self-scanned, self-honored, self-secure."

Reading the proposed claimants should be enough to settle the issue. Lord Bacon, for instance, on the basis of his acknowledged works, could not possibly have written the plays. On the other hand, Shakespeare, with his tongue in his cheek, *might* have ghost-written the *Essays.*

30. *Was it the proud full sail of his great verse*
WILLIAM SHAKESPEARE

Was it the proud full sail of his great verse,
Bound for the prize of all-too-precious you,
That did my ripe thoughts in my brain inhearse,
Making their tomb the womb wherein they grew?
Was it his spirit, by spirits taught to write
Above a mortal pitch, that struck me dead?
No, neither he, nor his compeers by night
Giving him aid, my verse astonishèd.
He, nor that affable familiar ghost,
Which nightly gulls him with intelligence,
As victors, of my silence cannot boast;
I was not sick of any fear from thence:
  But when your countenance filled up his line,
  Then lacked I matter; that enfeebled mine.

Out-topping Arnold, Shakespeare provides a further mystery in Sonnet LXXXVI.

Shakespeare's sonnets are to begin with a Sherlock Holmes' despair: all motive and no clue. To whom are they addressed? in what order? and by whom? Even if it *is* Shakespeare there is little, outside of his work, to identify him.

Critics who object that "obscurity" and "private allusion" are alienating the audience for poetry can scarcely have taken into account these enormously popular poems. Are they intended for the eyes and ears of two or three friends alone? for a coterie? for the world? Is it a sequence? a scrambled series of sequences? an assortment of individual poems? Why do they vary so in inspiration? Do they include some that his friend, his mistress or Lord Bacon wrote to *him?*

This sonnet is the core of a story whose details are withheld. The "rival poet" is alluded to in several adjacent sonnets, then disappears forever. Speculation—there is nothing else to go on—has run through Christopher Marlowe, Samuel Daniel, George Chapman and many other poets of the time. It remains a beautiful enigma.

Apart from identity, what does the sonnet say? Is Shakespeare admitting to a greater than himself? Neither the rival nor his supernatural crony—suggesting Mephistopheles in Marlowe's *Doctor Faustus*—gives Shakespeare pause. It is only "when your countenance filled up his line" that Shakespeare is, he says, silenced.

Here is an ambiguity worthy of William Empson's *Seven Types*. Is Shakespeare saying, "When he succeeded in describing you better than I"? Such an admission undermines the earlier boast. "When his verse is so filled up with you that I realize you're *his* friend"? This seems more likely; but there is still a third possibility.

"Your countenance" may be taken in the sense of "your countenancing it": "When you think his verse good, that knocks the wind out of *my* sail." This completes the image of the first line. The rival poet's "great verse" is not a "proud full sail" until the friend's approval puffs it up.

The ghost of Shakespeare chuckles in the wings.

31. *Whoever you are holding me now in hand*

WALT WHITMAN

Whoever you are holding me now in hand,
Without one thing all will be useless,
I give you fair warning before you attempt me further,
I am not what you supposed, but far different.

Who is he that would become my follower?
Who would sign himself a candidate for my affections?

The way is suspicious, the result uncertain, perhaps destructive,
You would have to give up all else, I alone would expect to be your sole
and exclusive standard,

Your novitiate would even then be long and exhausting,
The whole past theory of your life and all conformity to the lives around you would have to be abandoned,
Therefore release me now before troubling yourself any further, let go your hand from my shoulders,
Put me down and depart on your way.

Or else by stealth in some wood for trial,
Or back of a rock in the open air,
(For in any roof's room of a house I emerge not, nor in company,
And in libraries I lie as one dumb, a gawk, or unborn, or dead,)
But just possibly with you on a high hill, first watching lest any person for miles around approach unawares,
Or possibly with you sailing at sea, or on the beach of the sea or some quiet island,
Here to put your lips upon mine I permit you,
With the comrade's long-dwelling kiss, or the new husband's kiss,
For I am the new husband and I am the comrade.

Or if you will, thrusting me beneath your clothing,
Where I may feel the throbs of your heart or rest upon your hip,
Carry me when you go forth over land or sea;
For thus merely touching you is enough, is best,
And thus touching you would I silently sleep and be carried eternally.

But these leaves conning you con at peril,
For these leaves and me you will not understand,
They will elude you at first and still more afterward, I will certainly elude you,
Even while you should think you had unquestionably caught me, behold!
Already you see I have escaped from you.

For it is not for what I have put into it that I have written this book,
Nor is it by reading it you will acquire it,
Nor do those know me best who admire me and vauntingly praise me,
Nor will the candidates for my love (unless at most a very few) prove victorious,

Nor will my poems do good only, they will do just as much evil, perhaps
 more,
For it is useless without that which you may guess at many times and not
 hit, that which I hinted at;
Therefore release me and depart on your way.

This poem from the group called *Calamus* (a reed pen), first published in the third edition (1860) of *Leaves of Grass*, is, like most of Whitman's poetry, a self-portrait. Is he a supreme egotist? He appears in nearly all of his poems; nearly all could be called "Song of Myself."

What do they say about "myself"? Who is the "I" of his poems? They give us his name, sometimes where he is living, and that is about all. Little biography of Walt Whitman, the man, can be extracted from Walt Whitman, the poet. Rather less, I should think, than from Shakespeare in his sonnets. As to facts, in his poems at least, Whitman is reticent.

The "I" in his poems is the poem. That is his mask; what Ezra Pound would call his *persona:* a personality assumed, not as disguise, but to release and realize a poetic potentiality. Pound has many masks; he calls his poems (apart from the *Cantos*) *Personae.* In one of them, "A pact" (page 89), he outgrows his detestation of Whitman: "Let there be commerce between us."

Whitman has the one mask. He identifies with his poems, and his poems identify with everything. Their "I" is curiously like the editorial "we." At intervals an editor on several newspapers, among them the Brooklyn *Eagle*, he is writing in many of his poems emotional editorials. They publicize emotions very much as the editorial writer publicizes opinions.

This is what gives them, I feel, their unique tone of an American speaking to Americans. His "free verse" has been justified as deriving from the King James Version of the Bible. Some of his rhythms are undoubtedly inspired by it, but the language seldom.

Whitman's chief editorial opinion is a belief in democracy. He transmutes this into poetry by taking it literally; as Marianne Moore, quoting Yeats, might put it, he is a "literalist of the imagination." We are all "leaves of grass." As one leaf, Whitman would express what is common to all.

The "I" in "Whoever you are holding me now in hand" is clearly his book. Its wish is for the closest possible contact with the reader: to be held by the shoulders; to be read secretly; to be put under his clothes. This desire for nearness extends to most of Whitman's poems. They approach intimately all conditions of men, all qualities of experience. Baseball teams that embrace each other and shed tears of victory might consider some of his expressions "unmanly."

Like nearly all great poets, Whitman can be tiresome. When we return to him, the astonishing thing is his great variety within singleness of purpose. Expectation never quite catches up with his performance. "Already you see I have escaped from you." His identifications go deeper, often, than we would like to admit about ourselves. "The way is suspicious, the result uncertain, perhaps destructive."

His poems *have* had a destructive effect on later writing. This is true, to a degree, of any great style, especially one so thoroughly self-devised. While reading him, it imposes itself. It seems to supersede all other styles: "I alone would expect to be your sole and exclusive standard."

Taking this at its face value, his imitators execute the manner without comprehending the standard. Bulk, they seem to think, the undigested *material* of poetry, is enough. Get close to unshaped life; the shapes will emerge.

This is partly true. But there is a saturation point for Indian place names and the cataloguing of rivers, battlegrounds, and industrial equipment. What makes Whitman's style so compelling, especially to American writers, is its obvious difference, its almost complete break with what goes before it. It seems so easy and natural; a "mere" outpouring.

It is not, for Whitman, as effortless and spontaneous as it may appear. His notes and preparations for *Leaves of Grass* are revealing. They indicate the *ideal* of spontaneity, and crafty ways for snaring it.

"Make no quotations," he writes, "and no reference to any other writers. Lumber the writing with nothing—let it go as lightly as the bird flies in the air or a fish swims in the sea. Avoid all poetical similes; be faithful to the perfect likelihoods of nature—healthy, exact, simple, disdaining ornaments. Do not go into criticisms or arguments at all; make full-blooded, rich, flush, natural works. Insert natural things, indestructibles, idioms, characteristics, rivers, states, persons, &c. Be full of *strong sensual germs. . . .* Poet! beware lest your poems are made in the spirit that comes from the study of pictures of things—and not from the spirit that comes from the contact with real things themselves."

32. *In my craft or sullen art*

DYLAN THOMAS

In my craft or sullen art
Exercised in the still night
When only the moon rages
And the lovers lie abed
With all their griefs in their arms,
I labour by singing light
Not for ambition or bread
Or the strut and trade of charms
On the ivory stages
But for the common wages
Of their most secret heart.

Not for the proud man apart
From the raging moon I write
On these spindrift pages
Nor for the towering dead
With their nightingales and psalms
But for the lovers, their arms
Round the griefs of the ages,
Who pay no praise or wages
Nor heed my craft or art.

This autobiography of a poem throws light on the incomparable lyric gifts of the Welsh poet Dylan Thomas, tragically dead in 1953.

It begins with four expressions of increasing effort; this is no "unpremeditated art." It is a "craft." It is "sullen." It is "exercised." "I labour," he says, "by singing light."

"Singing light" is the culmination of the effort. Like Shelley's skylark, it is at once inspiration and achievement.

He has said that "the moon rages." The moon is the traditional light of lovers and poets: a good light for making love and to sing by. It is also a transforming light. As it "rages"—being, too, associated with madness—it emerges fitfully from behind clouds. The appearance of everything is magically altered and intensified. How shall such moments of vision, such sudden transformations, be put into words?

The prose writer might describe it: "I was working at my desk and looked out the window and the moonlight suddenly shone so brightly it was as if I could hear it." This would be a true but lengthy account of something that has happened instantaneously.

"Singing light" does more than tell us, "I have had a feeling of beauty and mystery." It crystallizes this feeling. It communicates the intensity with which it has been felt. As nearly as possible, it *is* the feeling.

Alternately sullen and exultant, like the night sky, the poem follows the course of the poet's emotion and his struggle to express it. The two become one: a triumph of craft.

For whom is he writing? As he says, the poem serves no practical purpose: "ambition or bread / Or the strut and trade of charms." It is not written for practical or ambitious people: "the proud man apart / From the raging moon." Like Cummings' poet, Thomas is "no man,if men are gods."

Nor is he writing "for the towering dead / With their nightingales and psalms." The allusion is unspecific but suggests two currents of poetry, the romantic and the religious: I think of Keats and of David of Israel. But the lines serve to tell us that his poems do not compete with anyone, living or dead. They are addressed to "the lovers, their arms / Round the griefs of the ages."

Why should lovers, who if anyone is are happy, be holding grief in their arms? Is each the other's grief? It does not sound like a bitter poem; but if this is the interpretation, nothing could be more bitter.

Like the crystallization of "singing light," the phrase calls for loving attention. Who suffers grief? Everyone. How is grief comforted? By being taken in the arms. The lovers are the only people who, by taking each other in their arms, assuage all grief, "the griefs of the ages."

What is the poem saying? Love. Not the word "love." The action, love; that intimate rapport that is inexpressible: "the common wages /

Of their most secret heart." The poem's rapports with the moon, with the lovers, with the very "spindrift pages" on which it is written, are all examples of love in action.

The poem itself is a very special and paradoxical example. Love permeates it, like the rhymes that weave in and out. Love is its motive. Love is its hoped-for reward. But the lovers will pay no attention to it.

Why should they? They are themselves experiencing what the poet wishes for. This is at once the paradox and the triumph of the poem. It has so truly expressed the rapport of love that it knows such expression is impossible.

When Dylan Thomas speaks of his art as "sullen," he reveals an impatience that is common to most poets. Their longing, in solitude—to which "sullen" also refers—is to reach the "most secret heart"; there to divulge some experience that has transcended the ordinary. Their "labour" is to find expression that will *seem* as direct and spontaneous as the feelings that inspire them. As Marianne Moore says in "The past is the present" (*Collected Poems*, page 93): "Ecstasy affords / the occasion and expediency determines the form."

Keats expresses a similar impatience in the fourth stanza of his "Ode to a nightingale":

Away! away! For I will fly to thee,
Not charioted by Bacchus and his pards,
But on the viewless wings of poesy,
Though the dull brain perplexes and retards:
Already with thee! tender is the night . . .

Another "literalist of the imagination," Keats cannot be content with thinking of the nightingale as merely a symbol of that freedom of song he desires for himself. In the excess of his emotion he would be instantly, actually transported: "Already with thee!"

For the moment, the imagination's "viewless wings" have triumphed over the reasoning mind, the "dull brain" that "perplexes and retards." As with Shakespeare's lark (poem 105), their flight is all the more believable for the moment of profound doubt that has preceded it.

Perhaps all poets share in this urgency, the impulse to "build that dome in air." But poets are as various as people. The direction of the impulse, its degree of intensity, its emotional climate are different for each.

Cummings' arc describes the infinite potentialities of the poet. The poems that follow represent realized segments of the arc. Each poet approaches his own "mountain's heartbeat" by a unique route, widely or narrowly diverging: from the cool, detached amusement of Carew to the absorbed identification of Keats and Shelley; from the temperate serenity of Chaucer to the tropic tempests of Webster; from the merriment of Herrick to the wistful humor of Lear and the savagery of Swift; from the public intimacy of Whitman to the intimate rapport of Dylan Thomas; from the dreaming music of Coleridge to the all-inclusive awareness of Shakespeare.

PART THREE

"May I be there to see"

In Section XIV of "Variations on a summer day" (*Collected Poems*, page 234), Wallace Stevens writes:

Words add to the senses. The words for the dazzle
Of mica, the dithering of grass,
The Arachne integument of dead trees,
Are the eye grown larger, more intense.

The enlargement or intensification of sensuous experience is common to all the arts. Each art makes its predominant appeal to one or another of the senses, but there are many interrelationships and interminglings. At one time or another poetry comes close to them all.

Surely the inescapable connection of poetry is with sound. A poem enters through the ear, including the inner ear of the silent reader. What the ear hears is a combination—always a different combination, a new proportion—of speech and music.

These two poles, speech and music, are themselves inconstant. There are many kinds of speech and many kinds of music. Consequently the ratios between them are incalculable.

The poems that follow explore some of these ratios, not systematically but rather in a series of forays in one direction or another. For convenience, not to imply an "order of merit" or any absolute distinction, these forays are divided into four groups: ballads in this section; songs in Part Four; lyrics in Part Five; and in Part Six, harmonic or orchestral poems. These musical analogies, it will be seen, are suggestive rather than definitive.

The ballad springs out of music and dancing. Like epic and other narrative poems and poetic drama, it has affinities as well with prose. They all overlap with what nowadays more customarily satisfies the narrative appetite: the short story, the novel, the prose play, and the motion picture.

A primary narrative interest is in what is going to happen next. The simplest stories—and ballads are usually that—satisfy this curiosity quickly and continuously.

But where prose is more apt to "get on with the story," poetry tends to dwell on, to "present" the sensations, images, thoughts, feelings that accompany narrative action. Prose need not be *without* such presentation, any more than poetry need be without narrative interest. It is rather a shift in the center of interest.

Hamlet is not without detective-story interest, though the unraveling of its plot, as such, scarcely competes with *The Adventures of Sherlock Holmes*. Nor would the latter be improved or "lifted" by giving extended soliloquies to the detective, to Dr. Watson, or to the foiled villain. The main interest is *in* the plot. That, in the all-embracing sense of the word, is its poetry; its "making."

The ballad has a double, interwoven center of interest: its story, and the way the story is carried forward by singing and dancing rhythms.

33. *The laily worm and the machrel of the sea*

ANONYMOUS

"I was but seven year auld
  When my mither she did dee;
My father married the ae warst woman
  The warld did ever see.

"For she has made me the laily worm,
  That lies at the fit of the tree,
An' my sister Masery she's made
  The machrel of the sea.

"An' every Saturday at noon
  The machrel comes to me,
An' she takes my laily head
  An' lays it on her knee,
She kaims it wi' a siller kaim,
  An' washes it in the sea.

"Seven knights hae I slain,
  Sin I lay at the fit of the tree,
An' ye war na my ain father,
  The eighth ane ye should be."

"Sing on your song, ye laily worm,
  That ye did sing to me."
"I never sung that song but what
  I would sing it to thee.

"I was but seven year auld,
  When my mither she did dee;
My father married the ae warst woman
  The warld did ever see.

"For she changed me to the laily worm,
  That lies at the fit o' the tree,
And my sister Masery
  To the machrel of the sea.

"And every Saturday at noon
  The machrel comes to me,
An' she takes my laily head
  And lays it on her knee,
An' she kames it wi' a siller kame,
  An' washes it i' the sea.

"Seven knights have I slain
  Sin I lay at the fit o' the tree;
An' ye war na my ain father,
  The eighth ane ye should be."

He sent for his lady,
  As fast as send could be:
"Whar is my son that ye sent frae me,
  And my daughter, Lady Masery?"

"Your son is at our king's court,
  Serving for meat an' fee,
An' your daughter's at our queen's court,
  The queen's maiden to be."

"Ye lee, ye lee, ye ill woman,
  Sae loud as I hear ye lee;
My son's the laily worm
  That lies at the fit o' the tree,

And my daughter, Lady Masery,
  Is the machrel of the sea!"

She has tane a siller wan',
  An' gi'en him strokès three,
And he's started up the bravest knight
  That ever your eyes did see.

She has ta'en a small horn,
  An' loud and shrill blew shee,
An' a' the fish came her until
  But the machrel of the sea:
"Ye shapeit me ance an unseemly shape,
  An' ye's never mare shape me."

He has sent to the wood
  For whins and for hawthorn,
An' he has ta'en that gay lady,
  An' there he did her burn.

laily: loathly; *dee:* die; *ae:* one, or very; *fit:* foot; *kaim:* comb; *siller:* silver; *sin:* since; *war:* were; *ain:* own; *ane:* one; *lee:* lie; *tane:* taken; *whins:* gorse

The word "ballad" comes from an old French verb *baller*, "to dance." Certainly the beat of this early ballad suggests stamping or strumming accompaniment. Taking a stock incident of legend, the dragon that lays waste the countryside, it acts it out like a children's game: "You must be the serpent and I must be your father."

Carried away by the action, some of the players seem to have improvised. There are other versions in which "my father married the warst woman." Even then, the bad mother—or, as here, stepmother—is recognized as a powerful source of mischief. In this version the Worm throws in "ae"—"one" or "very"—for good measure; this particular stepmother was *really* bad.

But it's his sister, Lady Masery, that has the last word. In other variants she resumes her rightful shape. Here one senses the sudden inspiration of a character actress playing a two-line bit. She springs a Celtic surprise on them; she's *too angry* to be changed back from a mackerel.

If some of the old ballads are composite in origin, they also go back and forth in time, having been handed down—so to speak—from mouth to mouth. It's a collaboration between the centuries. This gives them their unique quality; at once remote and yet very near, as if they were happening around us.

34. *Sir Eglamour, that worthy knight*

SAMUEL ROWLANDS

Sir Eglamour, that worthy knight,
He took his sword and went to fight;
And as he rode both hill and dale,
Armèd upon his shirt of mail
A dragon came out of his den,
Had slain, God knows how many men!

When he espied Sir Eglamour,
Oh, if you had but heard him roar,
And seen how all the trees did shake,
The knight did tremble, horse did quake,
The birds betake them all to peeping—
It would have made you fall a weeping!

But now it is in vain to fear,
Being come unto, "fight dog! fight bear!"
To it they go and fiercely fight
A live-long day from morn till night.
The dragon had a plaguy hide,
And could the sharpest steel abide.

No sword will enter him with cuts,
Which vexed the knight unto the guts;
But, as in choler he did burn,
He watched the dragon a good turn;
And, as a yawning he did fall,
He thrust his sword in, hilts and all.

Then, like a coward, he to fly
Unto his den that was hard by;
And there he lay all night and roared.
The knight was sorry for his sword,
But, riding thence, said, "I forsake it,
He that will fetch it, let him take it!"

Too many ballads on the same theme can be cloying. Like a child glutted with fairy tales, Samuel Rowlands, early in the seventeenth century, appears to be surfeited by an overrich diet of chivalric derring-do. In this poem he sets out to slay the dragon ballad.

Like a reverse archaism, some of the lines are peculiarly modern in flavor: "Which vexed the knight unto the guts" and "The knight was sorry for his sword." The rhythms are close to those of prose: "The dragon came out of his den"; it would seem intended to be spoken rather than sung.

Rowlands' travesty finds echoes in a fine modern ballad that is not, however, satirizing the *ballad:* John Crowe Ransom's "Captain Carpenter" (*Selected Poems*, page 31). It achieves its shifting sense of time—a silghtly obliterated quality—not by any great use of archaic words, but by sly anachronisms, as if conflicting versions of an old legend were merging.

The gallant gentleman, Captain Carpenter, carries pistols but successively fights and is fought with swords, clubs, teeth, tongue, and heart. He is cast at once in dimly delineated historic and mythological eras, which add up to an eternal past.

Does he symbolize the continual defeat of chivalry? His eulogy does not fail to note, if affectionately, a certain idiotic streak in the old boy: "I wish he had delivered half his blows."

Two very different ironic uses of the ballad are W. H. Auden's on the approach of war, "O what is that sound which so thrills the ear" (*Collected Poetry*, page 222), and E. E. Cummings' savage ballad of the conscientious objector, "i sing of Olaf glad and big" (*Poems 1923–1954*, page 244).

35. *Sir Patrick Spens*

ANONYMOUS

The king sits in Dumferling toune,
  Drinking the blude-reid wine:
"O whar will I get guid sailor,
  To sail this schip of mine?"

Up and spak an eldern knicht,
  Sat at the king's richt knee:
"Sir Patrick Spens is the best sailor
  That sails upon the se."

The king has written a braid letter,
  And signed it wi his hand,
And sent it to Sir Patrick Spens,
  Was walking on the sand.

The first line that Sir Patrick red,
  A loud lauch lauched he;
The next line that Sir Patrick red,
  The teir blinded his ee.

"O wha is this has don this deid,
  This ill deid don to me,
To send me out this time o' the yeir,
  To sail upon the se?

"Mak hast, mak hast, my mirry men all,
  Our guid schip sails the morne":
"O say na sae, my master deir,
  For I fear a deadlie storme.

"Late late yestreen I saw the new moone,
  Wi the auld moone in hir arme,
And I feir, I feir, my deir master,
  That we will cum to harme."

O our Scots nobles were richt laith
  To weet their cork-heild schoone:
But lang owre a' the play wer playd,
  Their hats they swam aboone.

O lang, lang may their ladies sit,
  Wi their fans into their hand,
Or ere they se Sir Patrick Spens
  Cum sailing to the land.

O lang, lang may the ladies stand
  Wi their gold kems in their hair,
Waiting for their ain deir lords,
  For they'll see thame na mair.

Haf owre, haf owre to Aberdour,
  It's fifty fadom deip,
And their lies guid Sir Patrick Spens,
  Wi the Scots lords at his feit.

braid: broad

This ballad, supposedly commemorating a twelfth-century shipwreck, has curious anticipations of moving-picture technique. The scene, the pace, even the tense, keep changing.

It opens with a long shot: "The king sits in Dumferling toune," drinking technicolor wine. Truck to elderly knight, who "up and *spak*." Quick dissolve to king, finishing a letter: "The king *has* written a braid letter." Does he use wide stationery? broad, rather than courtly, speech? Is he issuing extensive commands? "braid" or deceitful orders, sending his lords and his best sailor to their certain doom? The overtones of all the possible ways it may have been heard coalesce; an audible palimpsest.

Flash to Sir Patrick Spens, "Was walking on the sand" (sometimes "strand"). Close-up of tear blinding his eye. And later the future comes into the picture: "For they'll see thame na mair."

This constant change of focus creates the illusion of a great deal happening. Yet for all its momentum, doesn't it have a quality of arrested motion, like an old woodcut of a wave? All its action is about to take place or has already gone by. The shipwreck is hats bobbing on the water.

Other versions include more incident: a trip to "Norroway" to bring back a bride for the king; a quarrel in Norway; the decision to return in the teeth of a storm. But except for one memorable line, "And gurly grew the sea," these details seem to relax the mounting tension. The ballad travels at us through a mist of years, alternately vivid and dim, like flashes of memory, until its strangely triumphant ending, fading out to eternity.

36. *John Gilpin*

WILLIAM COWPER

John Gilpin was a citizen
  Of credit and renown.
A train-band captain eke was he
  Of famous London town.

John Gilpin's spouse said to her dear,
  "Though wedded we have been
These twice ten tedious years, yet we
  No holiday have seen.

"Tomorrow is our wedding-day,
  And we will then repair
Unto *The Bell* at Edmonton,
  All in a chaise and pair.

"My sister, and my sister's child,
  Myself, and children three
Will fill the chaise; so you must ride
  On horseback after we."

He soon replied, "I do admire
  Of womankind but one,
And you are she, my dearest dear;
  Therefore it shall be done.

"I am a linen-draper bold,
  As all the world doth know,
And my good friend, the Callender,
  Will lend his horse to go."

Quoth Mrs. Gilpin, "That's well said;
  And for that wine is dear,
We will be furnished with our own,
  Which is both bright and clear."

John Gilpin kissed his loving wife.
  O'erjoyed was he to find
That though on pleasure she was bent,
  She had a frugal mind.

That morning came, the chaise was brought,
  But yet was not allowed
To drive up to the door, lest all
  Should say that she was proud.

So three doors off the chaise was stayed,
  Where they did all get in;
Six precious souls, and all agog
  To dash through thick and thin.

Smack went the whip, round went the wheels;
  Were never folk so glad;
The stones did rattle underneath
  As if Cheapside were mad.

John Gilpin at his horse's side
  Seized fast the flowing mane,
And up he got, in haste to ride,
  But soon came down again.

For saddle-tree scarce reached had he,
  His journey to begin,
When, turning round his head, he saw
  Three customers come in.

So down he came; for loss of time,
  Although it grieved him sore,
Yet loss of pence, full well he knew,
  Would trouble him much more.

'Twas long before the customers
 Were suited to their mind,
When Betty screaming came downstairs:
 "The wine is left behind!"

"Good lack!" quoth he, "yet bring it me;
 My leathern belt likewise,
In which I bear my trusty sword
 When I do exercise."

Now Mistress Gilpin, careful soul,
 Had two stone bottles found
To hold the liquor that she loved,
 And keep it safe and sound.

Each bottle had a curling ear,
 Through which the belt he drew,
And hung a bottle on each side
 To make his balance true.

Then over all, that he might be
 Equipped from top to toe,
His long red cloak, well brushed and neat,
 He manfully did throw.

Now see him mounted once again
 Upon his nimble steed,
Full slowly pacing o'er the stones
 With caution and good heed.

But finding soon a smoother road
 Beneath his well-shod feet,
The snorting beast began to trot,
 Which galled him in his seat.

So, "Fair and softly!" John, he cried,
 But John he cried in vain;
The trot became a gallop soon,
 In spite of curb and rein.

So stooping down, as needs he must
  Who cannot sit upright,
He grasped the mane with both his hands,
  And eke with all his might.

His horse, who never in that sort
  Had handled been before,
What thing upon his back had got
  Did wonder more and more.

Away went Gilpin neck or nought,
  Away went hat and wig,
He little dreamt when he set out
  Of running such a rig.

The wind did blow, the cloak did fly
  Like streamer long and gay,
Till loop and button failing both,
  At last it flew away.

Then might all people well discern
  The bottles he had slung;
A bottle swinging at each side,
  As hath been said or sung.

The dogs did bark, the children screamed,
  Up flew the windows all;
And every soul cried out, "Well done!"
  As loud as he could bawl.

Away went Gilpin—who but he?
  His fame soon spread around:
"He carries weight, he rides a race,
  'Tis for a thousand pound!"

And still as fast as he drew near,
  'Twas wonderful to view
How in a trice the turnpike-men
  Their gates wide open threw.

And now as he went bowing down
His reeking head full low,
The bottles twain behind his back
Were shattered at a blow.

Down ran the wine into the road,
Most piteous to be seen,
Which made his horse's flanks to smoke
As they had basted been.

But still he seemed to carry weight,
With leathern girdle braced;
For all could see the bottle-necks
Still dangling at his waist.

Thus all through merry Islington
These gambols he did play,
And till he came unto the Wash
Of Edmonton so gay.

And there he threw the Wash about!
On both sides of the way,
Just like unto a trundling mop
Or a wild goose at play.

At Edmonton his loving wife
From the balcony spied
Her tender husband, wondering much
To see how he did ride.

"Stop, stop, John Gilpin!—Here's the house!"
They all at once did cry;
"The dinner waits and we are tired."
Said Gilpin, "So am I!"

But yet his horse was not a whit
Inclined to tarry there;
For why?—his owner had a house
Full ten miles off, at Ware.

So like an arrow swift he flew,
  Shot by an archer strong;
So did he fly—which brings me to
  The middle of my song.

Away went Gilpin, out of breath
  And sore against his will,
Till at his friend's the Callender's
  His horse at last stood still.

The Callender, amazed to see
  His neighbor in such trim,
Laid down his pipe, flew to the gate,
  And thus accosted him:

"What news? what news? your tidings tell,
  Tell me you must and shall—
Say why bare-headed you are come,
  Or why you come at all?"

Now Gilpin had a pleasant wit
  And loved a timely joke,
And thus unto the Callender
  In merry guise he spoke:

"I came because your horse would come
  And if I well forebode,
My hat and wig will soon be here,
  They are upon the road."

The Callender, right glad to find
  His friend in merry pin,
Returned him not a single word,
  But to the house went in.

Whence straight he came with hat and wig;
  A wig that flowed behind,
A hat not much the worse for wear,
  Each comely in its kind.

He held them up, and in his turn
   Thus showed his ready wit:
"My head is twice as big as yours,
   They therefore needs must fit.

"But let me scrape the dirt away
   That hangs upon your face;
And stop and eat, for well you may
   Be in a hungry case."

Said John, "It is my wedding day,
   And all the world would stare
If wife should dine at Edmonton
   And I should dine at Ware."

So turning to his horse, he said,
   "I am in haste to dine;
'Twas for your pleasure you came here,
   You shall go back for mine."

Ah, luckless speech, and bootless boast!
   For which he paid full dear;
For, while he spake, a braying ass
   Did sing most loud and clear.

Whereat his horse did snort as he
   Had heard a lion roar,
And galloped off with all his might,
   As he had done before.

Away went Gilpin, and away
   Went Gilpin's hat and wig;
He lost them sooner than at first;
   For why? they were too big.

Now Mistress Gilpin, when she saw
   Her husband posting down
Into the country far away,
   She pulled out half a crown;

And thus unto the youth she said
  That drove them to *The Bell,*
"This shall be yours when you bring back
  My husband safe and well."

The youth did ride, and soon did meet
  John coming back amain;
Whom in a trice he tried to stop
  By catching at his rein;

But not performing what he meant,
  And gladly would have done,
The frighted steed he frighted more,
  And made him faster run.

Away went Gilpin, and away
  Went post-boy at his heels,
The post-boy's horse right glad to miss
  The lumbering of the wheels.

Six gentlemen upon the road,
  Thus seeing Gilpin fly,
With post-boy scampering in the rear,
  They raised the hue and cry:

"Stop thief! stop thief! a highwayman!"
  Not one of them was mute;
And all and each that passed that way
  Did join in the pursuit.

And now the turnpike gates again
  Flew open in short space,
The toll-men thinking as before
  That Gilpin rode a race.

And so he did, and won it too,
  For he got first to town,
Nor stopped till where he had got up
  He did again get down.

Now let us sing, Long live the king,
  And Gilpin long live he;
And when he next doth ride abroad,
  May I be there to see!

The ballad's rousing beat and mounting excitement are put at the service here of an eighteenth-century comedy of manners, if rather less modish than most. This is a society of small tradesmen—the Callender probably presses clothes—who are members of the citizens' army. The poem is believable because it draws on the rhythms of action; funny because it treats the action momentously.

Horses' hoofs enter very differently into Robert Browning's "How they brought the good news from Ghent to Aix," T. S. Eliot's "Triumphal march" from "Coriolan" (*Collected Poems*, page 135), E. E. Cummings' "what a proud dreamhorse" (poem 121).

37. *In good King Charles's golden days*

ANONYMOUS

In good King Charles's golden days,
  When loyalty no harm meant,
A furious High-Church man I was,
  And so I gained preferment.
Unto my flock I daily preached:
  "Kings are by God appointed,
And damned are those who dare resist,
  Or touch the Lord's anointed."
    And this is law, I will maintain
      Unto my dying day, sir,
    That whatsoever king shall reign,
      I will be Vicar of Bray, sir!

When royal James possessed the crown,
  And Popery grew in fashion,
The Penal Law I hunted down
  And read the Declaration:

The Church of Rome, I found, would fit
  Full well my constitution,
And I had been a Jesuit,
  But for the Revolution.
    And this is law . . .

When William our deliverer came,
  To heal the nation's grievance,
I turned the cat in pan again
  And swore to him allegiance:
Old principles I did revoke,
  Set conscience at a distance,
Passive obedience is a joke,
  A jest is non-resistance.
    And this is law . . .

When glorious Ann became our Queen,
  The Church of England's glory,
Another face of things was seen
  And I became a Tory:
Occasional Conformists base,
  I damned, and moderation,
And thought the church in danger was
  From such prevarication.
    And this is law . . .

When George in pudding time came o'er,
  And moderate men looked big, sir,
My principles I changed once more
  And so became a Whig, sir:
And thus preferment I procured
  From our Faith's great defender,
And almost every day abjured
  The Pope and the Pretender.
    And this is law . . .

The illustrious House of Hanover
  And Protestant Succession,
To these I lustily will swear
  While they can keep possession:

For in my faith and loyalty
I never once will falter,
But George my lawful King shall be,
Except the times should alter.
And this is law . . .

The manners of still another class of English society are illustrated in this eighteenth-century popular ballad, whose off-stage action includes the political ferment of the latter half of the seventeenth century. It apes the rhythms of high resolve and unswerving loyalty.

38. *Little Musgrave and Lady Barnard*

ANONYMOUS

As it fell out on a high holy day,
As many be in the year,
When young men and maids together do go,
Their masses and matins to hear,

Little Musgrave came to the church door,
The priest was at the mass;
But he had more mind of the fine women,
Than he had of Our Lady's grace.

And some of them were clad in green,
And others were clad in pall;
And then came in my Lord Barnard's wife,
The fairest among them all.

She cast an eye on little Musgrave
As bright as the summer sun:
O then bethought him little Musgrave,
"This lady's heart I have won."

Quoth she, "I have loved thee, little Musgrave,
Full long and many a day."
"So have I loved you, lady fair,
Yet word I never durst say."

"I have a bower at Bucklesford-Bury,
  Full daintily bedight,
If thou'lt wend thither, my little Musgrave,
  Thou'lt lig in mine arms all night."

Quoth he, "I thank ye, lady fair,
  This kindness ye show to me;
And whether it be to my weal or woe,
  This night will I lig with thee."

All this beheard a little foot-page,
  By his lady's coach as he ran:
Quoth he, "Though I am my lady's page,
  Yet I'm my Lord Barnard's man.

"My Lord Barnard shall know of this,
  Although I lose a limb."
And ever whereas the bridges were broke,
  He laid him down to swim.

"Asleep or awake, thou Lord Barnard,
  As thou art a man of life,
Lo! this same night at Bucklesford-Bury
  Little Musgrave's in bed with thy wife."

"If it be true, thou little foot-page,
  This tale thou hast told to me,
Then all my lands in Bucklesford-Bury
  I freely will give to thee.

"But and it be a lie, thou little foot-page,
  This tale thou hast told to me,
On the highest tree in Bucklesford-Bury
  All hangèd shalt thou be.

"Rise up, rise up, my merry men all,
  And saddle me my good steed;
This night must I to Bucklesford-Bury;
  God wot, I had never more need."

Then some they whistled, and some they sang,
  And some did loudly say,
Whenever Lord Barnard's horn it blew,
  "Away, Musgrave, away."

"Methinks I hear the throstle cock,
  Methinks I hear the jay,
Methinks I hear Lord Barnard's horn:
  I would I were away."

"Lie still, lie still, thou little Musgrave,
  And huggle me from the cold;
For it is but some shepherd's boy
  A-whistling his sheep to the fold.

"Is not thy hawk upon the perch,
  Thy horse eating corn and hay?
And thou a gay lady within thine arms:
  And wouldst thou be away?"

By this Lord Barnard was come to the door,
  And lighted upon a stone:
And he pullèd out three silver keys,
  And opened the doors each one.

He lifted up the coverlet,
  He lifted up the sheet;
"How now, how now, thou little Musgrave,
  Dost find my gay lady sweet?"

"I find her sweet," quoth little Musgrave,
  "The more is my grief and pain;
I'd gladly give three hundred pounds
  That I were on yonder plain."

"Arise, arise, thou little Musgrave,
  And put thy clothes now on,
It shall never be said in my country,
  That I killed a naked man.

"I have two swords in one scabbard,
Full dear they cost my purse;
And thou shalt have the best of them,
And I will have the worse."

The first stroke that little Musgrave struck,
He hurt Lord Barnard sore;
The next stroke that Lord Barnard struck,
Little Musgrave never struck more.

With that bespake the lady fair,
In bed whereas she lay,
"Although thou art dead, my little Musgrave,
Yet for thee I will pray:

"And wish well to thy soul will I,
So long as I have life;
So will I not do for thee, Barnard,
Though I am thy wedded wife."

He cut her paps from off her breast;
Great pity it was to see
The drops of this fair lady's blood
Run trickling down her knee.

"Wo worth, wo worth ye, my merry men all,
You never were born for my good:
Why did you not offer to stay my hand,
When you saw me wax so wood?

"For I have slain the fairest sir knight,
That ever rode on a steed;
So have I done the fairest lady,
That ever ware woman's weed.

"A grave, a grave," Lord Barnard cried,
"To put these lovers in;
But lay my lady o' the upper hand,
For she comes o' the better kin."

lig: lie; *wood*: mad

So many of the early ballads are collaborations in which time has had a hand that it is refreshing to come upon "Little Musgrave and Lady Barnard." Elements of it appear elsewhere; there are several that "fall out" or "befall" on a "high holy day." The swimming foot-page turns up in more than one situation. But there is an individuality of tone and dramatic development that suggests a single, though unknown, poet.

"Little Musgrave" seems spoken rather than sung. At least it suggests a freely modified beat rather than a fixed melody. The final line in each quatrain usually reaches a climactic point. Their rhythms are subtly varied according to the nature of the climax, especially in the breathless speech of the page: "Little Musgrave's in bed with thy wife."

The point of view, too, is comparatively rare. There is no real villain, as there usually is in ballads of star-crossed lovers. There is no feckless hero, either, although one's sympathies naturally go out to the hapless Musgrave. But it is impossible to detest Lord Barnard, acting by instinct and immediately regretting his action. The ballad brings to mind George Meredith's line in *Modern Love:* "No villain need be; passions spin the plot."

39. *Wha is that at my bower door?*

ROBERT BURNS

Wha is that at my bower door?
  O wha is it but Findlay;
Then gae your gate, ye'se nae be here!
  Indeed maun I, quo' Findlay.
What make ye sae like a thief?
  O come and see, quo' Findlay;
Before the morn ye'll work mischief;
  Indeed will I, quo' Findlay.

Gif I rise and let you in;
  Let me in, quo' Findlay;
Ye'll keep me waukin wi' your din;
  Indeed will I, quo' Findlay.

In my bower if ye should stay;
  Let me stay, quo' Findlay;
I fear ye'll bide till break o' day;
  Indeed will I, quo' Findlay.

Here this night if ye remain;
  I'll remain, quo' Findlay;
I dread ye'll learn the gate again;
  Indeed will I, quo' Findlay.
What may pass within this bower—
  Let it pass, quo' Findlay;
Ye maun conceal till your last hour;
  Indeed will I, quo' Findlay.

maun: must; *waukin:* waking

The rewards of persistence are celebrated in this song-ballad of the often-awakened mistress. As is true of so many of Burns' poems, it is set to an old tune; but, says Burns, "the words are mine."

Sometimes he redoes the words of an existing song or ballad, as in "The Carle of Kellyburn Braes," recounting the carrying off of an ill-tempered wife by the devil and her subsequent return. Speaking of it, Mrs. Burns is quoted as saying, "Robert gae this ane a terrible brushing."

40. *La belle Dame sans merci*

JOHN KEATS

O what can ail thee, knight-at-arms,
  Alone and palely loitering?
The sedge has withered from the lake
  And no birds sing.

O what can ail thee, knight-at-arms,
  So haggard and so woe-begone?
The squirrel's granary is full,
  And the harvest's done.

I see a lily on thy brow
  With anguish moist and fever dew
And on thy cheeks a fading rose
  Fast withereth too.

I met a lady in the meads,
  Full beautiful—a faery's child;
Her hair was long, her foot was light,
  And her eyes were wild.

I made a garland for her head,
  And bracelets too, and fragrant zone;
She looked at me as she did love,
  And made sweet moan.

I set her on my pacing steed,
  And nothing else saw all day long,
For sidelong would she bend, and sing
  A faery's song.

She found me roots of relish sweet,
  And honey wild, and manna-dew,
And sure in language strange she said,
  "I love thee true."

She took me to her elfin grot,
  And there she wept and sighed full sore,
And there I shut her wild, wild eyes
  With kisses four.

And there she lullèd me asleep,
  And there I dreamed—ah! woe betide!
The latest dream I ever dreamed
  On the cold hill side.

I saw pale kings, and princes too,
  Pale warriors, death-pale were they all;
They cried—"La belle Dame sans merci
  Hath thee in thrall!"

I saw their starved lips in the gloom,
With horrid warning gapèd wide;
And I awoke, and found me here
On the cold hill side.

And this is why I sojourn here,
Alone and palely loitering,
Though the sedge is withered from the lake,
And no birds sing.

Even if we didn't know this is by John Keats, it is unmistakably personal. Its rhythms are clearly designed: they do not come about by chance; they do not follow a tune; they make a music.

The haunting sense of time, which in old ballads is put there *by* time, is here a deliberate evocation. Isn't it a ballad of *no* time; the romantic dream of a region for which Keats is continually longing?

In the airless, soundless realm created for him by ballad and romance, it is possible to believe that "beauty is truth, truth beauty." This is not Keats's "philosophy," though he wishes it could be; it is what the figures on the "Grecian urn" say to him.

He returns from that dream, here, into a reality that is by comparison pallid and lusterless: "And no birds sing." The sorceress, "La belle Dame," seems to be the imagination of other ages, sealed into song and vase.

Another, possibly earlier, version substitutes "wretched wight" for "knight-at-arms." This identifies more closely with Keats himself, although it shows, like his line "Young Callidore was paddling o'er the lake," that when his ear deserted him it could fail magnificently.

A modern version of the romantic ballad translating, among other things, erotic love into a fantastic allegory of kaleidoscopic imagery is Dylan Thomas' "Ballad of the long-legged bait" (*Collected Poems*, page 166).

41. *The sisters*

ALFRED, LORD TENNYSON

We were two daughters of one race:
She was the fairst in the face:
  The wind is blowing in turret and tree.
They were together, and she fell;
Therefore revenge became me well.
  O the Earl was fair to see!

She died: she went to burning flame:
She mixed her ancient blood with shame.
  The wind is howling in turret and tree.
Whole weeks and months, and early and late,
To win his love I lay in wait:
  O the Earl was fair to see!

I made a feast; I bade him come;
I won his love, I brought him home.
  The wind is roaring in turret and tree.
And after supper, on a bed,
Upon my lap he laid his head:
  O the Earl was fair to see!

I kissed his eyelids into rest:
His ruddy cheek upon my breast.
  The wind is raging in turret and tree.
I hated him with the hate of hell,
But I loved his beauty passing well.
  O the Earl was fair to see!

I rose up in the silent night:
I made my dagger sharp and bright.
  The wind is raving in turret and tree.
As half-asleep his breath he drew,
Three times I stabbed him through and through.
  O the Earl was fair to see!

I curled and combed his comely head,
He looked so grand when he was dead.

The wind is blowing in turret and tree.
I wrapt his body in the sheet,
And laid him at his mother's feet.
O the Earl was fair to see!

Tennyson's Gothic tale is parody-proof, it comes so close to parodying itself. But what magnificent fustian! It leaves a question hovering in the air: is it tongue-in-cheek cloak-and-dagger?

T. S. Eliot tops its most Victorian line in his poem "Burbank with a Baedeker: Bleistein with a Cigar" (*Collected Poems,* page 40), where the hero, at a small hotel, encounters Princess Volupine: "They were together, and he fell."

But I shall be forever haunted by the image of the avenging sister, in the silent night, furtively whetting her knife. Tennyson is seldom *deliberately* funny.

42. *A Ballad upon a wedding*

SIR JOHN SUCKLING

I tell thee, Dick, where I have been,
Where I the rarest things have seen;
O, things without compare!
Such sights again cannot be found
In any place on English ground,
Be it at wake or fair.

At Charing Cross, hard by the way,
Where we (thou know'st) do sell our hay,
There is a house with stairs:
And there did I see coming down
Such folk as are not in our town,
Forty at least, in pairs.

Amongst the rest, one pest'lent fine
(His beard no bigger though than thine)
Walked on before the rest:

Our landlord looks like nothing to him:
The King (God bless him) 'twould undo him,
   Should he go still so drest.

At Course-a-Park, without all doubt,
He should have first been taken out
   By all the maids i' th' town:
Though lusty Roger there had been,
Or little George upon the Green,
   Or Vincent of the Crown.

But wot you what? the youth was going
To make an end of all his wooing;
   The parson for him stayed:
Yet by his leave (for all his haste)
He did not so much wish all past
   (Perchance) as did the maid.

The maid (and thereby hangs a tale),
For such a maid no Whitsun-ale
   Could ever yet produce:
No grape, that's kindly ripe, could be
So round, so plump, so soft as she,
   Nor half so full of juice.

Her finger was so small, the ring
Would not stay on, which they did bring,
   It was too wide a peck:
And to say truth (for out it must)
It looked like the great collar (just)
   About our young colt's neck.

Her feet beneath her petticoat,
Like little mice, stole in and out,
   As if they feared the light:
But O she dances such a way!
No sun upon an Easter-day
   Is half so fine a sight.

He would have kissed her once or twice,
But she would not, she was so nice,
  She would not do't in sight,
And then she looked as who should say:
I will do what I list today,
  And you shall do't at night.

Her cheeks so rare a white was on,
No daisy makes comparison
  (Who sees them is undone),
For streaks of red were mingled there,
Such as are on a Catherine pear
  (The side that's next the sun).

Her lips were red, and one was thin,
Compared to that was next her chin
  (Some bee had stung it newly);
But (Dick) her eyes so guard her face;
I durst no more upon them gaze
  Than on the sun in July.

Her mouth so small, when she does speak,
Thou'dst swear her teeth her words did break,
  That they might passage get;
But she so handled still the matter,
They came as good as ours, or better,
  And are not spent a whit.

If wishing should be any sin,
The parson himself had guilty been
  (She looked that day so purely);
And did the youth so oft the feat
At night, as some did in conceit,
  It would have spoiled him surely.

Just in the nick the cook knocked thrice,
And all the waiters in a trice
  His summons did obey;

Each serving-man, with dish in hand,
Marched boldly up, like our trained band,
   Presented, and away.

When all the meat was on the table,
What man of knife or teeth was able
   To stay to be entreated?
And this the very reason was,
Before the parson could say grace,
   The company was seated.

The business of the kitchen's great,
For it is fit that men should eat;
   Nor was it there denied:
Passion o' me, how I run on!
There's that that would be thought upon
   (I trow) besides the bride.

Now hats fly off, and youths carouse;
Healths first go round, and then the house,
   The bride's came thick and thick:
And when 'twas named another's health,
Perhaps he made it hers by stealth;
   And who could help it, Dick?

On the sudden up they rise and dance;
Then sit again and sigh, and glance:
   Then dance again and kiss:
Thus several ways the time did pass,
Whilst every woman wished her place,
   And every man wished his.

By this time all were stolen aside
To counsel and undress the bride;
   But that he must not know:
But yet 'twas thought he guessed her mind,
And did not mean to stay behind
   Above an hour or so.

When in he came (Dick), there she lay
Like new-fall'n snow melting away
  ('Twas time, I trow, to part);
Kisses were now the only stay,
Which soon she gave, as who would say,
  God b' w' ye, with all my heart.

But, just as heaven would have, to cross it,
In come the bridesmaids with the posset:
  The bridegroom ate in spite;
For had he left the women to't,
It would have cost two hours to do't,
  Which were too much that night.

At length the candle's out, and now
All that they had not done they do.
  What that is, who can tell?
But I believe it was no more
Than thou and I have done before
  With Bridget and with Nell.

This sprightly period piece of the seventeenth century is full of the worldly airs and mannerisms associated with the Cavalier poets ("passion o' me!"). One can almost see Sir John, from time to time, taking a pinch of snuff as he follows the proceedings.

All men are potential rivals; the bridegroom is "pest'lent fine." This is surely a spoken ballad, slightly through the nose. For all that, what keen observation and unforced description it achieves, both of the scene and its details:

Her feet beneath her petticoat,
Like little mice, stole in and out . . .

43. *The arrest of Oscar Wilde at the Cadogan Hotel*

JOHN BETJEMAN

He sipped a weak hock and seltzer
  As he gazed at the London skies

Through the Nottingham lace of the curtains
  Or was it his bees-winged eyes?

To the right and before him Pont Street
  Did tower in her new built red,
As hard as the morning gaslight
  That shone on his unmade bed.

"I want some more hock in my seltzer,
  And Robbie, please give me your hand—
Is this the end or beginning?
  How can I understand?

"So you've brought me the latest *Yellow Book:*
  And Buchan has got in it now:
Approval of what is approved of
  Is as false as a well-kept vow.

"More hock, Robbie—where is the seltzer?
  Dear boy, pull again at the bell!
They are all little better than *cretins,*
  Though this *is* the Cadogan Hotel.

"One astrakhan coat is at Willis's—
  Another one's at the Savoy:
Do fetch my morocco portmanteau,
  And bring them on later, dear boy."

A thump, and a murmur of voices—
  ("Oh why must they make such a din?")
As the door of the bedroom swung open
  And Two Plain Clothes POLICEMEN came in:

"Mr. Woilde, we 'ave come for tew take yew
  Where felons and criminals dwell:
We must ask yew tew leave with us quoietly
  For this *is* the Cadogan Hotel."

He rose, and he put down *The Yellow Book.*
  He staggered—and, terrible-eyed,
He brushed past the palms on the staircase
  And was helped to a hansom outside.

An historical ballad with a difference, this deftly re-creates the decline and fall of a period and a personality. The nineties wane and change: "new built red" on Pont Street, Buchan in *The Yellow Book*. Against this exterior-interior backdrop the last flickering scene of a personal drama is played out as the asbestos curtain of propriety descends: the fumbling distraction, threatened pathos, and quick recovery in an epigram; petulance and mislaid coats; the intrusion; the mock horror and real shock; the tragedy. The ballad rhythms, with their forward drive, contribute a quality of inevitability.

44. The listeners

WALTER DE LA MARE

"Is there anybody there?" said the Traveler,
  Knocking on the moonlit door;
And his horse in the silence champed the grasses
  Of the forest's ferny floor.
And a bird flew up out of the turret,
  Above the Traveler's head:
And he smote upon the door again a second time;
  "Is there anybody there?" he said.
But no one descended to the Traveler;
  No head from the leaf-fringed sill
Leaned over and looked into his gray eyes,
  Where he stood perplexed and still.
But only a host of phantom listeners
  That dwelt in the lone house then
Stood listening in the quiet of the moonlight
  To that voice from the world of men:
Stood thronging the faint moonbeams on the dark stair
  That goes down to the empty hall,
Hearkening to an air stirred and shaken
  By the lonely Traveler's call.
And he felt in his heart their strangeness,
  Their stillness answering his cry,
While his horse moved, cropping the dark turf,
  'Neath the starred and leafy sky;

For he suddenly smote on the door, even
  Louder, and lifted his head—
"Tell them I came, and no one answered,
  That I kept my word," he said.
Never the least stir made the listeners,
  Though every word he spake
Fell echoing through the shadowiness of the still house
  From the one man left awake:
Aye, they heard his foot upon the stirrup,
  And the sound of iron on stone,
And how the silence surged softly backward,
  When the plunging hoofs were gone.

Part of the enchantment of this ballad lies in what it doesn't tell us. Who is the Traveler? Where does he come from? What promise is he keeping?

The answers it suggests to us tremble between the ordinary and the eerie. The Traveler could be anyone stopping by night at a deserted house. His question is thoroughly commonplace: "Is there anybody there?" Why does it set up premonitory reverberations?

Isn't it because the strong ballad beat is interspersed by a flock of little syllables? The pattering rhythm—here and throughout the poem —anticipates a scurry of feet; a scurry that is never quite audible.

It's a perfect ghost story with, I think, a new twist. Who are the ghosts? They are never specifically revealed, and yet we are made to sense them even if we don't guess. After the hoofbeats have died away, going as mysteriously as they came, who are left listening, wondering?

We are; the listeners. It's as if we had awakened to find ourselves in the middle of a recurrent dream—or an old ballad—and were trying to remember.

45. *Three young rats with black felt hats*

ANONYMOUS (MOTHER GOOSE)

Three young rats with black felt hats,
Three young ducks with new straw flats,
Three young dogs with curling tails,
Three young cats with demi-veils,

Went out to walk with two young pigs
In satin vests and sorrel wigs.
But suddenly it chanced to rain
And so they all went home again.

The anonymous poet or poets writing under the *nom de plume* of Mother Goose first appear, according to some accounts, in a collection published in London around 1760 by John Newbery.

There are rumors that some of these verses have concealed political implications. This one seems very subversive to me. It takes a dim child's-eye view of the grownup world: elaborate preparations for an event that never quite comes off.

The ballad is often thought of as a distinct variety of poetry. Especially the folk ballad is alleged to be "simple," based on a real or imaginary event and characterized by a pronounced beat with interesting irregularities or "crudities."

Don't they, however, differ as widely among themselves as they do with other poems? Even in their anonymous form they can be complex in their dealings with time, place, and personality. In the hands of individual poets they are susceptible of subtle, intensely personal variation. The event may be reduced to a minimum. The pronounced beat may be modified hauntingly, as in "The listeners" (poem 44), or modulated to the lyric intensity of "La belle Dame sans merci" (poem 40).

Released from their category, all of them would find places in the groups to follow, beginning in Part Four with song.

PART FOUR

"Ah, wanton, will ye?"

There is no strict dividing line between ballad and song. Many songs are called ballads whether they involve a story or not. And frequently songs imply a story situation.

I am taking as songs poems that, for me, suggest musical accompaniment; that either have been, or might be, set to music.

Of the preceding poems, John Ford's "Can you paint a thought?" (poem 6) would find a place here. Perhaps James Stephens' "The rivals" (poem 8) might be included too, although I can imagine music interfering with the imagined music of the bird. Similarly Blake's "Piping down the valleys wild" (poem 12) would be ruined by pipes imitating piping.

George Herbert may have provided a setting for "A true hymn" (poem 11). But it seems more spoken than his "Virtue" in this group. Several, though by no means all, of the ballads are singable.

46. *It fell upon a holy eve*

EDMUND SPENSER

PERIGOT: It fell upon a holy eve,
WILLIE: Hey, ho, holiday!
P: When holy fathers wont to shrieve;
W: Now ginneth this roundelay.
P: Sitting upon a hill so high,
W: Hey, ho, the high hill!
P: The while my flock did feed thereby;
W: The while the shepherd self did spill;
P: I saw the bouncing Bellibone,
W: Hey, ho, Bonibell!
P: Tripping over the dale alone,
W: She can trip it very well!
P: Well deckèd in a frock of gray,

W: Hey, ho, gray is greete!
P: And in a kirtle of green saye,
W: The green is for maidens meet.
P: A chapelet on her head she wore,
W: Hey, ho, chapelet!
P: Of sweet violets therein was store,
W: She sweeter than the violet.
P: My sheep did leave their wonted food,
W: Hey, ho, silly sheep!
P: And gazed on her as they were wood,
W: Wood as he that did them keep!
P: As the bonilasse passèd by,
W: Hey, ho, bonilasse!
P: She roved at me with glancing eye,
W: As clear as the crystal glass:
P: All as the sunny beam so bright,
W: Hey, ho, the sun beam!
P: Glanceth from Phoebus' face forthright,
W: So love into thy heart did stream:
P: Or as the thunder cleaves the clouds.
W: Hey, ho, the thunder!
P: Wherein the lightsome levin shrouds,
W: So cleaves thy soul asunder:
P: Or as Dame Cynthia's silver ray,
W: Hey, ho, the moonlight!
P: Upon the glittering wave doth play,
W: Such play is a piteous plight.
P: The glance into my heart did glide;
W: Hey, ho, the glider!
P: Therewith my soul was sharply gryde.
W: Such wounds soon waxen wider.
P: Hasting to raunch the arrow out,
W: Hey, ho, Perigot!
P: I left the head in my heart-root,
W: It was a desperate shot.
P: There it rankleth, ay more and more,
W: Hey, ho, the arrow!

P: Ne can I find salve for my sore:
W: Love is a cureless sorrow.
P: And though my bale with death I bought,
W: Hey, ho, heavy cheer!
P: Yet should thilk lass not from my thought,
W: So you may buy gold too dear.
P: But whether in painful love I pine,
W: Hey, ho, pinching pain!
P: Or thrive in wealth, she shall be mine,
W: But if thou can her obtain.
P: And if for graceless grief I die
W: Hey, ho, graceless grief!
P: Witness she slew me with her eye,
W: Let thy folly be prief.
P: And you that saw it, simple sheep,
W: Hey, ho, the fair flock!
P: For prief thereof, my death shall weep,
W: And moan with many a mock.
P: So learned I love on a holy eve,
W: Hey, ho, holiday!
P: That ever since my heart did grieve,
W: Now endeth our roundelay.

spill: destroy, injure; *greete:* mourning; *saye:* fine cloth; *wood:* mad; *roved:* shot, as with an arrow; *levin:* lightning; *gryde:* pierced; *raunch:* wrench; *prief:* proof

Close to ballad, as a group performance with real or imaginary accompaniment, is this roundelay from Spenser's first book, *The Shepherd's Calendar*, published in 1579.

A rollicking song of unrequited—or so far unreciprocated—love, it is in the vaudeville tradition. Perigot is the "straight man"; his companion Willie, if not entirely the "comic," often twists or tops his lines.

47. *Oh, what a plague is love!*

ANONYMOUS

Oh, what a plague is love! How shall I bear it?
She will unconstant prove, I greatly fear it.
She so molests my mind, that my wit faileth.
She wavers with the wind, as the ship saileth.
  Please her the best I may,
  She looks another way.
  Alack and well-a-day!
    Phyllida flouts me.

At the fair, yesterday, she would not see me,
But turned another way, when she came nigh me.
Dick had her in to dine; he might intreat her.
Will had her to the wine; I could not get her.
  With Daniel did she dance;
  At me she looked askance.
  O thrice unhappy chance!
    Phyllida flouts me.

I cannot work and sleep, both at all season:
Love wounds my heart so deep, without all reason.
I do consume, alas! with care and sorrow,
Even like a sort of beasts pinde in a meadow.
  I shall be dead, I fear,
  Within this thousand year;
  And all for very care:
    Phyllida flouts me.

She hath a clout of mine, wrought with good coventry,
Which she keeps for a sign of my fidelity;
But, in faith, if she flinch, she shall not wear it;
To Tib, my t'other wench, I mean to bear it.
  Yet it will kill my heart
  So quickly to depart.
  Death, kill me with thy dart!
    Phyllida flouts me.

Yesternight, very late, as I was walking,
I saw one in the gate, with my love talking.
Every word that she spoke, he gave her kissing,
Which she as kindly took as mother's blessing.
  But when I come to kiss,
  She very dainty is.
  Oh, what a hell is this!
    Phyllida flouts me.

Fair maid, be not so coy, never disdain me!
I am my mother's boy; sweet, entertain me!
She'll give me, when she dies, all things befitting:
Her poultry and her bees, with her goose sitting,
  A pair of mattress beds,
  A barrel full of shreds,—
  And yet, for all my goods,
    Phyllida flouts me.

I saw my face, of late, in a fair fountain;
I know there's none so feat, in all the mountain.
Lasses do leave their sheep and flock above me,
And for my love do weep, and fain would have me.
  Maidens in every place
  Strive to behold my face;
  And yet—O heavy case!—
    Phyllida flouts me.

Maiden, look what you do, and in time take me!
I can have other two, if you forsake me:
For Doll, the dairy-maid, laughed on me lately,
And wanton Winifred favours me greatly.
  One threw milk on my clothes;
  T'other plays with my nose:
  What loving signs be those!
    Phyllida flouts me.

Come to me, pretty peat, let me embrace thee!
Though thou be fair and feat, do not disgrace me;

For I will constant prove (make no denial!)
And be thy dearest love—proof maketh trial.
  If ought do breed thy pain,
  I can procure thy gain;
  Yet, bootless, I complain—
    Phyllida flouts me.

Thou shalt eat curds and cream, all the year lasting;
And drink the crystal stream, pleasant in tasting;
Whig and whey whilst thou burst, and bramble-berries,
Pie-lids and pasty-crust, pears, plums, and cherries.
  Thy garments shall be thin,
  Made of a wether's skin—
  Yet all not worth a pin!—
    Phyllida flouts me.

I found a stock-dove's nest, and thou shalt have it.
The cheese-cake, in my chest, for thee I save it.
I will give thee rush-rings, key-nobs, and cushnets,
Pence, purse, and other things, bells, beads, and bracelets.
  My sheep-hook, and my dog,
  My bottle, and my bag—
  Yet all not worth a rag!
    Phyllida flouts me.

Thy glorious beauty's gleam dazzles my eyesight,
Like the sun's brightest beam shining at midnight.
O my heart! O my heels! Fie on all wenches!
Pluck up thy courage, Giles; bang him that flinches!
  Back to thy sheep again,
  Thou silly shepherd's swain;
  Thy labour is in vain!
    Phyllida flouts me.

pinde: pinned (confined) or pined; *cushnets:* pincushions

This seventeenth-century song-with-a-story is more definitely a music-hall number, playing for laughs. There is more than one version, the bumpkin hero making just as big a fool of himself.

48. *Mark Antony*

JOHN CLEVELAND

When as the nightingale chanted her vespers,
And the wild forester couched on the ground,
Venus invited me in the evening whispers
Unto a fragrant field with roses crowned,
  Where she before had sent
  My wishes' complement,
  Unto my heart's content,
  Played with me on the green.
    Never Mark Antony
    Dallied more wantonly
    With the fair Egyptian Queen.

First on her cherry cheeks I mine eyes feasted,
Thence fear of surfeiting made me retire;
Next on her warmer lips, which when I tasted,
My duller spirits made active as fire.
  Then we began to dart
  Each at another's heart,
  Arrows that knew no smart,
  Sweet lips and smiles between.
    Never Mark Antony . . .

Wanting a glass to plait her amber tresses
Which like a bracelet rich deckèd mine arm,
Gaudier than Juno wears when as she graces
Jove with embraces more stately than warm;
  Then did she peep in mine
  Eyes' humor crystalline;
  I in her eyes was seen
  As if we one had been.
    Never Mark Antony . . .

Mystical grammar of amorous glances;
Feeling of pulses, the physic of love;
Rhetorical courtings and musical dances;
Numbering of kisses arithmetic prove;

Eyes like astronomy;
Straight-limbed geometry;
In her art's ingeny
Our wits were sharp and keen.
  Never Mark Antony
  Dallied more wantonly
  With the fair Egyptian Queen.

At one reading Cleveland's song, first published in 1647, seems like another Cavalier exercise in polished phrasing. I find myself wishing especially that the arts and sciences had been left to their own devices.

At the next it enforces its music so that I can almost hear it. It's not uncommon for the words of a song to evaporate on the page. Rather rarely, I think, do they virtually compose the score.

49. *With lullay, lullay, like a child*

JOHN SKELTON

  With lullay, lullay, like a child,
  Thou sleepest too long, thou art beguiled.

"My darling dear, my daisy flower,
  Let me," quod he, "lie in your lap."
"Lie still," quod she, "my paramour,
  Lie still hardely, and take a nap."
  His head was heavy, such was his hap,
All drowsy dreaming, drowned in sleep,
That of his love he took no keep,
        With hey, lullay, lullay . . .

With ba, ba, ba, and bas, bas, bas,
  She cherished him both cheek and chin,
That he wist never where he was;
  He had forgotten all deadly sin.
  He wanted wit her love to win:
He trusted her payment, and lost all his pay:
She left him sleeping, and stale away.

The rivers routh, the waters wan;
  She sparèd not to wet her feet;
She waded over, she found a man
  That halsid her heartily and kissed her sweet:
  Thus after her cold she caught a heat.
"My lefe," she said, "routith in his bed:
Ywis he hath an heavy head."

What dreamest thou, drunkard, drowsy pate!
  Thy lust and liking is from thee gone;
Thou blinkard blowbowl, thou wakest too late,
  Behold, thou liest, luggard, alone!
  Well may thou sigh, well may thou groan,
To deal with her so cowardly:
Ywis, poule-hachet, she bleared thine eye.

hardely (hardily): confidently; *routh:* rough; *halsid:* embraced (literally, "necked"); *lefe:* beloved; *routith:* snoreth; *blowbowl:* drinker; *ywis:* indeed; *poule-hachet:* hatchet-face (poll-hatchet) or blockhead(?); a man who gossips around an ale-pole, sign of an inn(?); perhaps, newly hatched chicken

This is not in typical Skeltonics, the delightfully gnarled metre of longer poems like "Philip Sparrow":

  Her kirtle so goodly lacèd,
And under that is bracèd
Such pleasure that I may
Neither write nor say.
  Yet though I write not with ink
No man can let me think,
For thought hath liberty,
Thought is frank and free . . .

("Let" here, meaning "prevent"—"No man can keep me from thinking"—survives today as a noun in the expression "without let or hindrance.")

All Skelton's poems use rather cross-grained, rocking rhythms, so refreshing after "smoother" versification. Not all melody is for the tenor voice; like John Donne, Skelton seems baritone.

Both poets have their ups and downs of critical esteem. By the end of the sixteenth century Skelton is thought a "rude railing rhymer." In the eighteenth, Alexander Pope calls him "beastly Skelton" and says: "Skelton's poems are all low and bad, there is nothing in them that is worth reading."

Since editors differ on his early spellings and their modern equivalents, we may be allowed a conjecture or two. The marvelous epithet "blinkard blowbowl" (one who blinks from blowing the bowl too often) is sometimes given as "blinkerd blowboll," although "drunkard," two lines earlier, retains its a (sometimes "drunchard"). This suggests, though early spellings have little consistency, that different words may be intended: "blinkered blowball." The guileless hero is provided with blinkers, like a horse, or "hoodwinked," while engaged in blowing the fluff off old dandelions.

"Poule-hachet" in the last line has almost as many spellings and interpretations, usually followed by question marks, as there are scholars of the period. So far as I know, no one previously has proposed a "hatched chicken." The chickenhearted lover is as easily "blerid" ("bleared" or deceived) as a baby chick.

But the nature of name-calling is to be grandly muzzy.

50. *You spotted snakes with double tongue*

WILLIAM SHAKESPEARE

You spotted snakes with double tongue,
  Thorny hedgehogs, be not seen;
Newts and blind-worms do no wrong,
  Come not near our fairy queen.
    Philomel, with melody,
    Sing in our sweet lullaby:
Lulla, lulla, lullaby; lulla, lulla, lullaby!
    Never harm, nor spell, nor charm,
    Come our lovely lady nigh;
    So good night, with lullaby.

Weaving spiders, come not here:
  Hence, you long-legged spinners, hence!
Beetles black, approach not near;
  Worm, nor snail, do no offence.
    Philomel, with melody,
    Sing in our sweet lullaby:
Lulla, lulla, lullaby; lulla, lulla, lullaby!
    Never harm, nor spell, nor charm,
    Come our lovely lady nigh,
    So good night, with lullaby.

Farther removed from the ballad tradition, or song-with-a-story, is the song *from* a story. Shakespeare sprinkles his plays with many, like this from *A Midsummer Night's Dream.*

They contribute to mood, gay or macabre, but seldom to plot. Sometimes written separately like "specialty numbers" in musical comedy, they usually have their own unity and are not excerpts like the soliloquies, whose meaning, out of context, is frequently distorted.

This song and the one that follows do something that elaborate settings tend to cancel out. They create an outdoor scene for an audience accustomed to the relatively bare Elizabethan stage. In this they approach painting as well as music.

The delicious humor here lies in a sly combination of magic and realism. The "lovely lady," preparing for the delights of sleeping under the sky, needs powerful enchantments to keep away the snakes and bugs.

51. *Over hill, over dale*

WILLIAM SHAKESPEARE

Over hill, over dale,
  Thorough bush, thorough brier,
Over park, over pale,
  Thorough flood, thorough fire,
I do wander everywhere,
Swifter than the moon's sphere;

And I serve the fairy queen,
To dew her orbs upon the green.
The cowslips tall her pensioners be;
In their gold coats spots you see,
Those be rubies, fairy favours,
In those freckles live their savours:
I must go seek some dewdrops here,
And hang a pearl in every cowslip's ear.

Here we are made to imagine first the flowers, then the placing of dew-drops in them. This is an interior spectator-sport denied us on the stage if the scenic designer is too explicit. Lifelike and imagined flowers do not always complement each other. This suggests that the more closely two arts approach each other the less easily they can be combined.

52. *Tom o'Bedlam's song*

ANONYMOUS

From the hag and hungry goblin
That into rags would rend ye,
And the spirit that stands by the naked man
In the book of moons, defend ye,
That of your five sound senses
You never be forsaken,
Nor wander from yourselves with Tom,
Abroad to beg your bacon.

While I do sing: Any food,
Any feeding, drink, or clothing?
Come, dame or maid, be not afraid,
Poor Tom will injure nothing.

Of thirty bare years have I
Twice twenty been enragèd,
And of forty been three times fifteen
In durance soundly cagèd

On the lordly lofts of Bedlam,
  With stubble soft and dainty,
Brave bracelets strong, sweet whips, ding-dong,
  With wholesome hunger plenty.

    And now I sing: Any food, . . .

With a thought I took for Maudlin,
  And a cruse of cockle pottage,
With a thing thus tall, sky bless you all,
  I befell into this dotage.
I slept not since the Conquest,
  Till then I never wakèd,
Till the roguish boy of love where I lay
  Me found and stripped me naked.

    And now I sing: Any food, . . .

When I short have shorn my sour-face,
  And swigged my horny barrel,
In an oaken inn I pound my skin,
  As a suit of gilt apparel.
The moon's my constant mistress,
  And the lovely owl my morrow,
The flaming drake and the night-crow make
  Me music to my sorrow.

    And now I sing: Any food, . . .

The palsy plagues my pulses,
  When I prig your pigs or pullen,
Your culvers take, or matchless make
  Your chanticleer or sullen.
When I want provant, with Humphry
  I sup, and when benighted,
I repose in Powles with waking souls,
  Yet never am affrighted.

    But I do sing: Any food, . . .

I know more than Apollo,
  For oft when he lies sleeping,
I see the stars at bloody wars
  In the wounded welkin weeping,
The moon embrace her shepherd,
  And the queen of love her warrior,
While the first doth horn the star of morn,
  And the next the heavenly Farrier.

While I do sing: Any food, . . .

The gypsy Snap and Pedro
  Are none of Tom's comradoes.
The punk I scorn, and the cutpurse sworn,
  And the roaring boys' bravadoes.
The meek, the white, the gentle,
  Me handle, touch, and spare not;
But those that cross Tom Rhinoceros
  Do what the panther dare not.

Although I sing: Any food, . . .

With an host of furious fancies
  Whereof I am commander,
With a burning spear and a horse of air
  To the wilderness I wander.
By a knight of ghosts and shadows
  I summoned am to tourney
Ten leagues beyond the wide world's end,
  Methinks it is no journey.

Yet will I sing: Any food, . . .

Powles: probably, St. Paul's churchyard

Realism and magic inhabit the world of Tom o'Bedlam, one of the vagrants or "Abraham-men" roaming the sixteenth- and seventeenth-century English roads. Discharged as harmlessly incurable from the Abraham ward of London's Hospital of St. Mary of Bethlehem (Bedlam), they wear badges permitting them to beg. Often they are taken for imposters, gypsies, criminals, or escaped, less harmless lunatics.

The song seems to be composed of snatches of the street cries with which they probably announce or embellish their condition and ask for alms. Its mounting fantasy suggests a single or principal shaper, an anonymous Villon of the roads and taverns.

In Shakespeare's *King Lear*, Edgar, banished son of the Earl of Gloster, disguises himself as a Tom o'Bedlam:

Poor Tom, that eats the swimming frog, the toad, the tadpole, the wall-newt, and the water; that in the fury of his heart, when the foul fiend rages, eats cow-dung for sallets; swallows the old rat and the ditch-dog; drinks the green mantle of the standing pool; who is whipped from tithing to tithing, and stocked, punished, and imprisoned; who hath had three suits to his back, six shirts to his body, horse to ride, and weapon to wear,—

But mice and rats, and such small deer,
Have been Tom's food for seven long year.

53. *Back and side go bare, go bare*

WILLIAM STEVENSON

Back and side go bare, go bare,
Both foot and hand go cold;
But, belly, God send thee good ale enough,
Whether it be new or old.

I cannot eat but little meat,
My stomach is not good;
But sure I think that I can drink
With him that wears a hood.
Though I go bare, take ye no care,
I am nothing a-cold;
I stuff my skin so full within
Of jolly good ale and old.
Back and side go bare, go bare, . . .

I love no roast but a nutbrown toast,
  And a crab laid in the fire;
A little bread shall do me stead,
  Much bread I not desire.
No frost nor snow, no wind, I trow,
  Can hurt me if I would,
I am so wrapt, and throughly lapt
  Of jolly good ale and old.
    Back and side go bare, go bare, . . .

And Tib my wife, that as her life
  Loveth well good ale to seek,
Full oft drinks she, till ye may see
  The tears run down her cheek.
Then doth she troll to me the bowl,
  Even as a maltworm should;
And saith, "Sweetheart, I took my part
  Of this jolly good ale and old."
    Back and side go bare, go bare, . . .

Now let them drink, till they nod and wink,
  Even as good fellows should do;
They shall not miss to have the bliss
  Good ale doth bring men to.
And all poor souls that have scourèd bowls,
  Or have them lustily trolled,
God save the lives of them and their wives,
  Whether they be young or old.
    Back and side go bare, go bare,
      Both foot and hand go cold;
    But, belly, God send thee good ale enough,
      Whether it be new or old.

This song, sometimes listed as anonymous, is from the sixteenth-century play *Gammer Gurton's Needle*, once attributed to James Still, later Bishop of Bath. More recent editors assign it to "one William Stevenson," of whom little seems to be known except that he died in 1575.

The song sounds as if it has a folk origin; perhaps in a somewhat coarser drinking-song of the period. "Back and side" may be a genteel substitution.

54. *There was a little woman*

ANONYMOUS (MOTHER GOOSE)

There was a little woman
  As I have heard tell,
She went to market
  Her eggs for to sell;
She went to market
  All on a market day
And she fell asleep
  On the king's highway.

There came by a peddler,
  His name was Stout,
He cut her petticoats
  All round about;
He cut her petticoats
  Up to her knees
Which made the little woman
  To shiver and sneeze.

When this little woman
  Began to awake,
She began to shiver,
  And she began to shake;
She began to shake,
  And she began to cry,
"Lawk a mercy on me,
  This is none of I!

"But if this be I,
  As I do hope it be,
I have a little dog at home
  And he knows me;

If it be I,
  He'll wag his little tail,
And if it be not I
  He'll loudly bark and wail."

Home went the little woman
  All in the dark,
Up starts the little dog,
  And he began to bark;
He began to bark
  And she began to cry,
"Lawk a mercy on me,
  This is none of I!"

This is another of the alleged productions of the famous Mother Goose. Her name comes apparently from the feigned narrator of the French fairy tales, *Contes de Ma Mère l'Oye*, by Charles Perrault, published in 1697. Seven of these are drawn from an earlier Italian collection, *Pentamerone*.

Mention is also made, for the English rhymes, of a *Mother Goose's Melodies* (1719) by an unknown grandmother, a native of Boston. Whatever their origins, there are by now numerous variants and additions.

Verses that are partly, at least, handed down from mother to child—or often, as in children's games, by children themselves—usually fall between speech and song. Like street cries and barkers' spiels, their rhythms are apt to be strong but erratic, bearing down heavily wherever the singsong tuneless tune dictates:

There was' a lit'tle wo'man
  As I' have heard' tell,'
She' went' to mar'ket
  Her eggs' for' to sell' . . .

The song is in tune with a child's mind. All speech is strange, and shouting makes it familiar. Reading it later brings back some of these sensations.

To repeat emphatically, "She went to market," makes it a fact.

Naming the peddler "Stout" makes him real. He's all the more real for rhyming with "about." Being grown up, he can have scissors and knives to cut people's clothes with.

And it doesn't have a moral. You feel sorry for the little woman, but Stout does have fun. He cuts and cuts and gets away with it.

He's real because he has a name. It's easy to see how the little woman gets confused. She doesn't have any.

55. *The son*

RIDGELY TORRENCE

I heard an old farm-wife,
  Selling some barley,
Mingle her life with life
  And the name "Charley."

Saying: "The crop's all in,
  We're about through now;
Long nights will soon begin,
  We're just us two now.

"Twelve bushel at sixty cents,
  It's all I carried—
He sickened making fence;
  He was to be married—

"It feels like frost was near—
  His hair was curly.
The spring was late that year,
  But the harvest early."

Ridgely Torrence's comparatively few poems, posthumously re-collected in 1952, include the somber song of a lynching bee, "The bird and the tree" (*Poems*, page 91), with its premonitory line, "The minutes crawl like last year's flies."

In "The son" the rather flat voice of a midwestern farm woman is transmuted into song. In her community, "It feels like frost was near" would be a commonplace autumn greeting. In a story it would suggest character and locale. Here it does more:

"It feels like frost was near—
His hair was curly. . ."

An underlying rhythm has been released, a quality of muted song latent in the everyday words. The emotion is intensified by the echo of "Charley" in "curly" and "early"; a subdued refrain.

56. *Adieu! farewell earth's bliss!*

THOMAS NASHE

Adieu! farewell earth's bliss!
This world uncertain is:
Fond are life's lustful joys,
Death proves them all but toys.
None from his darts can fly:
I am sick, I must die.
Lord, have mercy on us!

Rich men, trust not in wealth!
Gold cannot buy you health;
Physic himself must fade;
All things to end are made;
The plague full swift goes by:
I am sick, I must die.
Lord, have mercy on us!

Beauty is but a flower
Which wrinkles will devour:
Brightness falls from the air;
Queens have died young and fair;
Dust hath closed Helen's eye:
I am sick, I must die.
Lord, have mercy on us!

Strength stoops unto the grave:
Worms feed on Hector brave;
Swords may not fight with fate;
Earth still holds ope her gate;
Come! come! the bells do cry.
I am sick, I must die.
Lord, have mercy on us!

Wit with his wantonness
Tasteth death's bitterness:
Hell's executioner
Hath no ears for to hear
What vain art can reply:
I am sick, I must die.
Lord, have mercy on us!

Haste, therefore, each degree
To welcome destiny:
Heaven is our heritage,
Earth but a player's stage:
Mount we unto the sky.
I am sick, I must die.
Lord, have mercy on us!

This song is from Nashe's satirical masque, *Summer's Last Will and Testament*, written outside London during the plague year of 1592.

Few songs of calamity have quite the pace, almost verve, of these lines. Their speed suggests both the vitality of the life being overtaken and the inescapable rapidity of approaching death. There is time only to make peace with destiny before "Brightness falls from the air."

57. *Virtue*

GEORGE HERBERT

Sweet day, so cool, so calm, so bright,
The bridal of the earth and sky:
The dew shall weep thy fall tonight;
For thou must die.

Sweet rose, whose hue angry and brave
Bids the rash gazer wipe his eye:
Thy root is ever in its grave,
And thou must die.

Sweet spring, full of sweet days and roses,
A box where sweets compacted lie;
My music shows ye have your closes,
And all must die.

Only a sweet and virtuous soul,
Like seasoned timber, never gives;
But though the whole world turn to coal,
Then chiefly lives.

Read aloud, this song imposes its phrasing, so closely does it follow the natural tempo of breathing. The music Herbert must have set for it seems to accompany it in ghostly echo. One imagines the music adding still further dimension to the harmony between his poetic technique and his religious belief.

A further apprehension of the music lies in the play of his phrase, "My music shows ye have your closes." A "close" in music is a cadence: "a subsiding of melody or chord sequence . . . to a harmonic close or point of rest." The first three stanzas end in "die." But the fourth employs what is sometimes call a suspended cadence: "ending on an unexpected chord, evading the final close."

58. *Sumer is icumen in*

ANONYMOUS

Sumer is icumen in,
Lhude sing cuccu;
Groweth sed and bloweth med,
And springeth the wude nu.
Sing cuccu!

Awe bleteth after lomb,
  Lhouth after calve cu;
Bulluc sterteth, bucke verteth,
  Murie sing cuccu.

Cuccu, cuccu, wel singes thu, cuccu:
  Na swike thu naver nu;
Sing cuccu, nu, sing cuccu,
  Sing cuccu, sing cuccu, nu!

Summer is a-coming in,
  Loudly sing cuckoo;
Groweth seed and bloweth mead
  And springeth the wood anew.
    Sing cuckoo!

Ewe a-bleateth after lamb,
  Loweth after calf the cow;
Bullock starteth, buck averteth,
  Merrily sing cuckoo.

Cuckoo, cuckoo, well singest thou, cuckoo:
  Nor cease thou never now;
Sing cuckoo, now, sing cuckoo,
  Sing cuckoo, sing cuckoo, now!

Thought to be from the twelfth or thirteenth century, this paean of joy over the change of the seasons can no more be "translated" than Chaucer.

Rather than notes on the unfamiliar spellings, I follow it with an adaptation, staying as close as possible to the original while trying to use the same number of syllables in each line.

"Sumer is icumen in" means literally "Summer is (has) come in." "Nu" probably means "now" throughout, but "now" and "new" are related.

59. *Westron winde, when will thou blow?*
ANONYMOUS

Westron winde, when will thou blow,
  The smalle raine downe can raine?
Crist, if my love wer in my armis,
  And I in my bed againe.

Western wind, when will thou blow,
  The small rain down can rain?
Christ, if my love were in my arms
  And I in my bed again.

In "Sumer is icumen in" the terminal e, as in "wude," "awe," "calve," "murie," is probably pronounced. I doubt if this is so by the time of "Westron winde, when will thou blow," usually attributed to the sixteenth century. However, I've given two versions, original and respelled.

60. *Whenas the rye reach to the chin*
GEORGE PEELE

Whenas the rye reach to the chin,
And chopcherry, chopcherry ripe within,
Strawberries swimming in the cream,
And schoolboys playing in the stream;
Then oh, then oh, then oh, my true love said,
Till that time come again
She could not live a maid.

This is from Peele's play *The Old Wife's Tale*, written toward the end of the sixteenth century. The delicately bawdy allusion in "chopcherry" is to a game similar to "bobbing for apples."

61. *The Crier*

MICHAEL DRAYTON

Good folk, for gold or hire,
But help me to a Crier!
For my poor heart is run astray
After two eyes, that passed this way.
O yes! O yes! O yes!
If there be any man,
In town or country can
Bring my heart again,
I'll please him for his pain.
And by these marks I will you show
That only I this heart do owe:
It is a wounded heart,
Wherein yet sticks the dart;
Every piece sore hurt throughout it,
Faith and troth writ round about it;
It was a tame heart, and a dear,
And never used to roam:
But having got this haunt, I fear
'Twill hardly stay at home.
For God's sake, walking by the way
If you my heart do see,
Either impound it for a stray,
Or send it back to me!

owe: own

The desire of the poet to incorporate the action of the subject into his poem is charmingly illustrated in the fifth line. Wishing for a Crier, Drayton becomes one by echoing the anglicized triple "Oyez!" ("Hear ye!") used in court and for attracting attention to proclamations. The play is as light as those on "hart" and "deer" throughout this bantering Elizabethan song.

62. *Come, oh, come, my life's delight*

THOMAS CAMPION

Come, oh, come, my life's delight,
  Let me not in languor pine!
Love loves no delay: thy sight
  The more enjoyed the more divine:
Oh, come, and take from me
The pain of being deprived of thee!

Thou all sweetness dost enclose
  Like a little world of bliss.
Beauty guards thy looks: the rose
  In them pure and eternal is.
Come then, and make thy flight
As swift to me as heavenly light!

Like Herbert, Thomas Campion sets music to his songs. The words themselves make a melody, with their beautifully matched vowels and subtly repeated consonants.

In spite of his 1602 diatribe against rhyme, he seems perfectly at home with it. This song is from his *Third Booke of Ayres*, published about 1617.

63. *Rosalind's madrigal*

THOMAS LODGE

Love in my bosom like a bee
  Doth suck his sweet;
Now with his wings he plays with me,
  Now with his feet.
Within mine eyes he makes his nest,
His bed amidst my tender breast;
My kisses are his daily feast,
And yet he robs me of my rest:
  Ah, wanton, will ye?

And if I sleep, then percheth he
  With pretty flight,
And makes his pillow of my knee
  The livelong night.
Strike I my lute, he tunes the string;
He music plays if so I sing;
He lends me every lovely thing;
Yet cruel he my heart doth sting:
  Whist, wanton, still ye!—

Else I with roses every day
  Will whip you hence,
And bind you, when you long to play,
  For your offence.
I'll shut mine eyes to keep you in,
I'll make you fast it for your sin,
I'll count your power not worth a pin,—
Alas! what hereby shall I win
  If he gainsay me?

What if I beat the wanton boy
  With many a rod?
He will repay me with annoy,
  Because a god.
Then sit thou safely on my knee,
And let thy bower my bosom be;
Lurk in mine eyes, I like of thee.
O Cupid, so thou pity me,
  Spare not, but play thee!

This is one of the lyric interludes of Lodge's romance, *Rosalynde*, written toward the end of the sixteenth century. As a poetic form "madrigal" is quite loosely defined as a lyric adaptable to music. Its musical definition, too, seems rather tenuous, although it is frequently applied to polyphonic or counterpointed songs.

"Rosalind's madrigal" is obviously for one voice. Yet there are contrapuntal suggestions, particularly in the four successive lines rhyming together in each stanza. These sound like one melody overlaying another. They are followed by terminal resolving lines rhyming only with each other: "Ah, wanton, will ye?" with "Whist, wanton, still ye!" and "If he gainsay me?" with "Spare not, but play thee!"

64. *A red, red rose*

ROBERT BURNS

O, my luve's like a red, red rose,
  That's newly sprung in June:
O, my luve's like the melodie
  That's sweetly played in tune.

As fair art thou, my bonie lass,
  So deep in luve am I:
And I will luve thee still, my dear,
  Till a' the seas gang dry.

Till a' the seas gang dry, my dear,
  And the rocks melt wi' the sun:
I will luve thee still, my dear,
  While the sands o' life shall run.

And fare thee weel, my only luve,
  And fare thee weel awhile!
And I will come again, my luve,
  Tho' it were ten thousand mile.

In my copy of Burns, edited by Alexander Smith and bearing no date, a notation under this title reads: "TUNE—'Wishaw's favourite.'" The Notes in the back of the book add: "The foundation of this song was a short ditty, written, it is said, by one Lieutenant Hinches, as a farewell to his sweetheart."

Existing Scottish airs are often the inspiration of Burns' songs, as he tells us, and the original lyric may serve as a point of departure. It's interesting how frequently they end on a note of parting—"And fare thee weel, my only luve." They seem happiest then, vowing to return.

The opening line is sometimes printed, "My love is like a red, red rose." Whether this is Burns' own variant or not, it sounds flat by comparison; possibly a singing version to fit the tune. But I should expect *my* to be lightly stressed, with a proud lilt, in "O, my luve's like a red, red rose."

65. *Alone*

JAMES JOYCE

The moon's greygolden meshes make
All night a veil,
The shorelamps in the sleeping lake
Laburnum tendrils trail.

The sly reeds whisper to the night
A name—her name—
And all my soul is a delight,
A swoon of shame.

To anyone who reads only the "big" works of James Joyce, *Ulysses* and *Finnegans Wake*, his poems in *Chamber Music* and *Pomes Penyeach* are apt to come as a surprise. Less so, I should think, to readers of *A Portrait of the Artist as a Young Man* and *Dubliners*. The poems seem more related to the moods of the younger Stephen Dedalus in the former, and to the Irish tenor in the latter, in the story called "The Dead."

Unlike all of these, however, the poems are so fragilely constructed as to seem "unplotted," even in the sense in which lyrics may be said to lead from point to point, to prepare their climaxes. Each phrase, sometimes a single word, seems to be savored for itself.

Why, from the rest of the song, should "Alone" end with "A swoon of shame"? Doesn't it come with all the greater conviction because unforeseen? Only later do we realize that its "rightness"—even its unexpectedness—has been subtly and indirectly anticipated by the word "veil." At first it may seem purely descriptive. It is its emotional association with concealment, with modesty, that anticipates adolescent longing and formless shame.

66. *Dear, though the night is gone*

W. H. AUDEN

Dear, though the night is gone,
Its dream still haunts today,
That brought us to a room
Cavernous, lofty as
A railway terminus,
And crowded in that gloom
Were beds, and we in one
In a far corner lay.

Our whisper woke no clocks,
We kissed and I was glad
At everything you did,
Indifferent to those
Who sat with hostile eyes
In pairs on every bed,
Arms round each other's neck,
Inert and vaguely sad.

O but what worm of guilt
Or what malignant doubt
Am I the victim of,
That you then, unabashed,
Did what I never wished,
Confessed another love;
And I, submissive, felt
Unwanted and went out?

Dream as a mirror of reality figures in this fourth of Auden's "Songs and Other Musical Pieces" in *The Collected Poetry*. A series of reflections, only slightly distorted, of modern life, its central image is at once natural and bizarre: a railway terminus filled with beds.

Crowded into a corner of this public-private ménage, the interior life of love, doubt, and anguish exists in complete isolation. The paradoxical condition of agoraphobic claustrophobia, since popularized in such books as *The Lonely Crowd*, is intensified in each stanza by the action of the rhymes and half-rhymes, revolving about a couplet.

67. *A birthday*

CHRISTINA ROSSETTI

My heart is like a singing bird
  Whose nest is in a watered shoot;
My heart is like an apple-tree
  Whose boughs are bent with thickset fruit;
My heart is like a rainbow shell
  That paddles in a halcyon sea;
My heart is gladder than all these
  Because my love is come to me.

Raise me a dais of silk and down;
  Hang it with vair and purple dyes;
Carve it in doves and pomegranates,
  And peacocks with a hundred eyes;
Work it in gold and silver grapes,
  In leaves and silver fleurs-de-lys;
Because the birthday of my life
  Is come, my love is come to me.

One of the hazards of allying poetry and music is illustrated by this fixture of sopranistic repertoire. As a poem, its imagery is at once simple and lush. As it is usually sung, the second quality submerges the first, so indefatigable is the desire to give each image its full, rich, expressive value.

68. *She moved through the fair*

PADRAIC COLUM

My young love said to me, "My brothers won't mind,
And my parents won't slight you for your lack of kind."
Then she stepped away from me, and this she did say
"It will not be long, love, till our wedding day."

She stepped away from me and she moved through the fair,
And fondly I watched her go here and go there,

Till she went her way homeward with one star awake,
As the swan in the evening moves over the lake.

The people were saying no two were ere wed
But one had a sorrow that never was said,
And I smiled as she passed with her goods and her gear,
And that was the last that I saw of my dear.

I dreamed it last night that my young love came in,
So softly she entered, her feet made no din;
She came close beside me, and this she did say
"It will not be long, love, till our wedding day."

In a note on "She moved through the fair" and other songs in his *Collected Poems*, Padraic Colum writes that they "are restorations of Irish traditional songs of which one or two lines were in existence; they were written for traditional music collected by Herbert Hughes and published with the words given here in one of his collections."

As with Burns' songs, the words follow the melody, a familiar and haunting one. There is an interesting comparison with my supposition as to how the line, "O, my luve's like a red, red rose" may be sung. An American reader is apt to stress the word "said" in "My young love said to me" and "away" in "She stepped away from me." In the song each phrase is sung smoothly, with almost equal value on every word. The time beat, unemphasized but present, falls on "to" and on "from."

"To" and "from" are the important words; the heart of this drifting, ballad-like song, with its possibly inimical brothers, its premonition, its ghostly finale.

69. *O thou that sleep'st like pig in straw*

SIR WILLIAM DAVENANT

O thou that sleep'st like pig in straw,
  Thou lady dear, arise!
Open, to keep the sun in awe,
  Thy pretty pinking eyes:

And, having stretched each leg and arm,
  Put on your clean white smock,
And then, I pray, to keep you warm,
  A petticoat on dock.

Arise, arise! Why should you sleep
  When you have slept enough?
Long since, French boys cried "Chimney-sweep,"
  And damsels "Kitchen-stuff."
The shops were opened long before,
  And youngest prentice goes
To lay at's mistress' chamber-door
  His master's shining shoes.

Arise, arise! Your breakfast stays—
  Good water-gruel warm,
Or sugar-sops, which Galen says
  With mace will do no harm.
Arise, arise! When you are up
  You'll find more to your cost—
For morning's-draught in caudle-cup,
  Good nut-brown ale and toast.

The delicate art of name-calling as a form of endearment permeates this song by the seventeenth-century dramatist who would like to believe himself Shakespeare's son. Davenant Senior kept an inn on the road between London and Stratford.

"Thy pretty pinking eyes" is a slyly turned compliment. At first it emphasizes the insult in "pig" and the lady's drowsiness—"pinking" also means "blinking." As a courtly afterthought it alludes as well to drawing blood in a fencing bout. In their love duel he is no match for her.

However, he reserves the last thrust for himself. Surely the lady's breakfast is a slimming diet.

70. *Think of dress in every light*

JOHN GAY

Think of dress in every light
  'Tis woman's chiefest duty;
Neglecting that, ourselves we slight
  And undervalue beauty.
That allures the lover's eye,
  And graces every action;
Besides, when not a creature's by,
  'Tis inward satisfaction.

Gay is chiefly famous for *The Beggar's Opera*. This song, which helps account for the circulation of women's magazines, is from another opera, *Achilles*, posthumously produced in 1733.

71. *Damon and Celimena*

JOHN DRYDEN

D: Celimena, of my heart
None shall e'er bereave you,
If with your good leave I may
Quarrel with you once a day,
I will never leave you.

C: Passion's but an empty name
Where respect is wanting:
Damon, you mistake your aim;
Hang your heart, and burn your flame,
If you must be ranting.

D: Love as dull and muddy is
As decaying liquor:
Anger sets it on the lees,
And refines it by degrees,
Till it works it quicker.

C: Love by quarrels to beget
Wisely you endeavor,
With a grave physician's wit,
Who to cure an ague-fit
Put me in a fever.

D: Anger rouses love to fight,
And his only bait is;
'Tis the spur to dull delight,
And is but an eager bite
When desire at height is.

C: If such drops of heat can fall
In our wooing weather,
If such drops of heat can fall
We shall have the Devil and all
When we come together.

Dryden's *An Evening's Love, or the Mock Astrologer* (1668), adapted from *Le Feint Astrologique* by Thomas Corneille, younger brother of the tragedian, draws from Samuel Pepys the comment, "Very smutty."

In this duet from it, the celebrated wit that in the satires, couplet after clever couplet, comes to be expected is neatly turned. Much of it depends on fourth-line surprises: "Quarrel with you once a day"; "Hang your heart, and burn your flame."

72. *O goodly hand*

SIR THOMAS WYATT

O goodly hand
Wherein doth stand
My heart distract in pain!
Fair hand, alas!
In little space
My life that doth restrain.

O fingers slight
Departed right,
So long, so small, so round;
Goodly begone,
And yet alone
Most cruel in my wound!

With lilies white
And roses bright
Doth strive thy color fair;
Nature did lend
Each finger's end
A pearl for to repair.

Consent at last,
Since that thou hast
My heart in thy demesne,
For service true
On me to rue
And reach me love again.

And if not so,
Then with more woe
Enforce thyself to strain
This simple heart
That suffereth smart,
And rid it out of pain.

Wyatt (sometimes spelled Wyat), poet and statesman of the first half of the sixteenth century, probably accompanies himself on the lute, an instrument to which he addresses several of his poems.

Richard Puttenham, reputed author of *Arte of English Poesie* (1589), speaks of him as in the "company of courtly makers who . . . having travelled in Italie and there tasted the sweet and stately measures and stile of the Italian Poesie, as novices newly crept out of the schoole of Dante, Arioste and Petrarche, greatly polished our rude and homely maner of vulgar Poesie, from that it had been before."

Along with his friend Henry Howard, Earl of Surrey, Wyatt is credited with introducing the sonnet and other Italian forms into English. Surrey has sometimes been preferred for "smoother" versification, while Wyatt retains some of the texture and mocking flavor of Skelton. Many of his poems seem written in code, amatory rather than political. But as here, the surface meaning is lovely enough.

73. *Song*

JOHN DONNE

Sweetest Love, I do not go
For weariness of thee,
Nor in hope the world can show
A fitter love for me;
But since that I
Must die at last, 'tis best
To use myself in jest
Thus by feigned deaths to die.

Yesternight the sun went hence,
And yet is here today;
He hath no desire nor sense,
Nor half so short a way:
Then fear not me,
But believe that I shall make
Speedier journeys, since I take
More wings and spurs than he.

Oh, how feeble is man's power,
That, if good fortune fall,
Cannot add another hour,
Nor a lost hour recall!
But come bad chance,
And we join to it our strength,
And we teach it art and length,
Itself o'er us to advance.

When thou sigh'st, thou sigh'st not wind,
  But sigh'st my soul away;
When thou weep'st, unkindly kind,
  My life's blood doth decay.
    It cannot be
That thou dost love me as thou say'st,
If in thine my life thou waste,
  Thou art the best of me.

Let not thy divining heart
  Forethink me any ill;
Destiny may take thy part,
  And may thy fears fulfil.
    But think that we
Are but turned aside to sleep:
They who one another keep
  Alive, ne'er parted be.

This is musical in quite a different way from Campion's "Come, oh, come, my life's delight" (poem 62). Its music is of the speaking voice, its rhythms heightened but colloquial. One of the most exalted poems of shared love, its ornamentation arises out of direct address:

Let not thy divining heart
  Forethink me any ill;
Destiny may take thy part,
  And may thy fears fulfil.

A curious circumstance surrounds these lines. The poem is supposed to have been written to his wife, the former Anne More, when Donne was on the point of leaving for France. At Amiens he is said to have had a vision of his wife, with her hair over her shoulders, carrying a dead child in her arms. Twelve days later, in Paris, news reached him of the still-birth of the infant, their eighth, and of his wife's recovery.

In music, a song may be anything from a hum to grand opera. Poetry does not parallel music, but its range is as great. Its singing quality runs from being an accompaniment of music to making a music of its own. It includes the natural voice and the trained voice; colloquial speech and the calculated phrases of rhetoric.

So the songs included here have included opposites. Some seem based on folk music, like Spenser's roundelay, or on popular ditties, like the anonymous "Oh, what a plague is love!" At the other extreme is the polished phrasing of Campion, of Herbert, of John Cleveland. In between are any number of variations and gradations: the seeming artlessness of "Sumer is icumen in," of "Westron winde," of Shakespeare's fairy songs; the wit of Dryden, Gay, and Davenant; the haunting qualities, in very different ways, of "She moved through the fair" and "Dear, though the night is gone."

Besides all these are the songs based, not on music or the evocation of music, but on colloquial speech; such as "There was a little woman" and Torrence's "The son." Perhaps these, with John Donne's song, "Sweetest love, I do not go," might have been included as appropriately in the lyrics that follow. But the distinctions seem less valuable than the variety to be found within them and the relationships between them.

PART FIVE

"Washing the water with her beauties white"

Just as there is no clear dividing line between ballad and song, so song and what I am calling "lyric" are often interchangeable. Everyone will have his own ideas of these greater or lesser proximities.

Many of the poems in this group suggest musical phrasing; some may have been set to music. But to me at least, their verbal music is so definite as to make actual music seem superfluous. They create poetic tunes of their own.

74. *Everyone sang*

SIEGFRIED SASSOON

Everyone suddenly burst out singing;
And I was filled with such delight
As prisoned birds must find in freedom
Winging wildly across the white
Orchards and dark-green fields; on—on—and out of sight.

Everyone's voice was suddenly lifted;
And beauty came like the setting sun;
My heart was shaken with tears; and horror
Drifted away . . . O, but Everyone
Was a bird; and the song was wordless; the singing will never be done.

This is unquestionably song, and about song. But it captures the action of this song and translates it, in the image of the birds, for the eye as well as for the ear. We hear the song more clearly because we see its flight.

This mélange of the senses, their happy confusion, intensifies the poem's feeling of exultation. Literal music would be anticlimactic, drowning out the poem's evocation of "the singing" that "will never be done."

Coming as it does in Sassoon's *Collected Poems* after some of his bitterest attacks on war—he once withdrew from combat at a time when it was most courageous to do so—"Everyone sang" seems to refer to the upsurge of joy at the ending of the first of the world wars.

75. *To Helen*

EDGAR ALLAN POE

Helen, thy beauty is to me
  Like those Nicaean barks of yore,
That gently, o'er a perfumed sea,
  The weary, wayworn wanderer bore
  To his own native shore.

On desperate seas long wont to roam,
  Thy hyacinth hair, thy classic face,
Thy Naiad airs have brought me home
  To the glory that was Greece
  And the grandeur that was Rome.

Lo! in yon brilliant window-niche
  How statue-like I see thee stand,
The agate lamp within thy hand!
  Ah, Psyche, from the regions which
  Are Holy Land!

Part of the verbal magic here lies in rhythmic recurrences. In the first stanza the e sounds, some stressed, some unstressed, in "beauty," "me," "Nicaean," "gently," "sea," "weary" are played against "yore," "o'er," "wayworn," "bore," and "shore" to create a dreamy, lapping motion.

Such correspondences, throughout, intensify the poem's nostalgia for a past "that never was on land or sea." Like Coleridge's "Kubla Khan" (poem 1), "To Helen" has sometimes been called "pure poetry." Yet its theme, shimmery and shadowy as it is, is contained in its musical pattern. The melody does carry like a ship.

This evocative quality of Poe's traveled to France via Charles

Baudelaire's translations and greatly influenced the French Symbolist poets. They were not bothered by his use of identical rhyme—"roam" with "Rome"; as "rime riche" it is one of the graces of French poetry.

76. *Villon's straight tip to all cross coves*
(*"Tout aux tavernes et aux filles"*)

W. E. HENLEY

Suppose you screeve? or go cheap-jack?
  Or fake the broads? or fig a nag?
Or thimble-rig? or knap a yack?
  Or pitch a snide? or smash a rag?
  Suppose you duff? or nose and lag?
Or get the straight, and land your pot?
  How do you melt the multy swag?
Booze and the blowens cop the lot.

Fiddle, or fence, or mace, or mack;
  Or moskeneer, or flash the drag;
Dead-lurk a crib, or do a crack;
  Pad with a slang, or chuck a fag;
  Bonnet, or tout, or mump and gag;
Rattle the tats, or mark the spot;
  You cannot bank a single stag;
Booze and the blowens cop the lot.

Suppose you try a different tack,
  And on the square you flash your flag?
At penny-a-lining make your whack,
  Or with the mummers mug and gag?
  For nix, for nix the dibbs you bag!
At any graft, no matter what,
  Your merry goblins soon stravag:
Booze and the blowens cop the lot.

THE MORAL

It's up the spout and Charley Wag
With wipes and tickers and what not.
Until the squeezer nips your scrag,
Booze and the blowens cop the lot.

This adaptation from Villon is not only free. What would be, literally, "Everything to the taverns and the girls" is rendered "Booze and the blowens cop the lot." In a sense it's a double translation, into a thieves' jargon of nineteenth-century London's underworld.

Even partially negotiable, the cant terms are marvelously expressive. The list that follows is drawn mainly from *A Dictionary of Slang and Colloquial English,* which Henley edited with John S. Farmer. Not all the terms are to be found there. Eric Partridge's dictionaries and others have eked out the lacunae more or less, I hope, accurately.

cross coves: thieves (lit., men on the cross)
screeve: draw in chalk on a sidewalk, to attract passers-by for begging
go cheap-jack: become a peddling tradesman
fake the broads: stack the deck, or work a three-card trick
fig a nag: ginger a horse
thimble-rig: run a variety of shell-game
knap a yack: steal a watch
pitch a snide: pass a base coin
smash a rag: pass counterfeit money
duff: sell flashy goods as if contraband or stolen
nose and lag: inform on and send to penal servitude
get the straight: win at poker; various other meanings
land your pot: strike it rich
melt: spend
multy: very (from Italian *molto*)
blowens: wenches
cop the lot: take everything
fiddle: swindle
fence: receive stolen goods
mace: swindle by dressing up and borrowing a watch, etc.
mack: pimp
moskeneer: pawn above value
flash the drag: wear women's clothes for immoral purposes
dead-lurk a crib: rob a lodging during divine services
do a crack: burgle (crack a safe?)
pad with a slang: give false weight
chuck a [illegible]: your guess is as good as mine
bonnet: act as a stooge
tout: spy out information on race horses
mump and gag: beg and hoax
rattle the tats: shake dice
mark the spot: pick out a crib to rob
stag: a shilling
dibbs: money in small amounts, from *diobolon,* a classic coin worth 2½ d
merry goblins: sovereigns (coins)
stravag: abscond; wander off
up the spout: in pawn; done for
Charley Wag: play truant; disappear
wipes: handkerchiefs
tickers: watches
squeezer: hangman's noose
nips your scrag: pinches your neck

77. *ballade of the under side*

DON MARQUIS

by archy
the roach that scurries
skips and runs
may read far more than those
that fly
i know what family skeletons
within your closets
swing and dry
not that i ever
play the spy
but as in corners
dim i bide
i can t dodge knowledge
though i try
i see things from
the under side

the lordly ones the
haughty ones
with supercilious
heads held high
the up stage stiff
pretentious guns
miss much that meets
my humbler eye
not that i meddle
perk or pry
but i m too small
to feel great pride
and as the pompous world
goes by
i see things from
the under side

above me wheel
the stars and suns
but humans shut
me from the sky
you see their eyes as pure
as nuns
i see their wayward
feet and sly
i own and own it with
a sigh
my point of view
is somewhat wried
i am a pessimistic
guy
i see things from the
under side

l envoi
prince ere you pull a bluff
and lie
before you fake
and play the snide
consider whether
archy s nigh
i see things from
the under side

The ballade form, with its strict rhyme-and-rhythm pattern and its one-line refrain, is nevertheless susceptible of variation.

Don Marquis' alter ego, archy the cockroach of the old New York *Sun*, usually does his pieces in free verse. In a radio interview he is asked by "mars":

who has influenced you most in a
literary way

archy

theodore dreiser and bernard shaw
they taught me how far an author can go
if he never loses patience with himself

On the same program ("archy on the radio" from *the lives and times of archy and mehitabel*, page 237) he describes himself: "i am over six feet and go everywhere."

Archy owes his literary style to the office typewriter. Hopping from letter to letter as he must, he doesn't carry enough weight to lock the shift key. Yet in "ballade of the under side," for all its irregularity on the page, he achieves the strict form with a classic twist.

Each stanza rings a change on the idea of "lowness." In the first it's his low stature; in the second, his lowliness of spirit, his humility; in the third, his low opinion of mankind. And the *envoi* is his warning: "Watch out for me, I have the lowdown."

78. *The oftener seen, the more I lust*

BARNABE GOOGE

The oftener seen, the more I lust,
  The more I lust, the more I smart,
The more I smart, the more I trust,
  The more I trust, the heavier heart,
The heavy heart breeds mine unrest,
Thy absence therefore like I best.

The rarer seen, the less in mind,
  The less in mind, the lesser pain,
The lesser pain, less grief I find,
  The lesser grief, the greater gain,
The greater gain, the merrier I,
Therefore I wish thy sight to fly.

The further off, the more I joy,
  The more I joy, the happier life,
The happier life, less hurts annoy,
  The lesser hurts, pleasure most rife,
Such pleasures rife shall I obtain
When distance doth depart us twain.

Elizabeth's gentleman-pensioner may be taking his eminently logical conclusion quite seriously, though the rhythms that lead up to it seem tongue-in-cheek. In one of what he calls his "Eglogs" he asserts a preference for heavenly as against earthly love. This does not keep him, somewhat later, from bringing great pressure to bear when his future father-in-law withholds consent to his marriage with Mary Darrell. A knight has to intercede with an archbishop before the matter is—happily?—settled.

79. *Thou art not fair*

THOMAS CAMPION

Thou art not fair, for all thy red and white,
   For all those rosy ornaments in thee.
Thou art not sweet, though made of mere delight,
   Nor fair nor sweet unless thou pity me.
I will not soothe thy fancies. Thou shalt prove
That beauty is no beauty without love.

Yet love not me, nor seek thou to allure
   My thoughts with beauty, were it more divine.
Thy smiles and kisses I can not endure,
   I'll not be wrapped up in those arms of thine.
Now show it, if thou be a woman right,
Embrace, and kiss, and love me in despite.

Campion himself gives me the lie for including this as "lyric" rather than "song." It appears in *A Booke of Ayres*, the first of that name, brought out in 1601 in collaboration with his friend, the composer Philip Rosseter.

The poem, too, pretending to disdain "all those rosy ornaments in thee," gives itself the lie: a lovely variant of the double-negative love poem.

80. I pray thee leave, love me no more
MICHAEL DRAYTON

I pray thee leave, love me no more,
  Call home the heart you gave me!
I but in vain that saint adore
  That can but will not save me.
These poor half-kisses kill me quite;
  Was ever man thus servèd,
Amidst an ocean of delight,
  For pleasure to be stervèd?

Show me no more those snowy breasts
  With azure rivers branchèd,
Where, whilst mine eye with plenty feasts,
  Yet is my thirst not stanchèd.
O Tantalus, thy pains ne'er tell!
  By me thou art prevented:
'Tis nothing to be plagued in Hell,
  But thus in Heaven tormented!

Clip me no more in those dear arms,
  Nor thy life's comfort call me!
Oh, these are but too powerful charms,
  And do but more enthral me.
But see, how patient I am grown
  In all this coil about thee!
Come, nice thing, let thy heart alone!
  I cannot live without thee!

Perhaps Drayton, too, would give me the lie, in this rather more leisurely and explicit development of a theme similar to Campion's in poem 79.

"These poor half-kisses kill me quite," he says. I don't remember a more realistic statement of this amorous predicament prior to D. H. Lawrence's very different treatment of it in his dialect poem, "Whether or not" (*Collected Poems*, vol. I, page 80).

81. The lark now leaves his watery nest

SIR WILLIAM DAVENANT

The lark now leaves his watery nest
  And, climbing, shakes his dewy wings;
He takes this window for the east;
  And to implore your light, he sings,
Awake, awake, the morn will never rise,
Till she can dress her beauty at your eyes.

The merchant bows unto the seaman's star,
  The ploughman from the sun his season takes;
But still the lover wonders what they are,
  Who look for day before his mistress wakes.
Awake, awake, break through your veils of lawn!
Then draw your curtains, and begin the dawn.

Again the tenuous line between song and lyric quite disappears. Very similar in theme to "O thou that sleep'st like pig in straw" (poem 69), this is a more typically Cavalier compliment: the day can't begin without you. Rather than sprightly, its melodic line is longer and more sustained.

How Davenant must have wished, on this particular morning, that the sun would rise for once in the west.

82. When you are old

W. B. YEATS

When you are old and grey and full of sleep,
And nodding by the fire, take down this book,
And slowly read, and dream of the soft look
Your eyes had once, and of their shadows deep;

How many loved your moments of glad grace,
And loved your beauty with love false or true,
But one man loved the pilgrim soul in you,
And loved the sorrows of your changing face;

And bending down beside the glowing bars,
Murmur, a little sadly, how Love fled
And paced upon the mountains overhead
And hid his face amid a crowd of stars.

This, possibly inspired by Ronsard, is in Yeats's early vein of misty loveliness, the so-called Celtic Twilight period. Everything is bathed in the remoteness of a dream, and life has the quality of legend; like the haunting refrain of his still earlier "The stolen child" (*Collected Poems*, page 18):

Come away, O human child!
To the waters and the wild
With a faery, hand in hand,
For the world's more full of weeping
than you can understand.

83. *All my senses, like beacon's flame*

FULKE GREVILLE, LORD BROOKE

All my senses, like beacon's flame,
Gave alarum to desire
To take arms in Cynthia's name,
And set all my thoughts on fire:
Fury's wit persuaded me,
Happy love was hazard's heir,
Cupid did best shoot and see
In the night where smooth is fair;
Up I start believing well
To see if Cynthia were awake;
Wonders I saw, who can tell?
And thus unto myself I spake;
Sweet God Cupid, where am I,
That by pale Diana's light
Such rich beauties do espy,
As harm our senses with delight?

Am I borne up to the skies?
See where Jove and Venus shine,
Showing in her heavenly eyes
That desire is divine:
Look where lies the Milken Way,
Way unto that dainty throne
Where while all the gods would play,
Vulcan thinks to dwell alone.
Shadowing it with curious art,
Nets of sullen golden hair,
Mars am I, and may not part,
Till that I be taken there.
There withal I heard a sound,
Made of all the parts of love,
Which did sense delight and wound;
Planets with such music move.
Those joys drew desires near.
The heavens blushed, the white showed red,
Such red as in the skies appear
When Sol parts from Thetis' bed.
Then unto myself I said
Surely I Apollo am,
Yonder is the glorious maid
Which men do Aurora name,
Who for joy she hath in me,
Blushing forth desire and fear,
While she would have no man see,
Makes the world know I am there.
I resolve to play my sun,
And misguide my chariot fire:
All the sky to overcome,
And enflame with my desire.
I gave reigns to this conceit,
Hope went on the wheels of lust:
Fancy's scales are false of weight,

Thoughts take thought that go of trust,
I stepped forth to touch the sky,
I a god by Cupid dreams,
Cynthia who did naked lie,
Runs away like silver streams;
Leaving hollow banks behind,
Who can neither forward move,
Nor if rivers be unkind,
Turn away or leave to love.
There stand I, like Arctic Pole,
Where Sol passeth o'er the line,
Mourning my benighted soul,
Which so loseth light divine.
There stand I like men that preach
From the execution place,
At their death content to teach
All the world with their disgrace:
He that lets his Cynthia lie,
Naked on a bed of play,
To say prayers ere she die,
Teacheth time to run away:
Let no love-desiring heart,
In the stars go seek his fate,
Love is only nature's art,
Wonder hinders love and hate.
None can well behold with eyes,
But what underneath him lies.

Skelton's wool-gathering lover (poem 49) turns up again, this time in the first person, in Greville's poem from *Caelica*, posthumously published in 1633.

Another delightful example of poetry mocking itself, it goes to show that a poet's overweening fancy can be his undoing. Like Edmund Waller's Thyrsis (poem 16), "He catched at love, and filled his arm with bays."

84. I, with whose colors Myra dressed her head

FULKE GREVILLE, LORD BROOKE

I, with whose colors Myra dressed her head,
I, that ware posies of her own hand-making,
I, that mine own name in the chimneys read
By Myra finely wrought ere I was waking,—
Must I look on, in hope time coming may
With change bring back my turn again to play?

I, that on Sunday at the church-stile found
A garland sweet, with true-love knots in flowers,
Which I to wear about mine arm was bound,
That each of us might know that all was ours,—
Must I now lead an idle life in wishes,
And follow Cupid for his loaves and fishes?

I, that did wear the ring her mother left,
I, for whose love she gloried to be blamed,
I, with whose eyes her eyes committed theft,
I, who did make her blush when I was named,—
Must I lose ring, flowers, blush, theft, and go naked,
Watching with sighs till dead love be awakèd?

I, that, when drowsy Argus fell asleep,
Like jealousy o'erwatchèd with desire,
Was even warnèd modesty to keep,
While her breath, speaking, kindled nature's fire,—
Must I look on a-cold, while others warm them?
Do Vulcan's brothers in such fine nets arm them?

Was it for this that I might Myra see
Washing the water with her beauties white?
Yet would she never write her love to me.
Thinks wit of change, while thoughts are in delight?
Mad girls must safely love as they may leave;
No man can print a kiss: lines may deceive.

A mystery is posed here. In another of his poems complaining of a fickle mistress, Greville makes a pun on his name, calling himself "Grieve-Ill."

Perhaps an Elizabethan scholar will know if there is a similar play on words concealed in the lines:

> *I, that mine own name in the chimneys read*
> *By Myra finely wrought ere I was waking . . .*

Does she send him smoke signals? Or does he read early-morning messages from her by the light of his own grates? He says she wouldn't write him love letters. Are they breakfast invitations? Or do the lines refer to a custom of writing the lover's name in soot?

It must be one of those "private allusions." But there is nothing unclear in his description of a bath, except the age's indifference to apostrophes. Is it "her beauties white" or "her beauty's white"?

85. *In truth, O Love, with what a boyish kind*

SIR PHILIP SIDNEY

In truth, O Love, with what a boyish kind
Thou dost proceed in thy most serious ways,
That when the heaven to thee his best displays,
Yet of that best thou leav'st the best behind!
For, like a child, that some fair book doth find,
With gilded leaves or colored vellum plays,
Or, at the most, on some fine picture stays,
But never heeds the fruit of writer's mind;
So, when thou saw'st, in nature's cabinet,
Stella, thou straight look'st babies in her eyes;
In her cheeks' pit thou didst thy pitfold set,
And in her breast, bo-peep or couching, lies,
  Playing and shining in each outward part;
  But, fool, seek'st not to get into her heart.

Sir Philip Sidney, born the same year as Greville but predeceasing him by forty-two, is eulogized by his old schoolfellow and lifelong friend in a beautiful change-of-pace metre used earlier by Surrey in his "Laid in my quiet bed, in study as I were" (poem 206). The "Epitaph" begins:

Silence augmenteth grief, writing increaseth rage,
Staled are my thoughts, which loved and lost the wonder of our age:
Yet quickened now with fire, though dead with frost ere now,
Enraged I write I know not what; dead, quick, I know not how.

"In truth, O Love, with what a boyish kind" is Sonnet XI of Sidney's *Astrophel and Stella*, published in 1591, five years after his death. The sequence set a vogue followed by Samuel Daniel, Edmund Spenser and many other Elizabethans, including Shakespeare.

Sidney's "Stella," Lady Rich, never reciprocates his passion. He lays the blame for her "coldness," in this sonnet, on the god of love, who inhabits all of her but her heart. Perhaps "thou straight look'st babies in her eyes" has an allusion to her age, twelve, when they first met some five or six years before her marriage. Sidney's wife was about fourteen.

86. *Fie, pleasure, fie!*

GEORGE GASCOIGNE

Fie, pleasure, fie! thou cloyest me with delight;
  Thou fill'st my mouth with sweetmeats overmuch;
I wallow still in joy both day and night:
  I deem, I dream, I do, I taste, I touch
No thing but all that smells of perfect bliss,
Fie, pleasure, fie! I cannot like of this.

To taste, sometimes, a bait of bitter gall,
  To drink a draught of sour ale, some season,
To eat brown bread with homely hands in hall,
  Doth much increase men's appetites, by reason,
And makes the sweet more sugared that ensues,
Since minds of men do still seek after news.

It might suffice that Love hath built his bower
  Between my lady's lively shining eyes;
It were enough that beauty's fading flower
  Grows ever fresh with her in heavenly wise;
It had been well that she were fair of face,
And yet not rob all other dames of grace.

To muse in mind, how wise, how fair, how good,
  How brave, how frank, how courteous, and how true
My lady is, doth but inflame my blood
  With humors such as bid my health adieu:
Since hap always when it is clomb on high,
Doth fall full low, though erst it reached the sky.

Lo, pleasure, lo! lo, thus I lead a life
  That laughs for joy and trembleth oft for dread;
Thy pangs are such as call for change's knife
  To cut the twist, or else to stretch the thread,
Which holds yfeer the bundle of my bliss:
Fie, pleasure, fie! I dare not trust to this.

news: new things; *yfeer:* together

George Gascoigne, intermittent debtor, Member of Parliament and soldier of fortune, charged with being "a defamed person and noted for manslaughter," "a common Rymer," "a notorious ruffianne" and an atheist, makes a strange complaint about his lot. Most poets disparaging pleasure do so from moral considerations: pleasure is vanity; seek rather the eternal rewards of the spirit. Not so Gascoigne. His only objection is that pleasure is too pleasant; it is ruining his health.

Gascoigne is commemorated by his friend George Whetstone in what is described as "a long dull poem": "A remembrance of the wel-imployed life and godly end of George Gaskoigne, Esquire."

87. *Whoso list to hunt, I know where is an hind*

SIR THOMAS WYATT

Whoso list to hunt, I know where is an hind,
  But as for me, helas, I may no more.
  The vain travail hath wearied me so sore
I am of them that furthest come behind.
Yet may I, by no means, my wearied mind
  Draw from the deer; but as she fleeth afore
  Fainting I follow. I leave off therefore,
Since in a net I seek to hold the wind.

Who list her hunt, I put him out of doubt,
As well as I, may spend his time in vain;
And graven with diamonds in letters plain
There is written, her fair neck round about,
"*Noli me tangere*, for Caesar's I am,
And wild for to hold, though I seem tame."

There is a rumor that the lady of this sonnet is Anne Boleyn, second wife of Henry VIII and mother of Queen Elizabeth. It dates probably from before the marriage.

The fact that Wyatt retains favor—more or less—with the King even after Anne's execution in 1536 on charges of multiple infidelity may have something to do with the spicy ambiguity of the poem, privately circulated among his friends. It has an air of saying one thing when it means another.

The line "Since in a net I seek to hold the wind" is echoed by John Webster at the end of a song from *The Devil's Law-Case*, produced in 1623:

Vain the ambition of kings
Who seek by trophies and dead things
To leave a living name behind,
And weave but nets to catch the wind.

88. *Tears, idle tears, I know not what they mean*

ALFRED, LORD TENNYSON

Tears, idle tears, I know not what they mean,
Tears from the depth of some divine despair
Rise in the heart, and gather to the eyes,
In looking on the happy autumn-fields,
And thinking of the days that are no more.

Fresh as the first beam glittering on a sail,
That brings our friends up from the underworld,
Sad as the last which reddens over one
That sinks with all we love below the verge;
So sad, so fresh, the days that are no more.

Ah, sad and strange as in dark summer dawns
The earliest pipe of half-awakened birds
To dying ears, when unto dying eyes
The casement slowly grows a glimmering square;
So sad, so strange, the days that are no more.

Dear as remembered kisses after death,
And sweet as those by hopeless fancy feigned
On lips that are for others, deep as love,
Deep as first love, and wild with all regret;
O Death in Life, the days that are no more.

Tennyson seldom says one thing when he means another. His nature is to be completely possessed by his mood, without reservation or qualification.

This has its advantages and its drawbacks. Both the poetry of "wit" and the poetry of "sincerity," imitated, can lead to banality; and Tennyson is one of his own worst imitators. It has become a commonplace to note how often he slips over into mawkishness or prolongs a mood beyond endurance.

Yet if even his best poems sometimes have overtones of his worst, they are seldom lacking in a rich vein of music. Among them, "Tears, idle tears" is unique. Rhymeless as it is, it seems to anticipate half-rhyme in its fluid interweavings of "tears," "despair," "more"; of "mean," "divine," "eyes," "fields"; of "underworld" and "verge" and other unforced, as-if-accidental modulations.

89. *Look, stranger, on this island now*

W. H. AUDEN

Look, stranger, on this island now
The leaping light for your delight discovers,
Stand stable here
And silent be,
That through the channels of the ear
May wander like a river
The swaying sound of the sea.

Here at the small field's ending pause
When the chalk wall falls to the foam and its tall ledges
Oppose the pluck
And knock of the tide,
And the shingle scrambles after the suck-
-ing surf,
And the gull lodges
A moment on its sheer side.

Far off like floating seeds the ships
Diverge on urgent voluntary errands,
And the full view
Indeed may enter
And move in memory as now these clouds do,
That pass the harbour mirror
And all the summer through the water saunter.

The melody of sea sounds is carried out in the play of rhyme, half-rhyme and interior rhyme, such as "island"—"silent"; some close, others caught as echo. To these the rhythms add their revolving motion, lengthening out, pausing and beginning again. They enter the ear's "channels" as the sauntering clouds enter the mirroring harbor.

90. *The dream*

JOHN DONNE

Dear Love, for nothing less than thee
Would I have broke this happy dream;
　　It was a theme
For reason, much too strong for fantasy;
Therefore thou wak'dst me wisely; yet
My dream thou brok'st not, but continued'st it;
Thou art so truth that thoughts of thee suffice
To make dreams truths, and fables histories;
Enter these arms, for since thou thought'st it best
Not to dream all my dream, let's act the rest.

As lightning, or a taper's light,
Thine eyes, and not thy noise, waked me;
    Yet I thought thee
(For thou lov'st truth) an angel, at first sight;
But when I saw thou saw'st my heart,
And knew'st my thoughts, beyond an angel's art,
When thou knew'st what I dreamt, when thou knew'st when
Excess of joy would wake me, and cam'st then,
I must confess, it could not choose but be
Profane, to think thee any thing but thee.

Coming and staying showed thee, thee,
But rising makes me doubt that now
    Thou art not thou.
That love is weak, where fear's as strong as he;
'Tis not all spirit, pure and brave,
If mixture it of fear, shame, honor, have.
Perchance as torches, which must ready be,
Men light and put out, so thou deal'st with me;
Thou cam'st to kindle, go'st to come; then I
Will dream that hope again, but else would die.

More complex in music and in thought than "Song" (poem 73), this might be interchanged with "The sun rising" (poem 92) in the group that follows. The last has even more of Donne's alternations of speaking and singing tones. Here the dream prolonging itself calls for a more continuously melodic line.

Donne rings every change on the motif of love. At one extreme is the early, rather fashionable cynicism of "Go and catch a falling star" ending:

Yet she
Will be
False, ere I come, to two, or three.

At the other are so many like this, with its "Thou art so truth," as to make Donne a supreme master of the theme of requited love.

What a tribute—from a man not much later to be Dean of St. Paul's—that it would be sacrilegious to *her* to compare his lady with an angel.

"Lyric" originally means "accompanying the lyre." In a pure sense it is indistinguishable from song. The words of a song are often called "the lyric."

My use of it here, then, is rather special and not at all definite. But it doesn't bother me that a pigeonhole is makeshift. I expect the pigeons to fly out.

I have said that the lyric is a poem that makes a music of its own. Perhaps my sense of it may be illustrated by another partial analogy: the formation, for an American, of the French vowel *u*. One purses one's lips to say o͞o. That corresponds to the impulse to sing. Through the lips so formed one says ē. That corresponds to the impulse to speak. The result is neither song nor speech. It is the lyric French *u*.

PART SIX

"Concent divinely framèd"

As some poems seem to come from or suggest a musical phrase and others to create a music of their own, so a third group appears to go beyond melody, to suggest harmony, counterpoint or orchestration.

The analogy can go only so far. It may suggest proximities with a neighboring art; it cannot offer point-by-point comparison. Nor is a more complex structure, for that reason, necessarily "better."

Even in music itself there is no such thing as pure melody with no overtones. A single note, a single word, has repercussions. But poems, like music, do tend toward melody or toward harmony; which is a way of describing, not a scale of values.

One of the paradoxes of the arts is that the more they resemble the less they are apt to accompany. Milton's lapidary tribute to Shakespeare, engraved on a monument, would enhance neither. Mendelssohn's suite to *A Midsummer Night's Dream* and the play tend to overpower each other.

The paradox is not without brilliant exceptions. But it helps account for the unique difficulties of opera, where several arts are clearly intended to make a unity.

The more complex the "music" of poetry becomes, the more it tends to depart from music proper. Although in our time T. S. Eliot's *Four Quartets* approaches sonata form in its varying movements and in its use of four "voices," separately and in combination, Eliot himself warns against too literal an analogy.

Of the poems that have gone before, a number might properly be included here; perhaps most of all Coleridge's "Kubla Khan" (poem 1) with its patterned arrangement of vowel sounds, its continual change of mood and tempo.

91. *Rose-cheeked Laura, come*

THOMAS CAMPION

Rose-cheeked Laura, come;
Sing thou smoothly with thy beauty's
Silent music, either other
Sweetly gracing.

Lovely forms do flow
From concent divinely framèd;
Heaven is music, and thy beauty's
Birth is heavenly

These dull notes we sing
Discords need for helps to grace them;
Only beauty purely loving
Knows no discord;

But still moves delight,
Like clear springs renewed by flowing,
Ever perfect, ever in them-
Selves eternal.

concent: concord

Epic, dramatic, and narrative poems by nature are apt to be orchestral. But the orchestral or harmonic poem does not have to be long.

Campion's sixteen lines could serve equally well to illustrate song, lyric, or harmony. They are eminently singable. Their marriage of sound and thought makes a "silent music." And this music, smoothly as it flows, is rich and complex.

Campion tosses them off, apparently, as one of the exercises to bolster his attack on rhyme in *Observations in the Art of English Poesie.* His prosodic theories are rather confusing today, largely because they carry over from the Latin tongue (he says the Greek too) ideas about syllabic weight that might possibly have applied to Elizabethan speech but certainly not to our own.

Theory apart, Campion's ear is impeccable. To make up for the absence of end-rhyme he cheats a little by introducing copious internal rhyme and assonance. And he so binds rhythm and thought as to make them most extraordinarily coincide.

"Concent divinely framèd" makes yet another definition of poetry.

92. *The sun rising*

JOHN DONNE

Busy old fool, unruly Sun,
Why dost thou thus,
Through windows, and through curtains call on us?
Must to thy motions lovers' seasons run?
Saucy pedantic wretch, go chide
Late schoolboys, and sour prentices,
Go tell court-huntsmen, that the King will ride,
Call country ants to harvest offices;
Love, all alike, no season knows, nor clime,
Nor hours, days, months, which are the rags of time.

Thy beams, so reverend, and strong
Why shouldst thou think?
I could eclipse and cloud them with a wink,
But that I would not lose her sight so long:
If her eyes have not blinded thine,
Look, and tomorrow late, tell me,
Whether both the Indias of spice and mine
Be where thou left'st them, or lie here with me.
Ask for those kings whom thou saw'st yesterday,
And thou shalt hear, all here in one bed lay.

She is all states, and all princes, I,
Nothing else is.
Princes do but play us, compared to this,
All honor's mimic; all wealth alchemy.

Thou sun art half as happy as we,
In that the world's constructed thus;
Thine age asks ease, and since thy duties be
To warm the world, that's done in warming us.
Shine here to us, and thou art everywhere;
This bed thy center is; these walls, thy sphere.

To say that this alternates between speaking and singing tones is to belittle neither them nor it. Donne's choice of words, like Skelton's, often brings out their grain rather than their smoothness. "Busy old fool, unruly Sun" has the deliberately rough quality of name-calling. The play on words (unruly son) goes even further to put the sun in its place.

It is "unruly" although it appears at regular intervals. This very regularity is contrary to the higher laws of love. It is "pedantic," like a schoolboy who has learned only by rote, not by reason, and "sauces" those who know better.

The interior playfulness, besides counterpointing the surface meaning of the poem, dramatizes its feeling. This might be stated: "I am absurdly happy." It scolds the sun, reads it a lecture, sets it impossible tasks; then, relenting, invites it to stay and share in the lovers' happiness.

The byplay and cajolery make all the more convincing those lines that sing out with pure joy: "Love, all alike, no season knows, nor clime"; "If her eyes have not blinded thine"; "Nothing else is"; and the resolving "This bed thy center is; these walls, thy sphere." As well as his very specific injunction: "Look, and tomorrow *late*, tell me . . ."

The counterpointing is carried further in the varying lengths of the lines. Carefully plotted throughout, they yet give the poem an air of saying whatever comes into its head.

One doesn't have to grasp these overtones, or undertones, all at once, any more than one distinguishes—except with a trained ear—all the notes in a chord. Yet, like the notes, they contribute to the total effect.

Often the initial resistance to what has been called "metaphysical" poetry is an uneasy recognition that there is more to it than first meets the ear. This can be true, too, of apparently "simple" poems.

93. *To autumn*

JOHN KEATS

Season of mists and mellow fruitfulness,
  Close bosom-friend of the maturing sun;
Conspiring with him how to load and bless
  With fruit the vines that round the thatch-eaves run;
To bend with apples the mossed cottage trees,
  And fill all fruit with ripeness to the core;
    To swell the gourd, and plump the hazel shells
  With a sweet kernel; to set budding more,
And still more, later flowers for the bees,
Until they think warm days will never cease,
    For summer has o'er-brimmed their clammy cells.

Who hath not seen thee oft amid thy store?
  Sometimes whoever seeks abroad may find
Thee sitting careless on a granary floor,
  Thy hair soft-lifted by the winnowing wind;
Or on a half-reaped furrow sound asleep,
  Drowsed with the fume of poppies, while thy hook
    Spares the next swath and all its twinèd flowers:
And sometimes like a gleaner thou dost keep
  Steady thy laden head across a brook;
  Or by a cider-press, with patient look,
    Thou watchest the last oozings, hours by hours.

Where are the songs of spring? Aye, where are they?
  Think not of them, thou hast thy music too:
While barrèd clouds bloom the soft-dying day,
  And touch the stubble-plains with rosy hue;
Then in a wailful choir the small gnats mourn
  Among the river sallows, borne aloft
    Or sinking as the light wind lives or dies;
And full-grown lambs loud bleat from hilly bourn;
  Hedge-crickets sing; and now with treble soft
  The red-breast whistles from a garden-croft;
    And gathering swallows twitter in the skies.

This is more patently sonorous music, with long rolling and swaying rhythms and dark, autumnal vowels. The weaving rhymes, too, have the quality of autumn winds, alternately steady and fitful, coming in premonitory gusts and dying away.

The personification of the season, something of a poetic standby, is reanimated by its judicious vagueness. The figure seen can be either a harvest god or a sleepy plowboy.

The melancholy associated with the impending of winter, felt subtly throughout the poem, is at once climaxed and thrown away in the curtain line: "And gathering swallows twitter in the skies."

94. *Ode*

Intimations of immortality from recollections of early childhood

WILLIAM WORDSWORTH

The child is father of the man;
And I could wish my days to be
Bound each to each by natural piety.

I

There was a time when meadow, grove and stream,
The earth, and every common sight,
To me did seem
Apparelled in celestial light,
The glory and the freshness of a dream.
It is not now as it hath been of yore;—
Turn wheresoe'er I may,
By night or day,
The things which I have seen I now can see no more.

II

The rainbow comes and goes,
And lovely is the rose;
The moon doth with delight
Look round her when the heavens are bare;

Waters on a starry night
Are beautiful and fair;
The sunshine is a glorious birth;
But yet I know, where'er I go,
That there hath passed away a glory from the earth.

III

Now, while the birds thus sing a joyous song,
And while the young lambs bound
As to the tabor's sound,
To me alone there came a thought of grief:
A timely utterance gave that thought relief,
And I again am strong.
The cataracts blow their trumpets from the steep;
No more shall grief of mine the season wrong;
I hear the echoes through the mountains throng,
The winds come to me from the fields of sleep,
And all the earth is gay;
Land and sea
Give themselves up to jollity,
And with the heart of May
Doth every beast keep holiday;—
Thou child of joy,
Shout round me, let me hear thy shouts, thou happy shepherd-boy!

IV

Ye blessèd Creatures, I have heard the call
Ye to each other make; I see
The heavens laugh with you in your jubilee;
My heart is at your festival,
My head hath its coronal.
The fullness of your bliss I feel—I feel it all.
Oh evil day! if I were sullen
While earth herself is adorning
This sweet May-morning,
And the children are culling
On every side,

In a thousand valleys far and wide,
Fresh flowers; while the sun shines warm,
And the babe leaps up on his mother's arm:—
I hear, I hear, with joy I hear!
—But there's a tree, of many, one,
A single field which I have looked upon,
Both of them speak of something that is gone:
The pansy at my feet
Doth the same tale repeat:
Whither is fled the visionary gleam?
Where is it now, the glory and the dream?

V

Our birth is but a sleep and a forgetting:
The soul that rises with us, our life's star,
Hath had elsewhere its setting,
And cometh from afar:
Not in entire forgetfulness,
And not in utter nakedness,
But trailing clouds of glory do we come
From God, who is our home:
Heaven lies about us in our infancy!
Shades of the prison-house begin to close
Upon the growing boy,
But he beholds the light, and whence it flows,
He sees it in his joy;
The youth, who daily farther from the east
Must travel, still is nature's priest,
And by the vision splendid
Is on his way attended;
At length the man perceives it die away,
And fade into the light of common day.

VI

Earth fills her lap with pleasures of her own;
Yearnings she hath in her own natural kind.

And even, with something of a mother's mind,
  And no unworthy aim,
 The homely nurse doth all she can
To make her foster-child, her inmate man,
 Forget the glories he hath known,
And that imperial palace whence he came.

VII

Behold the child among his new-born blisses,
A six years' darling of a pigmy size!
See, where 'mid work of his own hand he lies,
Fretted by sallies of his mother's kisses,
With light upon him from his father's eyes!
See, at his feet, some little plan or chart,
Some fragment from his dream of human life,
Shaped by himself with newly-learnèd art;
 A wedding or a festival,
 A mourning or a funeral;
  And this hath now his heart,
 And unto this he frames his song:
  Then will he fit his tongue
To dialogues of business, love, or strife;
  But it will not be long
  Ere this be thrown aside,
  And with new joy and pride
The little actor cons another part;
Filling from time to time his "humorous stage"
With all the persons, down to palsied age,
That life brings with her in her equipage:
  As if his whole vocation
  Were endless imitation.

VIII

Thou, whose exterior semblance doth belie
  Thy soul's immensity;

Thou best philosopher, who yet dost keep
Thy heritage, thou eye among the blind,
That, deaf and silent, read'st the eternal deep,
Haunted forever by the eternal mind,—
    Mighty prophet! Seer blest!
        On whom those truths do rest,
Which we are toiling all our lives to find,
In darkness lost, the darkness of the grave;
Thou, over whom thy immortality
Broods like the day, a master o'er a slave,
A presence which is not to be put by;
Thou little Child, yet glorious in the might
Of heaven-born freedom on thy being's height,
Why with such earnest pains dost thou provoke
The years to bring the inevitable yoke,
Thus blindly with thy blessedness at strife?
Full soon thy soul shall have her earthly freight,
And custom lie upon thee with a weight,
Heavy as frost, and deep almost as life!

IX

        O joy! that in our embers
        Is something that doth live,
        That nature yet remembers
        What was so fugitive!
The thought of our past years in me doth breed
Perpetual benediction: not indeed
For that which is most worthy to be blest—
Delight and liberty, the simple creed
Of childhood, whether busy or at rest,
With new-fledged hope still fluttering in his breast:—
        Not for these I raise
        The song of thanks and praise;
    But for those obstinate questionings
        Of sense and outward things,
    Fallings from us, vanishings;

Blank misgivings of a creature
Moving about in worlds not realized,
High instincts before which our mortal nature
Did tremble like a guilty thing surprised:
But for those first affections,
Those shadowy recollections,
Which, be they what they may,
Are yet the fountain-light of all our day,
Are yet a master-light of all our seeing;
Uphold us, cherish, and have power to make
Our noisy years seem moments in the being
Of the eternal silence: truths that wake,
To perish never;
Which neither listlessness, nor mad endeavor,
Nor man nor boy,
Nor all that is at enmity with joy,
Can utterly abolish or destroy!
Hence in a season of calm weather
Though inland far we be,
Our souls have sight of that immortal sea
Which brought us hither;
Can in a moment travel thither,
And see the children sport upon the shore,
And hear the mighty waters rolling evermore.

x

Then sing, ye birds, sing, sing a joyous song!
And let the young lambs bound
As to the tabor's sound!
We in thought will join your throng,
Ye that pipe and ye that play,
Ye that through your hearts today
Feel the gladness of the May!
What though the radiance which was once so bright
Be now forever taken from my sight;
Though nothing can bring back the hour
Of splendor in the grass, of glory in the flower;

We will grieve not, rather find
Strength in what remains behind;
In the primal sympathy
Which having been must ever be;
In the soothing thoughts that spring
Out of human suffering;
In the faith that looks through death,
In years that bring the philosophic mind.

XI

And O, ye Fountains, Meadows, Hills, and Groves,
Forebode not any severing of our loves!
Yet in my heart of hearts I feel your might;
I only have relinquished one delight
To live beneath your more habitual sway.
I love the brooks which down their channels fret,
Even more than when I tripped lightly as they;
The innocent brightness of a new-born day
Is lovely yet;
The clouds that gather round the setting sun
Do take a sober coloring from an eye
That hath kept watch o'er man's mortality;
Another race hath been, and other palms are won.
Thanks to the human heart by which we live,
Thanks to its tenderness, its joys, and fears,
To me the meanest flower that blows can give
Thoughts that do often lie too deep for tears.

Wordsworth's gift of song and his philosophic meditation both find, it seems to me, their fullest expression here.

The songs and shorter poems reach often for a simplicity, a child-likeness, that doesn't always come off. And his long ruminative poems, filled with beautiful passages, do go on. In the ode the two tendencies seem both to curb and release each other. He is at once a man remembering a child, a child speaking through a man. How directly and yet how subtly the two rhythms, of joyous song and of brooding, not quite melancholy speculation, alternate and interpenetrate.

The three lines that precede the poem come from his earlier and much-quoted

My heart leaps up when I behold
A rainbow in the sky.

This is affecting. But as if dissatisfied, he seems to have asked himself, "Why?" The ode is the answer. How much more moving, because more childlike and direct, is the passage beginning:

The rainbow comes and goes,
And lovely is the rose . . .

And how skillfully the poem develops. Into the first theme, the festivity of the early stanzas, come tentative intrusions of the second, the loss of pristine wonder. Gradually this gathers momentum, broadens out, making its philosophic point chiefly by *looking back* at childhood.

The freshness and delight continually reassert themselves, with such effective use of contrast that what the poem says is impossible comes to pass. Childhood is reawakened.

95. *A palinode*

EDMUND BOLTON

As withereth the primrose by the river,
As fadeth summer's sun from gliding fountains,
As vanisheth the light-blown bubble ever,
As melteth snow upon the mossy mountains:
So melts, so vanisheth, so fades, so withers
The rose, the shine, the bubble, and the snow
Of praise, pomp, glory, joy—which short life gathers—
Fair praise, vain pomp, sweet glory, brittle joy.
The withered primrose by the mourning river,
The faded summer's sun from weeping fountains,
The light-blown bubble vanishèd forever,
The molten snow upon the naked mountains,
  Are emblems that the treasures we up-lay
  Soon wither, vanish, fade, and melt away.

For as the snow, whose lawn did overspread
The ambitious hills, which giant-like did threat
To pierce the heaven with their aspiring head,
Naked and bare doth leave their craggy seat;
Whenas the bubble, which did empty fly
The dalliance of the undiscernèd wind,
On whose calm rolling waves it did rely,
Hath shipwreck made, where it did dalliance find;
And when the sunshine which dissolved the snow,
Colored the bubble with a pleasant vary,
And made the rathe and timely primrose grow,
Swarth clouds withdrawn (which longer time do tarry)—
  Oh, what is praise, pomp, glory, joy, but so
  As shine by fountains, bubbles, flowers, or snow?

rathe: early blooming

We tend to think of poetry in periods, with a dominant characteristic for each. The Elizabethan age is lusty; the seventeenth, courtly; the eighteenth, witty; the early nineteenth, romantic; the Victorian (for they double as they reach us), sentimental; the Georgian, dull and our own, confused.

Actually they are *all* confused; there is no one prevailing style in any. As its work comes down to us, the greatest bulk of any period disappears—the worst, we hope. Some leveling out occurs, too, in our perspective. We are only partly aware of the literary conflicts in other periods. They appear, therefore, more orderly than our own.

But even in what appears, the visible iceberg, there is less uniformity than we think. Surely nothing could be less lusty, more delicately patterned than Edmund Bolton's palinode, printed in *England's Helicon* in 1600.

A palinode is usually written in retraction of a former ode. In this double sonnet the word, whose root meaning implies repetition as well as reversal ("back" or "again"), seems to apply to its hauntingly modulated recurrences; its appearing, reappearing, and disappearing "primrose," "river," "sun," "fountains," "bubble," "snow" and "mountains." These repetitions are active. They dance and vanish, live, breathe and die before our eyes.

96. *God's grandeur*

GERARD MANLEY HOPKINS

The world is charged with the grandeur of God.
  It will flame out, like shining from shook foil;
  It gathers to a greatness, like the ooze of oil
Crushed. Why do men then now not reck his rod?
Generations have trod, have trod, have trod;
  And all is seared with trade; bleared, smeared with toil;
  And wears man's smudge and shares man's smell: the soil
Is bare now, nor can foot feel, being shod.

And for all this, nature is never spent;
  There lives the dearest freshness deep down things;
And though the last lights off the black West went
  Oh, morning, at the brown brink eastward, springs—
Because the Holy Ghost over the bent
  World broods with warm breast and with ah! bright wings.

More than most poets, Gerard Manley Hopkins overrides all boundaries. His "Wreck of the Deutschland," that amazingly triumphant account of the shipwrecked nuns that seems to have frightened his ecclesiastical superiors, is, among other things, an historical ballad, a prayer, a symphony, and a love poem or epithalamion celebrating the marriage of the nuns with Christ.

So too "God's grandeur" is at once a unique orchestration, a whorl of physical imagery—visual, auditory, kinetic, tactile—and an emotional vortex of wonder, rage, sorrow, and love.

Rather than dispensing with the conventional prosody of his day, Hopkins may be said to burst and remold it, all in the same breath. It is interesting to think in this connection of Whitman, a poet with whom Hopkins sometimes feels a shuddery affinity.

"But when you read it," he writes of one of his poems, "let me know if there is anything like it in Walt Whitman; as perhaps there may be, and I should be sorry for that." In another letter, admitting to certain resemblances between them, he adds: "As he is a very great scoundrel this is not a pleasant confession."

To Hopkins, Whitman, like Swinburne, is an apostle of "the new paganism." Yet Hopkins, writing to the glory of God—and, through God, man—cannot help but admire the expressiveness of Whitman, celebrating himself—and, through himself, man. To which of them belongs the line: "I kiss my hand to the stars"?

Both share an impulse of universality; develop it in almost opposite ways. Where Whitman relaxes the metre and form of his poems to "get everything in," to surround his material, Hopkins performs miracles of compression. Whitman's theory of "versification" might be called "unsprung rhythm"; but he has his compressions too. And his language, based as it is on American speech, is not without heightening.

Hopkins' theory of "sprung rhythm" seems designed to convince himself and a rather uncomprehending friend, Robert Bridges—one of the few people to see Hopkins' poems during his lifetime—that his prosodic innovations have a basis in orthodox principle. It is interesting chiefly as a reflection of his temperament and—*after* reading the poems—for the light it throws on the enormous craftsmanship that goes into them.

What strikes us on hearing the rhythms of "God's Grandeur" is their astonishing variety and flexibility within a clearly defined form. They follow the motion of the mind—what Hopkins calls "inscape" —as it dwells on "grandeur," flames out with the lightning of the "shook foil," "gathers to a greatness" like "oil / Crushed" or treads with the "generations."

They seem so natural, so inevitable, that we wonder at Hopkins' need to defend them. In his manuscript he has hieroglyphic squiggles meaning "counterpointed" over the first line. He knows it will bother his contemporaries that there seem to be only four stresses in what would ordinarily be a five-foot line.

Such "irregularities" are less alarming today. It's not necessary to think of an imaginary stress on "with"; the weight of the heavy syllables (their own weight, not a Latin precedent) fills out the line.

There is just a suggestion of Wildean paradox in "bent / World." (How wonderfully he makes use of the divisions *between* lines for an additional rhythmic emphasis; "oil / Crushed" is the other, and opposite, example in this poem.) What is expected, and is still working in the image, is "the Holy Ghost bent over the world." That is true but obvious: love always bends toward the object of love. The significant fact is that the *world* is bent. Physically, it bends away as a sphere. Spiritually, it bends away from love. It "follows its own bent."

This is suggestive of the amount of counterpointing there is, in rhythm and in idea: to Hopkins the two are one. How carefully observed his physical imagery is may be shown by a note he makes to the line "It will flame out, like shining from shook foil."

He has considered substituting "lightning" for "shining" but thinks better of it. Perhaps he feels it will overstress an effulgence already implicit in the image. Here is his observation: "Shaken goldfoil gives off broad glares like sheet lightning and also, and this is true of nothing else, owing to its zigzag dints and creasings and network of small many cornered facets, a sort of fork lightning too."

The poems in Parts Three, Four, Five and Six have shown poetry in relation to sound. This relationship is multiple and complex. It is not readily condensed into a formula, even if that were desirable.

The one characteristic all poems seem to share is that they are made up of *some* combination of speech and music. Perhaps the poems here that most closely approach music are "Kubla Khan" (poem 1), "La belle Dame sans merci" (poem 40), "Virtue" (poem 57), "To Helen" (poem 75), "Rose-cheeked Laura, come" (poem 91) and "A palinode" (poem 95). Few of them, I think, for all the musical interweaving of their sound-patterns (or, more likely, *because* of that), would be enhanced by music proper. "Virtue" does seem *designed* for singing. Yet "Virtue" too, along with "Kubla Khan," "To Helen" and the others, depends quite as much on speech, heightened as its rhythms and the arrangement of its words may be as compared with what we think of as ordinary conversation.

On the other hand, those poems that are least "musical" in this sense, that lie closest to speech—both written and spoken—are clearly distinguishable from prose. There is, of course, prose—like that of James Joyce, or the plays of Synge—that is so heightened as to seem a form of poetry. And there are poems so tedious that we call them "prosaic"—as if "prose" were a term of reproach. "Mechanical" might be the more accurate description, whether the mechanics is that of traditional verse forms or of so-called "free verse." Even Shakespeare, in some of his sonnets, can be mechanical.

By now there is no excuse to confuse the "free verse" of Whitman with prose. It has been with us long enough for its heightenings, its tensions, its "music" to be recognized. Music itself is not confined to set forms. Ironically, Whitman's worst poem, in my opinion, is his one attempt to write "orthodox" poetry: "O Captain, my captain." The sincerity is undeniable; the structure simply will not support it.

"Free verse" since Whitman, when it is Whitmanesque, tends to be as mechanical as any tired sonnet. When it is based on personal rhythms, like those of William Carlos Williams (see poems 116 and 117), it creates its own shapes, a new "music."

Poetry is not good or bad by virtue of being, on the one hand, "musical" or, on the other, "colloquial." Its qualities reside in those unique combinations of both that truly express a temperament. Since these combinations are incalculable, the future of poetry is unpredictable. It will continue to create new forms, and along with them to reanimate the old.

PART SEVEN

"Little low heavens"

Poetry makes its appeal through some of the senses to all of them. Passing through the eye, in silent reading, it is directed perhaps most of all to the ear, which it reaches more readily when read aloud. From there it may be deflected in all sorts and combinations of ways: to the inner ear, in its evocation of sounds other than its own (the song of a lark, for instance, or the rhythms of the sea); to the inner eye, in the pictures it conjures up; more elusively, perhaps, to taste and touch and smell; and, more strongly and more often than may be consciously realized, to what is sometimes called the kinesthetic sense: sensations of motion and muscular activity.

One or another or a combination of these appeals is apt to predominate in a poem, depending as it dwells on, or presents, one or another aspect of experience. These predominances—representations or echoes of the various sensations—are often called images.

The word "image," related to "imitation," most commonly suggests something that can be seen. It is apt to be associated most readily with an object, such as a painted, modeled or carved figure; or with the memory of an object in the mind's eye. For this reason, I think, the use of "Imagist" to describe a kind of poetry may cause confusion, although the founders of the school of poetry known by that name have no such exclusive preoccupation in mind. Their interest is in a focusing or heightening of every kind of image.

Images include anything that is given form. A song or lyric makes images of sound: patterns, recurrences, contrasts, which may resemble those in music, in speech, in nature. It is here, as the three preceding groups—and, to a lesser extent, the ballads—may have shown, that poetry most obviously departs from prose.

Not that prose is lacking in this kind of imagery. It is a difference in degree. Sound-images in prose are apt to be less definitely shaped; at least, less attended to.

In conversation, "It's a bright day" adequately describes a weather. It is heard, but not especially *listened* to. In a story, "The day was fine and bright" may help set a scene in which something is going to happen.

When George Herbert says, "Sweet day, so cool, so calm, so bright" (poem 57), the sound of the words enters into the image. They are perfectly ordinary words, but their arrangement makes us listen to them.

Not only is their sequence musically beautiful, especially in the variety of vowel sound; it creates a motion in the mind. "Coolness" is close: a feeling on the skin. "Calmness" is broad: a looking out to see that nothing is stirring. "Brightness" is high: a looking up toward the source of light. The complete action describes what might be called a full-arm gesture of emotion.

A sound image need not be a *different* arrangement of words. In Ridgely Torrence's "The son" (poem 55) identical words serve as commonplace greeting, characteristic description, and—by strategic location—song.

Poems are not limited to a single kind of image. Herbert's song contains, if fleetingly, images of motion. Many, if not all, of the poems previously grouped carry more or less definite shapes of other sorts: visual images, where poetry approaches painting and sculpture; images of touch and taste and smell, for poetry can overlap with the culinary arts too ("Good nut-brown ale, and toast"); and images of motion, where poetry approaches dancing, not only watching or describing it, but, in the internal action of its rhythms, engaging in it.

In this group a number of images other than sound are present. Many similar images are to be found in the poems that have gone before; and those that follow are not, by that token, unmusical. It is rather a shift in our attention reading them.

97. *Meeting at night*

ROBERT BROWNING

The grey sea and the long black land;
And the yellow half-moon large and low;

And the startled little waves that leap
In fiery ringlets from their sleep,
As I gain the cove with pushing prow,
And quench its speed i' the slushy sand.

Then a mile of warm sea-scented beach;
Three fields to cross till a farm appears;
A tap at the pane, the quick sharp scratch
And blue spurt of a lighted match,
And a voice less loud, through its joys and fears,
Than the two hearts beating each to each!

Like so many of Browning's poems, this has a strong narrative interest. With a minimum of event, it yet follows one of the classic patterns of the short story, building to climax and denouement.

It places the reader at once in the middle of an action. Imagery supplies the incidents; a series, mainly, of pictures. But the pictures include hushed sounds, the feel and smell of sea air, and continuous movement. This culminates in the wonderful cluster of images:

A tap at the pane, the quick sharp scratch
And blue spurt of a lighted match . . .

The rhythm and the play of consonants make us enter into the action of tapping and scratching. The flame, when it comes, lights up the poem.

This sudden illumination is carefully plotted. The earlier "fiery ringlets from their sleep" is not only convincing in itself, it prepares the eye for alternations of dark and light.

This is not *unlike* what may go on in excellent reporting, in fiction, in cinema technique. To the extent that they approach this vivid economy, this compression of action into the sensations that accompany it, they approach poetry.

Cinerama has yet to devise quite so intense an immediacy.

98. *The night-piece, to Julia*

ROBERT HERRICK

Her eyes, the glowworm lend thee,
The shooting stars attend thee
    And the elves also,
    Whose little eyes glow
Like the sparks of fire, befriend thee.

No Will-o'-th'-Wisp mislight thee,
Nor snake, or slowworm bite thee;
    But on, on thy way
    Not making a stay,
Since ghost there's none to affright thee.

Let not the dark thee cumber:
What though the moon does slumber?
    The stars of the night
    Will lend thee their light
Like tapers clear without number.

Then Julia let me woo thee,
Thus, thus to come unto me;
    And when I shall meet
    Thy silvery feet
My soul I'll pour into thee.

Herrick's song is exquisite in its little picking-out sounds, its light, pattering rhythms, all in scale with the small lights of night. It's as if shooting stars could be heard.

It's true that, reading the last stanza, one is inclined to say, "Oh, Herrick! you'd say that to *any* girl." Being no hypocrite, he'd reply, "Indeed I would. And have."

99. *The mower to the glowworms*

ANDREW MARVELL

Ye living lamps, by whose dear light
The nightingale does sit so late,
And studying all the summer night,
Her matchless songs does meditate:

Ye country comets, that portend
No war, nor prince's funeral,
Shining unto no higher end
Than to presage the grasses' fall;

Ye glowworms, whose officious flame
To wandering mowers shows the way,
That in the night have lost their aim,
And after foolish fires do stray;

Your courteous lights in vain you waste,
Since Juliana here is come,
For she my mind hath so displaced
That I shall never find my home.

Marvell's poem is supposedly written some five years after the publication of Herrick's *Hesperides* (1648), which includes the preceding "Night-piece." The lengthening of the name "Julia" to "Juliana" is typical of their contrasting treatments.

Herrick's pizzicato enumeration of flickering and wayward lights gives place in Marvell to a more sustained lyric line. The glowworms, appearing often along the sides of paths, are here a steadying influence. Instead of leading his lady to him, they would lead him away from her with their "officious flame." Their "good offices" are insistent, if unavailing.

The differences in temperament are clear. Herrick is almost too unreluctant. Marvell has his doubts, but they are far from insurmountable.

100. Composed upon Westminster Bridge, Sept. 3, 1802
WILLIAM WORDSWORTH

Earth has not anything to show more fair:
Dull would he be of soul who could pass by
A sight so touching in its majesty:
This city now doth like a garment wear
The beauty of the morning; silent, bare,
Ships, towers, domes, theaters, and temples lie
Open unto the fields, and to the sky;
All bright and glittering in the smokeless air.
Never did sun more beautifully steep
In his first splendor, valley, rock, or hill;
Ne'er saw I, never felt, a calm so deep!
The river glideth at his own sweet will:
Dear God! the very houses seem asleep;
And all that mighty heart is lying still!

This panoramic sonnet has affinities with the graphic arts and with photography. Like an etching of the time, it preserves period touches: London is no longer "Open unto the fields," nor is it likely to be "smokeless" at whatever hour.

Appropriately to early morning, the poem presents not so much color as tone, a feeling of mass, the suggestion of detail—conveyed in a single line, "Ships, towers, domes, theaters, and temples lie"—and what Hemingway likes to call, and is himself a master of, a "sense of the terrain." The poem takes us on a tour with the eye.

The only discordant note I find is a certain smug, self-congratulatory tone. "Dull would he be of soul who could pass by" what Wordsworth has noticed. In another sonnet, "The world is too much with us," he says: "Great God! I'd rather be / A pagan suckled on a creed outworn," as if this were the most outlandish thing that could happen to a Wordsworth.

101. *Schoolboys in winter*
JOHN CLARE

The schoolboys still their morning rambles take
To neighboring village school with playing speed,
Loitering with pastime's leisure till they quake;
Oft looking up the wild-geese droves to heed,
Watching the letters which their journeys make,
Or plucking haws on which the fieldfares feed,
And hips, and sloes! and on each shallow lake
Making glib slides, where they like shadows go
Till some fresh pastimes in their minds awake.
Then off they start anew and hasty blow
Their numbed and clumpsing fingers till they glow;
Then races with their shadows wildly run
That stride huge giants o'er the shining snow
In the pale splendor of the winter sun.

Clare's poem is quite Breughel-like in its loving observation. The scene seems to be viewed from above, as if he has hidden himself on the top of a hill. But there is no condescension. He is there to watch children behave without adult intrusion.

A distance in time enters, too, into his telescopic vision. "Watching the letters which their journeys make" evokes both the present scene and memories of his own childhood. His spontaneous delight in fields and woods, he realizes, was a "spelling out" of nature, as contrasted with the rote learning of school.

The point of view is at once distant and near. Memory and affection impel him to describe the scene through the children's eyes as well as his own. "Huge giants" is the way *they* see their shadows. "Clumpsing fingers" seems to be a childhood idiom for "frostbitten": both "clumsy" and "freezing into clumps." His images are double, or composite: his and theirs, past and present.

102. *Upon the body of our blessed Lord, naked and bloody*
RICHARD CRASHAW

They have left thee naked, Lord, O that they had!
This garment too I wish they had denied.
Thee with thyself they have too richly clad;
Opening the purple wardrobe in thy side.
O never could there be garment too good
For thee to wear, but this of thine own blood.

The impulse to give permanence to what is most transitory enters peculiarly into the seventeenth-century poems of Richard Crashaw. In one, "The tear," a drop of the Virgin Mary's sorrow is thought of as an eternal object and carried on a pillow.

This is like the extravagant dew of baroque sculpture. As in William Browne's epitaph (poem 5) and Milton's tribute to Shakespeare (poem 28), an image in the mind is regarded with such intensity and absorption that it becomes fixed, as if solid.

A motif of Surrealist painting is suggested here. "Opening the purple wardrobe in thy side" seems a literary counterpart, perhaps a suggestion, for the chest of drawers built into the human figure in some of the early paintings of Salvador Dali.

Exaggerated metaphor, or "conceit," is sometimes thought of as "being all out of proportion" or "going too far." Yet the arts are nowhere in absolute scale with what we think of as "reality." Every metaphor is hyperbole; all description, distortion. Like the dome of St. Peter's, said to have come within inches of collapse, they stand or fall in relation to the structure and intention of the poem.

Crashaw's poems create their own strange world of devotion. Everything in them is in scale with it.

103. *I heard a noise and wishèd for a sight*
ANONYMOUS

I heard a noise and wishèd for a sight
I looked for life and did a shadow see
Whose substance was the sum of my delight,
Which came unseen, and so did go from me.

Yet hath conceit persuaded my content
There was a substance where the shadow went.

I did not play Narcissus in conceit,
I did not see my shadow in a spring:
I know mine eyes were dimmed with no deceit,
I saw the shadow of some worthy thing:
For, as I saw the shadow glancing by,
I had a glimpse of something in mine eye.

But what it was, alas, I cannot tell,
Because of it I had no perfect view:
But as it was, by guess, I wish it well
And will until I see the same anew.
Shadow, or she, or both, or choose you whither:
Blest be the thing that brought the shadow hither!

Here the visual image is evanescent, all but nonexistent. But what a powerful suggestion of the half-formed thought behind the thought in the mind; like the conclusion of James Stephens' "The goat paths" (*Songs from the Clay*, page 25):

I would think until I found
Something I can never find,
Something lying on the ground,
In the bottom of my mind.

104. *Spring*

GERARD MANLEY HOPKINS

Nothing is so beautiful as spring—
When weeds, in wheels, shoot long and lovely and lush;
Thrush's eggs look little low heavens, and thrush
Through the echoing timber does so rinse and wring
The ear, it strikes like lightnings to hear him sing;
The glassy peartree leaves and blooms, they brush
The descending blue; that blue is all in a rush
With richness; the racing lambs too have fair their fling.

What is all this juice and all this joy?
  A strain of the earth's sweet being in the beginning
In Eden garden.—Have, get, before it cloy,
  Before it cloud, Christ, lord, and sour with sinning,
Innocent mind and Mayday in girl and boy,
  Most, O maid's child, thy choice and worthy the winning.

One of the images here that subtly and yet distinctly convey action is "Thrush's eggs look little low heavens." Among a throng of images, each directing the heart's attention to a fresh marvel, it can pass only half perceived. To arrest its action for a moment may give some insight into the others.

Not only are we made to see the eggs, with a power of visual description. The mind's eye is made to stoop, with Hopkins; to regard them so intently that, for an instant, for us as for him, they become the horizon.

105. *When in disgrace with fortune and men's eyes*

WILLIAM SHAKESPEARE

When in disgrace with fortune and men's eyes,
I all alone beweep my outcast state,
And trouble deaf heaven with my bootless cries,
And look upon myself, and curse my fate,
Wishing me like to one more rich in hope,
Featured like him, like him with friends possessed,
Desiring this man's art, and that man's scope,
With what I most enjoy contented least;
Yet in these thoughts myself almost despising,
Haply I think on thee, and then my state,
Like to the lark at break of day arising
From sullen earth, sings hymns at heaven's gate;
  For thy sweet love remembered such wealth brings
  That then I scorn to change my state with kings.

The "music" of poetry is sometimes thought of as apart from its meaning; an extra grace added to embellish a plain statement. What is the "plain statement" in these three lines from Sonnet XXIX?

Haply I think on thee, and then my state,
Like to the lark at break of day arising
From sullen earth, sings hymns at heaven's gate.

Part of what the lines say may be put in five words: "Remembering you makes me happy." Is that all there is to the meaning? Is all the rest merely decorative scrollwork?

Reading quickly and silently with the eye, as we are prone to do, we might think this is so. It is when the words are sounded—aloud or in the mind's ear—that the transformation begins to take place.

"Haply" launches the poem's change of mood, like a breath of happiness. The three *th*-sounds in "I think on thee, and then" build up a momentum and suspense like a quickening of the heartbeat. They may literally increase the pulse, preparing for the upsurge of feeling in "Like to the lark at break of day." Now it is as if the heart skips a beat among the *l*'s and *k*'s. The emotion, held back a moment by the weight and doubt of "sullen earth," rises directly as the flight of the lark and "sings hymns at heaven's gate."

This is more than the statement of an emotion. It is direct transference. For an instant we share the precise feeling of a man sometimes thought to be the actor, poet and dramatist, William Shakespeare. We may know few of the facts of his life, but we are part of his emotional autobiography.

When it occurs, this is quite literally poetic immortality. It recalls the enormous justice of his quiet boast (poem 3):

Nor shall death brag thou wanderest in his shade,
When in eternal lines to time thou growest:
So long as men can breathe, or eyes can see,
So long lives this, and this gives life to thee.

106. *A bird came down the walk*

EMILY DICKINSON

A bird came down the walk:
He did not know I saw:
He bit an angle-worm in halves
And ate the fellow, raw.

And then he drank a dew
From a convenient grass,
And then hopped sidewise to the wall
To let a beetle pass.

He glanced with rapid eyes
That hurried all abroad—
They looked like frightened beads, I thought;
He stirred his velvet head

Like one in danger; cautious,
I offered him a crumb,
And he unrolled his feathers
And rowed him softer home

Than oars divide the ocean,
Too silver for a seam,
Or butterflies, off banks of noon,
Leap, plashless, as they swim.

Lyric poetry is full of beautiful beginnings that dwindle away. In contrast, how matter-of-factly, almost we might think prosaically, this starts out.

Its quiet introduction is part of its lyric magic. The poem is staying very still, observing without betraying pleasure or surprise.

There is one out-of-key phrase, I feel: "And ate the fellow, raw." This adds a note of condescension; a kitchen-garden cuteness that on more than one occasion overtakes Emily Dickinson.

Apart from the coy intrusion, the poem follows the action sparely and brilliantly. Its climax, the literal failure, is a symbolic triumph. The bird flies away. And the poem flies off with it, in smooth, perfectly unswerving motion. The poem is an image of motion through space.

107. *Sweeney among the nightingales*

T. S. ELIOT

ὤμοι, πέπληγμαι καιρίαν πληγὴν ἔσω

Apeneck Sweeney spreads his knees
Letting his arms hang down to laugh,
The zebra stripes along his jaw
Swelling to maculate giraffe.

The circles of the stormy moon
Slide westward toward the River Plate,
Death and the Raven drift above
And Sweeney guards the hornèd gate.

Gloomy Orion and the Dog
Are veiled; and hushed the shrunken seas;
The person in the Spanish cape
Tries to sit on Sweeney's knees

Slips and pulls the table cloth
Overturns a coffee-cup,
Reorganised upon the floor
She yawns and draws a stocking up;

The silent man in mocha brown
Sprawls at the window-sill and gapes;
The waiter brings in oranges
Bananas figs and hothouse grapes;

The silent vertebrate in brown
Contracts and concentrates, withdraws;
Rachel *née* Rabinovitch
Tears at the grapes with murderous paws;

She and the lady in the cape
Are suspect, thought to be in league;
Therefore the man with heavy eyes
Declines the gambit, shows fatigue,

Leaves the room and reappears
Outside the window, leaning in,
Branches of wistaria
Circumscribe a golden grin;

The host with someone indistinct
Converses at the door apart,
The nightingales are singing near
The Convent of the Sacred Heart,

And sang within the bloody wood
When Agamemnon cried aloud,
And let their liquid siftings fall
To stain the stiff dishonoured shroud.

This takes off not so much into space as through time. An altering resonance in the last eight lines carries us from, possibly, South Boston after the first of the world wars to the scene of Aeschylus' *Agamemnon*. There another act of betrayal follows the Trojan War.

Agamemnon meets it with the cry of the epigraph: "Alas, I have been smitten deep with a mortal blow." Sweeney meets it with a grin. The wound is deeper; he is used to betrayal.

The two eras are bridged by "nightingales." These, in the first part of the poem, are Sweeney's companions, "ladies of the evening." The poem is an image of motion through time.

108. *The windhover:*
To Christ our Lord

GERARD MANLEY HOPKINS

I caught this morning morning's minion, king-
  dom of daylight's dauphin, dapple-dawn-drawn Falcon, in his riding
  Of the rolling level underneath him steady air, and striding
High there, how he rung upon the rein of a wimpling wing
In his ecstasy! then off, off forth on swing,
  As a skate's heel sweeps smooth on a bow-bend: the hurl and gliding
  Rebuffed the big wind. My heart in hiding
Stirred for a bird,—the achieve of, the mastery of the thing!

Brute beauty and valour and act, oh, air, pride, plume, here
   Buckle! AND the fire that breaks from thee then, a billion
Times told lovelier, more dangerous, O my chevalier!

   No wonder of it; shéer plód makes plough down sillion
Shine, and blue-bleak embers, ah my dear,
   Fall, gall themselves, and gash gold-vermilion.

A prodigiously complicated, dazzlingly clear series of flights are engineered into the rhythms of this sonnet. Its sestet takes a further flight, partly concealed because interior.

All things "here"—even the powerful windhover—at a certain point "buckle." It is at this precise point that Christ's perfection takes off, in fire "a billion / Times told lovelier."

For further confirmation the poem returns to the lowliest of things: "plough down sillion" (a furrow), which shines from "sheer plod," and "blue-bleak embers," a fire all but extinguished. If these yield a splendor, how much more his who is eternal.

109. *The frigate pelican*

MARIANNE MOORE

Rapidly cruising or lying on the air there is a bird
   that realizes Rasselas's friend's project
   of wings uniting levity with strength. This
      hell-diver, frigate-bird, hurricane-
bird; unless swift is the proper word
      for him, the storm omen when
   he flies close to the waves, should be seen
         fishing, although oftener
         he appears to prefer

to take, on the wing, from industrious cruder-winged species
   the fish they have caught, and is seldom successless.
   A marvel of grace, no matter how fast his
      victim may fly or how often may

turn, the dishonest pelican's ease
in pursuit, bears him away
with the fish that the badgered bird drops.
A kind of superlative
swallow, that likes to live

on food caught while flying, he is not a pelican. The toe
with slight web, air-boned body, and very long wings
with the spread of a swan's—duplicating a
bow-string as he floats overhead—feel
the changing V-shaped scissor swallow-
tail direct the rigid keel.
And steering back to windward always,
the fleetest foremost fairy
among birds, outflies the

aeroplane which cannot flap its wings nor alter any quill-
tip. For him, the feeling in a hand, in fins, is
in his unbent downbent crafty oar. With him
other pelicans aimlessly soar
as he does; separating, until
not flapping they rise once more,
closing in without looking and move
outward again to the top
of the circle and stop

and blow back, allowing the wind to reverse their direction.
This is not the stalwart swan that can ferry the
woodcutter's two children home; no. Make hay; keep
the shop; I have one sheep; were a less
limber animal's mottoes. This one
finds sticks for the swan's-down dress
of his child to rest upon and would
not know Gretel from Hänsel.
As impassioned Handel—

meant for a lawyer and a masculine German domestic
career—clandestinely studied the harpsichord
and never was known to have fallen in love,

the unconfiding frigate-bird hides
in the height and in the majestic
display of his art. He glides
a hundred feet or quivers about
as charred paper behaves—full
of feints; and an eagle

of vigilance, earns the term aquiline; keeping at a height
so great the feathers look black and the beak does not
show. It is not retreat but exclusion from
which he looks down and observes what went
secretly, as it thought, out of sight
among dense jungle plants. Sent
ahead of the rest, there goes the true
knight in his jointed coat that
covers all but his bat

ears; a-trot, with stiff pig gait—our tame armadillo, loosed by
his master and as pleased as a dog. Beside the
spattered blood—that orchid which the native fears—
the fer-de-lance lies sleeping; centaur-
like, this harmful couple's amity
is apropos. A jaguar
and crocodile are fighting. Sharp-shinned
hawks and peacock-freckled small
cats, like the literal

merry-go-round, come wandering within the circular view
of the high bird for whom from the air they are ants
keeping house all their lives in the crack of a
crag with no view from the top. And here,
unlikely animals learning to
dance, crouch on two steeds that rear
behind a leopard with a frantic
face, tamed by an Artemis
who wears a dress like his,

and hampering haymaker's hat. *Festina lente*. Be gay
civilly. How so? 'If I do well I am blessed

whether any bless me or not, and if I do
ill I am cursed.' We watch the moon rise
on the Susquehanna. In his way
this most romantic bird, flies
to a more mundane place, the mangrove
swamp, to sleep. He wastes the moon.
But he, and others, soon

Rise from the bough, and though flying are able to foil the tired
moment of danger, that lays on heart and lungs the
weight of the python that crushes to powder.
The tune's illiterate footsteps fail;
the steam hacks are not to be admired.
These, unturbulent, avail
themselves of turbulence to fly—pleased
with the faint wind's varyings,
on which to spread fixed wings.

The reticent lugubrious ragged immense minuet
descending to leeward, ascending to windward
again without flapping, in what seems to be
a way of resting, are now nearer,
but as seemingly bodiless yet
as they were. Theirs are sombre
quills for so wide and lightboned a bird
as the frigate pelican
of the Caribbean.

Fregata aquila. The Frigate Pelican of Audubon.
Giant tame armadillo. Photograph and description by W. Stephen Thomas of New York.
Red-spotted orchids. The blood, supposedly, of natives slain by Pizarro.
'If I do well, I am blessed', etc. Hindoo saying.

Marianne Moore's notes to this poem, which in her book come at the back, are partial testimony to her encyclopedic detail. If poetry, as William Blake says, is "Minute Particulars," hers can be the minutest, the most exacting of all. Yet how perfectly they complete the large design.

The verse structure is a mosaic, in which every syllable takes its inevitable place. The rhythms are free to develop, apparently, in any way they may wish. This freedom is paradoxical: they are at liberty to reproduce, with infinite precisions, the look and feel of things, their native characteristics. Her descriptions strike inward: "For him, the feeling in a hand, in fins, is / in his unbent downbent crafty oar."

Varied and sustained throughout the poem, the flight of the bird, alone and in company, merges finally, in a vast rhythmic metaphor, with the circling of a carrousel. Like it, the poem comes, not to an end, but to a momentary pause.

110. *Ametas and Thestylis making hay-ropes*

ANDREW MARVELL

A: Think'st thou that this love can stand
Whilst thou still dost say me nay?
Love unpaid does soon disband:
Love binds love, as hay binds hay.

T: Think'st thou that this rope would twine
If we both should turn one way?
Where both parties so combine
Neither love will twist, nor hay.

A: Thus you vain excuses find,
Which yourself and us delay:
And love ties a woman's mind
Looser than with ropes of hay.

T: What you cannot constant hope
Must be taken as you may.
A: Then let's both lay by our rope,
And go and kiss within the hay.

Winding and unwinding, weaving and unweaving, this finally binds its rhythms as lightly and as surely as the dancing couple.

111. Cobb would have caught it

ROBERT FITZGERALD

In sunburnt parks where Sundays lie,
Or the wide wastes beyond the cities,
Teams in grey deploy through sunlight.

Talk it up, boys, a little practice.

Coming in stubby and fast, the baseman
Gathers a grounder in fat green grass,
Picks it stinging and clipped as wit
Into the leather: a swinging step
Wings it deadeye down to first.
Smack. Oh, attaboy, attyoldboy.

Catcher reverses his cap, pulls down
Sweaty casque, and squats in the dust:
Pitcher rubs new ball on his pants,
Chewing, puts a jet behind him;
Nods past batter, taking his time.
Batter settles, tugs at his cap:
A spinning ball: step and swing to it,
Caught like a cheek before it ducks
By shivery hickory: socko, baby:
Cleats dig into dust. Outfielder,
On his way, looking over his shoulder,
Makes it a triple. A long peg home.

Innings and afternoons. Fly lost in sunset.
Throwing arm gone bad. There's your old ball game.
Cool reek of the field. Reek of companions.

This poem on a thoroughly contemporary American theme immerses us in a Sunday back-lots game with skillful, unforced use of baseball lingo. The consistency of tone keeps the colloquialism from seeming cute or quaint; there is neither condescension nor "local color." It is as if we were participating in the game.

The ending conveys that slightly dazed feeling after the excitement is over; like coming out of a matinee into daylight.

112. *Methinks 'tis pretty sport to hear a child*

THOMAS BASTARD

Methinks 'tis pretty sport to hear a child
Rocking a word in mouth yet undefiled;
The tender racket rudely plays the sound
Which, weakly bandied, cannot back rebound;
And the soft air the softer roof doth kiss
With a sweet dying and a pretty miss,
Which hears no answer yet from the white rank
Of teeth not risen from their coral bank.
The alphabet is searched for letters soft
To try a word before it can be wrought;
And when it slideth forth, it goes as nice
As when a man doth walk upon the ice.

This Elizabethan conceit involves an act of translation between the senses. The child's tongue is thought of as a tennis racket, with a play on the audible meaning of the word. Like any novice, he lobs too high or misses completely. The visual projection of sound is affectionately exact in the concluding couplet.

Chrestoleros: Seven Books of Epigrams (1598), of which this is Epigram 36 ("*De puero babutietiente*"), begins with a sonnet that antedates by some fifty years Herrick's "The argument of his book" (poem 10). "*De subiecto operis sui*" starts: "I speak of wants, of frauds, of policies," and after enumerating "unthrifts," "murtherers," "pick-thanks," and many other things under the sun, concludes:

This is my subject, reader, I confess,
From which I think seldom I do digress.

113. *Minnie and Mattie*

CHRISTINA ROSSETTI

Minnie and Mattie
  And fat little May,
Out in the country,
  Spending a day.

Such a bright day,
  With the sun glowing,
And the trees half in leaf,
  And the grass growing.

Pinky white pigling
  Squeals through his snout,
Woolly white lambkin
  Frisks all about.

Cluck! cluck! the nursing hen
  Summons her folk,—
Ducklings all downy soft,
  Yellow as yolk.

Cluck! cluck! the mother hen
  Summons her chickens
To peck the dainty bits
  Found in her pickings.

Minnie and Mattie
  And May carry posies,
Half of sweet violets,
  Half of primroses.

Give the sun time enough,
  Glowing and glowing,
He'll rouse the roses
  And bring them blowing.

Don't wait for roses
  Losing today,
O Minnie, Mattie,
  And wise little May.

Violets and primroses
  Blossom today
For Minnie and Mattie
  And fat little May.

Singularly affecting in its lack of affectation, this has an acute, rather than "cute," ear for baby talk. A genuine childlike gaiety suffuses the poem.

Like E. E. Cummings' realizations of childhood in "chansons innocentes" (*Poems 1923–1954*, pages 21, 22, 23, 140, 141), it is extremely difficult to read. One false inflection will turn sentiment to gush.

114. *Another grace for a child*

ROBERT HERRICK

Here a little child I stand,
Heaving up my either hand;
Cold as paddocks though they be,
Here I lift them up to Thee,
For a benison to fall
On our meat and on us all. Amen.

The personal note in Herrick's songs of love and wine is not lost in what he calls "His Noble Numbers, or His Pious Pieces," of which this is one. How easily he combines his clerical duties and his affections. The word "paddocks" is an old one for "frogs."

115. *A sick child*

RANDALL JARRELL

The postman comes when I am still in bed.
"Postman, what do you have for me today?"
I say to him. (But really I'm in bed.)
Then he says—what shall I have him say?

"This letter says that you are president
Of—this word here; it's a republic."
Tell them I can't answer right away.
"It's your duty." No, I'd rather just be sick.

Then he tells me there are letters saying everything
That I can think of that I want for them to say.
I say, "Well, thank you very much. Good-bye."
He is ashamed, and turns and walks away.

If I can think of it, it isn't what I want.
I want . . . I want a ship from some near star
To land in the yard, and beings to come out
And think to me: "So this is where you are!

Come." Except that they won't do,
I thought of them . . . And yet somewhere there must be
Something that's different from everything.
All that I've never thought of—think of me!

This contemporary American poem recaptures the desperate boredom of childhood when, with monomaniac logic, a thought like eternity or infinity has been pushed beyond endurance. It brings a hot, dry, salty taste to the mouth.

116. *The term*

WILLIAM CARLOS WILLIAMS

A rumpled sheet
of brown paper
about the length

and apparent bulk
of a man was
rolling with the

wind slowly over
and over in
the street as

a car drove down
upon it and
crushed it to

the ground. Unlike
a man it rose
again rolling

with the wind over
and over to be as
it was before.

Wallace Stevens has called Williams an "anti-poet." Many of his poems give rhythms to the idle, unspoken musings we have while watching something "no one will believe"—as he says in "Pastoral" (*Collected Earlier Poems*, page 121)—"of vast import to the nation."

He catches alive what we wouldn't be caught dead thinking aloud unless it could be "dressed up." Williams excels at "undressing" the mind. Consequently he can give permanence to such unvoiced speculations as this, concerning death ("the term" of life) and immortality.

117. *Poem*

WILLIAM CARLOS WILLIAMS

As the cat
climbed over
the top of

the jamcloset
first the right
forefoot

carefully
then the hind
stepped down

into the pit of
the empty
flowerpot

A completed action in just the number of words and no more time than it takes to tell it is a "Poem."

118. *Big wind*

THEODORE ROETHKE

Where were the greenhouses going,
Lunging into the lashing
Wind driving water
So far down the river
All the faucets stopped?—
So we drained the manure-machine
For the steam plant,
Pumping the stale mixture
Into the rusty boilers,
Watching the pressure gauge
Waver over to red,
As the seams hissed
And the live steam
Drove to the far
End of the rose-house,
Where the worst wind was,
Creaking the cypress window-frames,
Cracking so much thin glass
We stayed all night,
Stuffing the holes with burlap;
But she rode it out,
That old rose-house,
She hove into the teeth of it,
The core and pith of that ugly storm,
Ploughing with her stiff prow,
Bucking into the wind-waves
That broke over the whole of her,
Flailing her sides with spray,
Flinging long strings of wet across the roof-top,
Finally veering, wearing themselves out, merely
Whistling thinly under the wind-vents;
She sailed into the calm morning,
Carrying her full cargo of roses.

Somewhere in Michigan we are carried through a wild night in an old rose-house. Our view of the world is like that of a grease monkey, an oiler or wiper sweating away below decks to keep a leaky vessel afloat. We share in the final victory without quite knowing how it came about. "She" came through.

119. *See the chariot at hand here of Love*

BEN JONSON

See the chariot at hand here of Love,
   Wherein my lady rideth!
Each that draws is a swan or a dove,
   And well the car Love guideth.
As she goes, all hearts do duty
      Unto her beauty;
And enamored do wish, so they might
      But enjoy such a sight,
That they still were to run by her side,
Thorough swords, thorough seas, whither she would ride.

Do but look on her eyes, they do light
   All that Love's world compriseth!
Do but look on her hair, it is bright
   As Love's star when it riseth!
Do but mark, her forehead's smoother
      Than words that soothe her;
And from her arched brows such a grace
      Sheds itself through the face,
As alone there triumphs to the life
All the gain, all the good of the elements' strife.

Have you seen but a bright lily grow
   Before rude hands have touched it?
Have you marked but the fall of the snow
   Before the soil hath smutched it?
Have you felt the wool o' the beaver,
      Or swan's down ever?

Or have smelt o' the bud o' the brier,
    Or the nard i' the fire?
Or have tasted the bag o' the bee?
Oh so white, oh so soft, oh so sweet is she!

The last stanza, customarily the only one sung, brings rarely used comparisons to bear on the loveliness of his lady; a truly sensual feast of vision, touch, smell, and taste.

120. *A spirit haunts the year's last hours*

ALFRED, LORD TENNYSON

A spirit haunts the year's last hours
Dwelling amid these yellowing bowers:
    To himself he talks:
For at eventide, listening earnestly,
At his work you may hear him sob and sigh
    In the walks;
    Earthward he boweth the heavy stalks
Of the mouldering flowers:
  Heavily hangs the broad sunflower
    Over its grave i' the earth so chilly;
  Heavily hangs the hollyhock,
    Heavily hangs the tiger-lily.

The air is damp, and hushed, and close,
As a sick man's room when he takes repose
    An hour before death.
My very heart faints and my whole soul grieves
At the moist rich smell of the rotting leaves,
    And the breath
    Of the fading edges of box beneath,
And the year's last rose.
  Heavily hangs the broad sunflower
    Over its grave i' the earth so chilly;
  Heavily hangs the hollyhock,
    Heavily hangs the tiger-lily.

Tennyson's redolent lyric, like his "Tears, idle tears" (poem 88), is from *The Princess*, that curious medley of embarrassment and riches. How often Tennyson's best poems are permeated by a vivid sense of death and decay.

The year has passed the mellow prime of Keats' "To autumn" (poem 93). Both literally and figuratively, Keats' farm-boy harvest god is believable, while Tennyson's "spirit," as "To himself he talks," seems perfunctory; too patently a "figure of speech." Once he is out of the way, the imagery grows richer and ranker.

121. *what a proud dreamhorse*

E. E. CUMMINGS

what a proud dreamhorse pulling(smoothloomingly)through
(stepp)this(ing)crazily seething of this
raving city screamingly street wonderful

flowers And o the Light thrown by Them opens

sharp holes in dark places paints eyes touches hands with newness and these startled whats are a(piercing clothes thoughts kiss
-ing wishes bodies)squirm-of-frightened shy are whichs small
its hungry for Is for Love Spring thirsty for happens
only and beautiful
                                        there is a ragged beside the who limps
man crying silence upward
                                                        —to have tasted Beautiful to have known
Only to have smelled Happens—skip dance kids hop point at
red blue yellow violet white orange green-
ness

        o what a proud dreamhorse moving(whose feet
almost walk air). now who stops. Smiles.he
                                                                                    stamps

The first few lines of this sonnet may be paraphrased by putting them in their own words, rearranged: "what a proud dreamhorse, smooth-loomingly stepping, pulling wonderful flowers through this crazily seething street of this screamingly raving city." Why does the poet change this order?

The first rearrangement is of "smoothloomingly stepping," which is bracketed and dispersed. Isn't "smoothloomingly" precisely the way a horse enters a street? We notice first his floating dreamlike gait, contrasting with the erratic, jerky motion of taxis and trucks.

Then we hear his hoofbeats on the pavement: a soft heavy plod —"(stepp)"—followed by the metallic ring of his shoe scraping the asphalt—"(ing)."

This is more than description. It is more than saying, "A horse is coming down the street." The horse moves through the poem. The poem is itself a city street: "crazily seething of this / raving city screamingly street." The hubbub suddenly rises to a deafening roar, in contrast to the quiet aura in which the horse moves.

Only then do we see what the horse is pulling: "wonderful flowers." The flowers arrive as they would in the actual scene. The rearrangement is not, we realize, an arbitrary distortion of the normal order of words. Nor is it the conventional poetic inversion for the sake of a rhyme: "Oh to be with you / Under the heavens blue."

The placement of every word is strategic to the unfolding of the action. This is in the classical dramatic tradition of Latin verse, like Vergil's "Arma virumque cano": "Arms and the man I sing." The predicates, "arms and the man," are placed before the verb, "sing," because they are the subject of the poem: war and the hero. Vergil is not going to tell us about them; he is going to sing them into being.

Now the tone of Cummings' poem alters. The frenzied rhythms are stilled to a calm but intense serenity: "And o the Light thrown by Them opens / sharp holes in dark places."

The quality of worship in the rhythm is suggested by another visual device: "And," "Light" and "Them" are the first words to be capitalized. This restores meaning to the capital letter. Instead of its customary remark, "I am beginning a sentence, or a line of poetry," it now indicates and enhances the sense of mystery, of miracle. The beauty of the flowers has subjugated the confusion of the city.

Anonymous eyes moving along the street turn and light up. As the poem says, the light cast by the flowers paints them. Windows open —"sharp holes in dark places." Hands lean on their sills, touched "with newness." Wrapped in their everyday thoughts and clothes, people are as impersonal as objects. They are "whats," "whichs," small "its." The flowers reach through their protective coverings, touching for an instant their innermost wishes.

How do we feel such wishes? They come to us, usually, as fleeting sensations, not as words at all. In the poem these unspoken fragmentary experiences are suggested by six verbal equivalents taken from different parts of speech. "Love" and "Spring" are nouns; they are universal. "Beautiful" is an adjective. Beautiful what? Whatever is beautiful to each of us. "Is" and "happens" are verbs. Our sensations are of *being*, of being more than we are, and of something quite wonderful happening. And all these unspecific wishes are for something that will be uniquely ours. We are hungry and thirsty for "only."

The children—and one other character—fully realize the flowers. The children skip dance hop, pointing at their colors. And there is a ragged man "crying silence upward." For the moment let's leave him for what he is, the flower-wagon man, very likely Italian or Greek. Why does he cry silence? Is his voice lost in the din of the traffic? Or is it that the words he is calling out—the names of flowers—are so beautiful that, in contrast to the uproar, they are a kind of silence?

Now the horse draws up beside us, "stops. Smiles.he stamps." The pause and the emphasis are indicated visually, "stamps" being dropped a space from the end of the line. By itself, it puts a period to the poem. And it completes the materialization of the horse. Like a pinch to see if we are asleep or awake, it tells us that this is no dream. The horse is more than a symbol. He is realer than anything.

Now that we've looked at pieces of the meaning, what is the whole poem saying?

Why is the horse proud? Why is he a *dream*horse? Why does he loom? And especially why does he "almost walk air"?

I'd read this poem many times before questioning these characteristics. They seem natural enough to fit any big shambling, probably dirty-white dray horse. Perhaps they are more affectionate than we expect of realistic description. But why was I haunted by the sense of something more?

Walking air. What horse *did* walk air? Pegasus, the wingèd steed of the Muses.

Suddenly the poem takes on a new dimension. This is poetry in the modern world; an obsolete, almost extinct animal, who makes comparatively rare appearances in a city street. And what of the ragged limping man?

The Greek hero Bellerophon is sent to slay the Chimaera, a fire-breathing monster ravaging the country of Lycia. This he does with the aid of Pegasus, whom the gods allow him to bridle.

What in this poem is being conquered? A modern Chimaera: "this crazily seething of this raving city screamingly street." The mélange of adverbs, adjectives and nouns, echoing the confused cries of the street, mirrors too the construction of the she-monster: head of lion, body of goat, tail of serpent. The flower-wagon man is the poet silencing this monster: "crying silence upward."

Could there be, too, an ironic implication in "silence"? If the horse today is fast disappearing, isn't the poem all but unheard?

Why does the poet limp? Bellerophon, after slaying the Chimaera, grows presumptuous. He tries to fly to heaven. But losing control of the reins, he falls to earth, lamed.

A later story is told by Schiller, of how Pegasus, sold by a needy poet, is put to the cart. And the last word in the poem, "stamps," may recall another legend. Hippocrene, the fountain of inspiration, bursts forth when the ground is struck by the forehoof of Pegasus.

In exploring the ways in which poetry explores experience, the temptation is to overformularize. The itch to establish "invariable principles" did not die out with William Lisle Bowles. Critics of our own time have been known to propose rules governing the construction and use of similes, metaphors and symbols, as if these were so many shapes of chair leg to be turned on a lathe. Poets will continue to find new ways of making comparisons and to modify the old ones.

The word "image" is convenient in describing that sharpening of focus with which poets often regard the various sensations. But the word has its dangers too, as the school of poetry that drew on it for a name testifies. "Imagism" as a technique was productive but mercifully short-lived. Adhered to as theory, it would lead to verse quite as mechanical as the genteel conventions it opposed. Theories are valuable while they remain flexible; while they are susceptible of modification in practice.

I hope the preceding groups have suggested the variety of ways in which poets perceive, without implying that there is a right way or a limited number of ways, or that the perception of sensations precludes emotion and idea. As illustration I have mentioned three methods evolved by poets of different times and temperaments.

Shakespeare, in his sonnets, is essayist and imagist by turns. His images are apt to be similes, and he is fond of following their action step by step. Hopkins is more likely to condense his images, to seal their action into a phrase. For Cummings, the whole poem may be an image or a configuration of images.

These observations are not true for these poets at all times. But they illustrate differences of treatment so striking that any one of them might be taken as a "standard."

Equally striking "standards" might be extracted from still other poets. There is no single tradition. The sporadic snipings at modern poetry, along with art and music, seldom specify the tradition to which they are advocating a "return." "I am for Coleridge's musical vowel-patterns!" "I'm for heroic couplets!" "I'm for Shakespeare's expanded simile-image!" "I'm for Webster's nightmare world!"

The possibilities are inexhaustible. One advice poets of the past and present may have for the future. Thou shalt not make unto thee any given image. Or—since nothing is entirely new—if it is truly given, accept it freely.

PART EIGHT

"We two suffice"

To pass from sensations to emotions is another shift of attention. They are by no means mutually exclusive regions. Less specifically located, the emotions are reached through the senses and return to them, in a quickened pulse or a sharp intake of breath, in a sinus attack, in tears or in laughter. Perhaps these sensations, more or less internal, are the emotions.

We should scarcely expect to find a completely emotionless poem. All in the preceding groups would fit into the groups to follow. The greatest proportion, certainly, of the songs and lyrics relates to the emotion of love.

This is not a category exclusively of amatory verse, addressed by the lover to his lady. It would take in, obviously, such songs and lyrics as Campion's "Come, oh, come, my life's delight!" (poem 62), Burns' "A red, red rose" (poem 64), Donne's "Song" (poem 73), "The dream" (poem 90) and "The sun rising" (poem 92), Herrick's "The night-piece, to Julia" (poem 98), Marvell's "The mower to the glowworms" (poem 99).

Perhaps less obviously it would include Shakespeare's "Shall I compare thee to a summer's day?" (poem 3), although this, like his "As an unperfect actor on the stage" (poem 7), "Was it the proud full sail of his great verse" (poem 30) and "When in disgrace with fortune and men's eyes" (poem 105), may have been addressed to his friend rather than to his mistress.

To indicate the broadness of the area, it would include, too, Dylan Thomas' equation of poetry and love, "In my craft or sullen art" (poem 32), and Whitman's love song to his reader, "Whoever you are holding me now in hand" (poem 31).

122. *Corydon, arise, my Corydon!*

ANONYMOUS

PHYLLIDA: Corydon, arise, my Corydon!
Titan shineth clear.
CORYDON: Who is it that calleth Corydon?
Who is it that I hear?
P: Phyllida, thy true love, calleth thee,
Arise then, arise then,
Arise and keep thy flock with me!
C: Phyllida, my true love, is it she?
I come then, I come then,
I come and keep my flock with thee.

P: Here are cherries ripe, my Corydon;
Eat them for my sake.
C: Here's my oaten pipe, my lovely one,
Sport for thee to make.
P: Here are threads, my true love, fine as silk,
To knit thee, to knit thee
A pair of stockings white as milk.
C: Here are reeds, my true love, fine and neat,
To make thee, to make thee
A bonnet to withstand the heat.

P: I will gather flowers, my Corydon,
To set in thy cap.
C: I will gather pears, my lovely one,
To put in thy lap.
P: I will buy my true love garters gay
For Sundays, for Sundays,
To wear about his legs so tall.
C: I will buy my true love yellow say
For Sundays, for Sundays,
To wear about her middle small.

P: When my Corydon sits on a hill
Making melody—

C: When my lovely one goes to her wheel
Singing cheerily—
P: Sure methinks my true love doth excel
For sweetness, for sweetness,
Our Pan that old Arcadian knight.
C: And methinks my true love bears the bell
For clearness, for clearness,
Beyond the nymphs that be so bright.

P: Had my Corydon, my Corydon,
Been, alack! her swain—
C: Had my lovely one, my lovely one,
Been in Ida plain—
P: Cynthia Endymion had refused,
Preferring, preferring,
My Corydon to play withal.
C: The queen of love had been excused,
Bequeathing, bequeathing,
My Phyllida the golden ball.

P: Yonder comes my mother, Corydon,
Whither shall I fly?
C: Under yonder beech, my lovely one,
While she passeth by.
P: Say to her thy true love was not here;
Remember, remember,
Tomorrow is another day.
C: Doubt me not, my true love, do not fear;
Farewell then, farewell then,
Heaven keep our loves alway.

say: fine cloth

The sixteenth century especially abounds in anonymous songs celebrating love. One of the simplest and loveliest is this duet between Phyllida and Corydon, in which they exchange gifts, vows, compliments—all gracefully plaited—and the one fear they have in common.

123. *The lass that made the bed to me*

ROBERT BURNS

When Januar' wind was blawing cauld
  As to the north I took my way,
The mirksome night did me enfauld,
  I knew na where to lodge till day.

By my good luck a maid I met,
  Just in the middle o' my care:
And kindly she did me invite
  To walk into a chamber fair.

I bow'd fu' low unto this maid,
  And thank'd her for her courtesie;
I bow'd fu low unto this maid,
  And bade her mak a bed to me.

She made the bed baith large and wide,
  Wi' twa white hands she spread it down;
She put the cup to her rosy lips,
  And drank, "Young man, now sleep ye soun."

She snatch'd the candle in her hand,
  And frae my chamber went wi' speed;
But I call'd her quickly back again
  To lay some mair below my head.

A cod she laid below my head,
  And servèd me wi' due respect;
And to salute her wi' a kiss,
  I put my arms about her neck.

"Haud aff your hands, young man," she says,
  "And dinna sae uncivil be:
If ye hae onie love for me,
  O wrang na my virginitie!"

Her hair was like the links o' gowd,
  Her teeth were like the ivorie;

Her cheeks like lilies dipt in wine,
The lass that made the bed to me.

Her bosom was the driven snaw,
Twa drifted heaps sae fair to see;
Her limbs the polish'd marble stane,
The lass that made the bed to me.

I kiss'd her owre and owre again,
And aye she wist na what to say;
I laid her between me and the wa',—
The lassie thought na lang till day.

Upon the morrow when we rose,
I thank'd her for her courtesie;
But aye she blush'd, and aye she sigh'd,
And said, "Alas! ye've ruin'd me."

I clasp'd her waist, and kiss'd her syne,
While the tear stood twinkling in her ee;
I said, "My lassie, dinna cry,
For ye ay shall make the bed to me."

She took her mither's Holland sheets,
And made them a' in sarks to me:
Blythe and merry may she be,
The lass that made the bed to me.

The bonnie lass made the bed to me,
The braw lass made the bed to me;
I'll ne'er forget till the day I die,
The lass that made the bed to me!

cod: pillow; *stane:* stone; *syne:* then; *sarks:* shirts

Burns writes with genuine and equal affection to a number of eighteenth-century Scottish lasses. This song, a little more than affectionate, is founded on an old ballad, but the choice is not inappropriate to his volatile temperament. The conclusion of the song seems to imply another of Burns' inimitable leave-takings. Surely "I'll ne'er forget" is a sentiment expressed in absence.

124. *Nymph of the garden where all beauties be*

SIR PHILIP SIDNEY

Nymph of the garden where all beauties be,
Beauties which do in excellency pass
His who till death looked in a watery glass,
Or hers whom nak'd the Trojan boy did see;
Sweet garden-nymph, which keeps the cherry-tree
Whose fruit doth far the Hesperian taste surpass,
Most sweet-fair, most fair-sweet, do not, alas,
From coming near those cherries banish me.
For though, full of desire, empty of wit,
Admitted late by your best-gracèd grace,
I caught at one of them, and hungry bit,
Pardon that fault; once more grant me the place;
  And I do swear, even by the same delight,
  I will but kiss, I never more will bite.

This is Sonnet LXXXII of the series "Astrophel"—Sir Philip Sidney—writes to his "Stella." He is so resolutely kept at a distance by her that it's no wonder he has to write a particularly flattering one, after the episode hinted at here, to get back in her good, cool graces.

125. *Give me a kiss from those sweet lips of thine*

ANONYMOUS

Give me a kiss from those sweet lips of thine
And make it double by enjoining mine,
Another yet, nay yet and yet another,
And let the first kiss be the second's brother.
Give me a thousand kisses and yet more;
And then repeat those that have gone before;
Let us begin while daylight springs in heaven,
And kiss till night descends into the even,
And when that modest secretary, night,
Discolors all but thy heaven beaming bright,
We will begin revels of hidden love
In that sweet orb where silent pleasures move.

In high new strains, unspeakable delight,
We'll vent the dull hours of the silent night:
Were the bright day no more to visit us,
Oh, then forever would I hold thee thus,
Naked, enchainèd, empty of idle fear,
As the first lovers in the garden were.
I'll die betwixt thy breasts that are so white,
For, to die there, would do a man delight.
Embrace me still, for time runs on before,
And being dead we shall embrace no more.
Let us kiss faster than the hours do fly,
Long live each kiss and never know to die.
Yet, if that fade and fly away too fast,
Impress another and renew the last;
Let us vie kisses, till our eyelids cover,
And if I sleep, count me an idle lover;
Admit I sleep, I'll still pursue the theme,
And eagerly I'll kiss thee in a dream.
Oh! give me way: grant love to me thy friend!
Did hundred thousand suitors all contend
For thy virginity, there's none shall woo
With heart so firm as mine; none better do
Than I with your sweet sweetness; if you doubt,
Pierce with your eyes my heart, or pluck it out.

No reticent lover is this anonymous seventeenth-century poet. The first half of the poem especially—sometimes appearing separately—is most direct, specific, and delicate.

126. *Me happy, night, night full of brightness*
EZRA POUND (after PROPERTIUS)

Me happy, night, night full of brightness;
Oh couch made happy by my long delectations;
How many words talked out with abundant candles;
Struggles when the lights were taken away;

Now with bared breasts she wrestled against me,
Tunic spread in delay;
And she then opening my eyelids fallen in sleep,
Her lips upon them; and it was her mouth saying:
Sluggard!

In how many varied embraces, our changing arms,
Her kisses, how many, lingering on my lips.
"Turn not Venus into a blinded motion,
Eyes are the guides of love,
Paris took Helen naked coming from the bed of Menelaus,
Endymion's naked body, bright bait for Diana,"
—such at least is the story.

While our fates twine together, sate we our eyes with love;
For long night comes upon you
and a day when no day returns.
Let the gods lay chains upon us
so that no day shall unbind them.

For who would set a term to love's madness,
For the sun shall drive with black horses,
earth shall bring wheat from barley,
The flood shall move toward the fountain
Ere love know moderations,
The fish shall swim in dry streams.
No, now while it may be, let not the fruit of life cease.
Dry wreaths drop their petals,
their stalks are woven in baskets,
To-day we take the great breath of lovers,
to-morrow fate shuts us in.

Though you give all your kisses
you give but few.

Nor can I shift my pain to other,
Hers will I be dead,
If she confer such nights upon me,
long is my life, long in years,

If she give me many,
God am I for the time.

Many of Pound's translations and adaptations of Latin, Provençal and Chinese poetry have the ring, in English, of original poems.

This is number VII in his *Homage to Sextus Propertius*, now included in the volume of all his poems except *The Cantos*, *Personae*. Its mastery begins in the first line, with its effrontery in taking over a Latin gerund, "Me happy," and making it sound like colloquial speech.

127. *To his coy mistress*

ANDREW MARVELL

Had we but world enough, and time,
This coyness, lady, were no crime.
We would sit down, and think which way
To walk, and pass our long love's day.
Thou by the Indian Ganges' side
Shouldst rubies find: I by the tide
Of Humber would complain. I would
Love you ten years before the Flood,
And you should, if you please, refuse
Till the conversion of the Jews;
My vegetable love should grow
Vaster than empires and more slow;
An hundred years should go to praise
Thine eyes, and on thy forehead gaze;
Two hundred to adore each breast,
But thirty thousand to the rest;
An age at least to every part,
And the last age should show your heart.
For, lady, you deserve this state,
Nor would I love at lower rate.
But at my back I always hear
Time's wingèd chariot hurrying near,
And yonder all before us lie
Deserts of vast eternity.

Thy beauty shall no more be found
Nor, in thy marble vault, shall sound
My echoing song; then worms shall try
That long-preserved virginity,
And your quaint honor turn to dust,
And into ashes all my lust:
The grave's a fine and private place,
But none, I think, do there embrace.
   Now, therefore, while the youthful hue
Sits on thy skin like morning dew,
And while thy willing soul transpires
At every pore with instant fires,
Now let us sport us while we may,
And now, like amorous birds of prey,
Rather at once our time devour,
Than languish in his slow-chapped power.
Let us roll all our strength and all
Our sweetness up into one ball,
And tear our pleasure with rough strife
Thorough the iron gates of life;
Thus, though we cannot make our sun
Stand still, yet we will make him run.

This foray into amatory forensic should have won its plea. Despite its eminently logical rhetoric and its air of leisurely impatience, the arguments it advances are far from dispassionate.

128. *Arachne*

WILLIAM EMPSON

Twixt devil and deep sea, man hacks his caves;
Birth, death; one, many; what is true, and seems;
Earth's vast hot iron, cold space's empty waves:

King spider, walks the velvet roof of streams:
Must bird and fish, must god and beast avoid:
Dance, like nine angels, on pin-point extremes.

His gleaming bubble between void and void,
Tribe-membrane, that by mutual tension stands,
Earth's surface film, is at a breath destroyed.

Bubbles gleam brightest with least depth of lands
But two is least can with full tension strain,
Two molecules; one, and the film disbands.

We two suffice. But oh beware, whose vain
Hydroptic soap my meagre water saves.
Male spiders must not be too early slain.

Note: The caves of cavemen are thought of as by the sea to escape the savage creatures inland. "Man lives between the contradictory absolutes of philosophy, the one and the many, etc. As king spider man walks delicately between two elements, avoiding the enemies which live in both. Man must dance, etc. Human society is placed in this matter like individual men, the atoms who make up its bubble." The spider's legs push down the unbroken surface of the water like a soft carpet, which brings in the surface-tension idea. The bubble surface is called land, the thin fertile surface of the earth, because the bubble is of the globe of the world. The water saves the soap because the soap alone couldn't make a bubble. Arachne was a queen spider and disastrously proud.

The title refers to a Lydian girl skilled in weaving, who challenges Athena to a contest. For her presumption, she is turned into a spider.

The Greek myth is combined with philosophic speculation, twentieth-century theorems in natural science, plus the Elizabethan double sense of "death," to make an exceedingly, if indirectly, frank poem. It skates very deftly on a bubble.

In Empson's *Collected Poems* the accompanying note is found at the back of the book. Concerning such explanations he has this to say:

There is a feeling, often justified, that it is annoying when an author writes his own notes, so I shall give a note about these notes. It is impertinent to expect hard work from the reader merely because you have failed to show what you were comparing to what, and though to write notes on such a point is a confession of failure it seems an inoffensive one. A claim is implied that the poem is worth publishing though the author knows it is imperfect, but this has a chance of being true. Also there is no longer a reasonably small field which may be taken as general knowledge. It is impertinent to suggest that the reader ought to possess already any odd bit of information one may have picked up in a field where one is oneself ignorant; such a point may be explained in a note without trouble to anybody; and it does not require much fortitude to endure seeing what you already know in a note. Notes are annoying when they are attempts to woo admiration for the poem or the poet, but that I hope I can avoid. Of course there are queerer forces at work; to write notes at all is to risk making a fool of yourself, and the better poems tend to require fewer notes. But it seems to me that there has been an unfortunate suggestion of writing for a clique about a good deal of recent poetry, and that very much of it might be avoided by a mere willingness to explain incidental difficulties.

129. *Madrigal*

WILLIAM DRUMMOND OF HAWTHORNDEN

Like the Idalian queen,
Her hair about her eyne,
With neck and breasts' ripe apples to be seen,
At first glance of the morn
In Cyprus' gardens gathering those fair flowers
Which of her blood were born,
I saw, but fainting saw, my paramour's.
The Graces naked danced about the place,
The winds and trees amazed
With silence on her gazed,
The flowers did smile, like those upon her face;
And as their aspen stalks those fingers band,
That she might read my case,
A hyacinth I wished me in her hand.

Sigmund Freud has discovered erotic symbolism in some of our most ordinary thoughts. Perhaps it gets there through lack of the exquisite explicit imagery here.

130. *Help me to seek*

SIR THOMAS WYATT

Help me to seek, for I lost it there
And if that ye have found it, ye that be here,
And seek to convey it secretly,
Handle it soft and treat it tenderly,
Or else it will plain and then appear:

But rather restore it to me mannerly,
Since that I do ask it thus honestly:
For to lose it, it sitteth me too near.
Help me to seek.

Alas, and is there no remedy?
But have I thus lost it wilfully?
I wis it was a thing all too dear
To be bestowed and wist not where:
It was my heart, I pray you heartily
Help me to seek.

This seems, too, to imply more than it says. There is a light play in the word "plain": the heart's grief—it will "complain"—will give it away—make it "plain."

131. *Love in a life*

ROBERT BROWNING

I

Room after room,
I hunt the house through
We inhabit together.
Heart, fear nothing, for, heart, thou shalt find her,
Next time, herself!—not the trouble behind her
Left in the curtain, the couch's perfume!
As she brushed it, the cornice-wreath blossomed anew:
Yon looking-glass gleamed at the wave of her feather.

II

Yet the day wears,
And door succeeds door;
I try the fresh fortune—
Range the wide house from the wing to the center.
Still the same chance! she goes out as I enter.
Spend my whole day in the quest,—who cares?
But 'tis twilight, you see,—with such suites to explore,
Such closets to search, such alcoves to importune!

The boundless confidence and miasma-dispelling optimism that the character Robert Browning brings with him into the play *The Barretts of Wimpole Street* seem to be confirmed here. But this is more subtly dramatic.

Browning, no playwright, excels at presenting just enough of a situation to reveal character. Here the telltale point is the twice-admonished heart: "Heart, fear nothing, for, heart, thou shalt find her." The repetition is the very heartbeat of a man hoping against hope. This is like a play in capsule, with the curtain line withheld.

132. *Dear, if you change, I'll never choose again*

ANONYMOUS

Dear, if you change, I'll never choose again;
Sweet, if you shrink, I'll never think of love;
Fair, if you fail, I'll judge all beauty vain;
Wise, if too weak, moe wits I'll never prove.
Dear, sweet, fair, wise, change, shrink, nor be not weak;
And, on my faith, my faith shall never break!

Earth with her flowers shall sooner heaven adorn;
Heaven her bright stars through earth's dim globe shall move;
Fire heat shall lose, and frosts of flames be born;
Air, made to shine, as black as hell shall prove.
Earth, heaven, fire, air, the world transformed shall view,
Ere I prove false to faith, or strange to you.

moe: more

The series of impossibilities preceding unfaithfulness that turns up in the second stanza of this sixteenth-century song bears comparison with the fourth stanza of Pound's "Me happy, night, night full of brightness" (poem 126).

There are many variants of this age-old lover's vow. In this collection it is found as well in Burns' "A red, red rose" (poem 64). A few modern versions are Conrad Aiken's "When trout swim down Great Ormond Street" (*Collected Poems*, page 386), W. H. Auden's wry reflections in "As I walked out one evening" (*Collected Poetry*, page 197), E. E. Cummings' "as freedom is a breakfastfood" (*Poems 1923–1954*, page 366) and his reapplication in "when serpents bargain for the right to squirm" (page 441).

133. *The good-morrow*

JOHN DONNE

I wonder, by my troth, what thou and I
Did, till we loved: were we not weaned till then?
But sucked on country pleasures, childishly?
Or snorted we in the Seven Sleepers' den?
'Twas so; but this, all pleasures fancies be;
If ever any beauty I did see,
Which I desired, and got, 'twas but a dream of thee.

And now good-morrow to our waking souls
Which watch not one another out of fear;
For love all love of other sights controls,
And makes one little room an everywhere.
Let sea-discoverers to new worlds have gone;
Let maps to other, worlds on worlds have shown,
Let us possess one world; each hath one, and is one.

My face in thine eye, thine in mine appears,
And true plain hearts do in the faces rest;
Where can we find two better hemispheres
Without sharp north, without declining west?

> What ever dies, was not mixed equally;
> If our two loves be one, or thou and I
> Love so alike that none do slacken, none can die.

but this: except this

The order of Donne's poems, published after his death, is uncertain. Surely "The good-morrow," which comes first in some editions, is later than his caustic celebration of "Woman's constancy": "you / Can have no way but falsehood to be true."

It's not unlikely that this and other misogynous sentiments were inspired by early and fickle mistresses. As he says in "Air and angels":

> *Twice or thrice had I loved thee,*
> *Before I knew thy face or name.*

And in this, all other pleasures, he says, are by comparison quite unreal. There is no mistaking the fully expressed reciprocity in "our waking souls / Which watch not one another out of fear." This is the happiness that comes *after* disappointing experience. Its complete joyousness is matched by few poets except John Donne, in his "Sweetest love, I do not go" (poem 73); in "The dream" (poem 90); in "The sun rising" (poem 92); in many others. He says in "The anniversary":

> *All other things to their destruction draw,*
> *Only our love hath no decay.*

134. *darling!because my blood can sing*

E. E. CUMMINGS

> darling!because my blood can sing
> and dance(and does with each your least
> your any most very amazing now
> or here)let pitiless fear play host
> to every isn't that's under the spring
> —but if a look should april me,
> down isn't's own isn't go ghostly they

doubting can turn men's see to stare
their faith to how their joy to why
their stride and breathing to limp and prove
—but if a look should april me,
some thousand million hundred more
bright worlds than merely by doubting have
darkly themselves unmade makes love

armies(than hate itself and no
meanness unsmaller)armies can
immensely meet for centuries
and(except nothing)nothing's won
—but if a look should april me
for half a when, whatever is less
alive than never begins to yes

but if a look should april me
(though such as perfect hope can feel
only despair completely strikes
forests of mind,mountains of soul)
quite at the hugest which of his who
death is killed dead. Hills jump with brooks:
trees tumble out of twigs and sticks;

An anthology of love in all its moods, tender, satiric, carnal and exalted, could be made from E. E. Cummings' poems. This dancing song brings together two strands often separate in his poetry: the lyric and the satiric.

Like a song, it has a refrain: "but if a look should april me." Unlike most songs, the refrain roves through the stanzas, a perpetual surprise.

The dancing rhythms are given further impetus by the interplay of rhyme and half-rhyme. These, in the pattern "a-b-c-b-a-c-c," separate, approach and join hands. The lines themselves revolve on gaily repeated or echoed sounds; like the course, in the first stanza, of "least" to "most" to "host," softly re-echoed in "ghostly."

Displacements of the customary order of words restore point and release song in otherwise "unimportant" words: "with each your least / your any most very amazing now / or here." Nouns may be verbs ("april") and verbs nouns ("isn't").

From his satire, chiefly, comes the emphatically doubled double negative: "isn't's own isn't"; "than hate itself and no / meanness unsmaller"; "whatever is less / alive than never." His rage and scorn are always directed against negation; in this case, the war. Here it deepens and intensifies a joy that culminates in miracle: "Hills jump with brooks: / trees tumble out of twigs and sticks;" bringing the poem to a pause. The semicolon shows it has no closes.

135. *My Love, I cannot thy rare beauties place*

WILLIAM SMITH

My Love, I cannot thy rare beauties place
Under those forms which many writers use:
Some like to stones compare their mistress' face;
Some in the name of flowers do love abuse;
Some make their love a goldsmith's shop to be,
Where orient pearls and precious stones abound.
In my conceit these far do disagree
The perfect praise of beauty forth to sound.
O Chloris, thou dost imitate thyself!
Self's imitating passeth precious stones,
Or all the Eastern-Indian golden pelf:
Thy red and white with purest fair atones.
  Matchless for beauty nature hath thee framed,
  Only unkind and cruel thou art named.

Poetry feeds on hyperbole. But when exaggerated compliment becomes commonplace, as it does in a good many Elizabethan sonnets, a way must be found to out-top it. This is done here in the seemingly plain statement: "O Chloris, thou dost imitate thyself!"

Rather than completing the action of the sonnet, the concluding couplet seems to be an afterthought, put in to "round out" the form. William Carlos Williams' complaint against sonnets has at least this much justification. Indulged in too often, they tend either to impose predictable conclusions, so that the emotion "goes stale," or else—as here—to fall apart. Shakespeare does not always escape either hazard.

136. *So is it not with me as with that muse*

WILLIAM SHAKESPEARE

So is it not with me as with that muse,
Stirred by a painted beauty to his verse,
Who heaven itself for ornament doth use
And every fair with his fair doth rehearse,
Making a complement of proud compare,
With sun and moon, with earth and sea's rich gems,
With April's first-born flowers, and all things rare
That heaven's air in this huge rondure hems.
O! let me, true in love, but truly write;
And then believe me, my love is as fair
As any mother's child, though not so bright
As those gold candles fixed in heaven's air:
Let them say more that like of hearsay well;
I will not praise that purpose not to sell.

An impulse similar to William Smith's in the preceding sonnet motivates several of Shakespeare's sonnets. Here, in Sonnet XXI, the attitude is given a deft twist.

Shakespeare is well aware that the very act of denying "proud compare"—"heaven," "sun and moon," "earth and sea's rich gems," "April's first-born flowers"—puts them to work for him. His disclaimer of praise is tongue-in-cheek.

137. *Why is my verse so barren of new pride?*

WILLIAM SHAKESPEARE

Why is my verse so barren of new pride?
So far from variation or quick change?
Why, with the time, do I not glance aside
To new-found methods and to compounds strange?
Why write I still all one, ever the same,
And keep invention in a noted weed,
That every word doth almost tell my name,
Showing their birth, and where they did proceed?

Oh! know, sweet love, I always write of you,
And you and love are still my argument:
So all my best is dressing old words new,
Spending again what is already spent;
For as the sun is daily new and old,
Still is my love still telling what is told.

Another denial of denial proceeds from the rhetorical question that launches Sonnet LXXVI.

Shakespeare can hardly avoid some realization of his genius. It is not mock modesty but a sufficient if slightly masked pride that causes him to say: "That every word doth almost tell my name." Is he not defining the height of style in "dressing old words new"?

Puzzlers over acrostics who go out of their way to find Sir Francis Bacon or some other name woven into the works of William Shakespeare may be disheartened to learn that the first two lines of this sonnet begin "W S." In other sonnets he puns almost insufferably on "will."

138. *That you were once unkind befriends me now*

WILLIAM SHAKESPEARE

That you were once unkind befriends me now,
And for that sorrow, which I then did feel,
Needs must I under my transgression bow,
Unless my nerves were brass or hammered steel:
For if you were by my unkindness shaken,
As I by yours, you have passed a hell of time;
And I, a tyrant, have no leisure taken
To weigh how once I suffered in your crime.
Oh, that our night of woe might have remembered
My deeper sense, how hard true sorrow hits,
And soon to you, as you to me, then tendered
The humble salve which wounded bosoms fits!
But that your trespass now becomes a fee;
Mine ransoms yours, and yours must ransom me.

It is difficult to tell, in many of Shakespeare's sonnets, whether they are addressed to his friend or his mistress. On various occasions both offend him, sometimes with each other. Sonnet CXX might be to either.

"Fits" seems to fit Mary Fitton, maid of honor to Queen Elizabeth and sometimes identified as the "Dark Lady." This is a game any number can play.

In either case, how lovingly the sonnet says more than: "Since you were unkind to me, you should forgive my unkindness." Shakespeare goes beyond simple justice to a delicate balance of feeling: "Remembering my own sorrow, I should have realized the extent of yours." This is, too, a pinch of salt in the wound.

The "humble salve" that "fits" "wounded bosoms" may be related to the expression "to eat humble pie." Originally "umble-pie," it refers to a dish, served to hunters, of umbles or numbles, the lesser parts of venison, including the heart. A salve made from a wounded deer would fit the wounded heart.

139. *To live in hell, and heaven to behold*

HENRY CONSTABLE

To live in hell, and heaven to behold;
  To welcome life, and die a living death;
To sweat with heat, and yet be freezing cold;
  To grasp at stars, and lie the earth beneath;
To tread a maze that never shall have end;
  To burn in sighs, and strive in daily tears;
To climb a hill, and never to descend;
  Giants to kill, and quake at childish fears;
To pine for food, and watch th'Hesperian tree;
  To thirst for drink, and nectar still to draw;
To live accursed, whom men hold blest to be,
  And weep those wrongs which never creature saw:
    If this be love, if love in these be founded,
    My heart is love, for these in it are grounded.

The paradoxes of love are convincingly enumerated here to make a balanced rhetoric of contrast. Almost continually exiled in France because of his Catholicism, Constable is another early participant in the Elizabethan vogue for sonnet sequences, his *Diana* being published in 1592.

140. *Needs must I leave, and yet needs must I love*

HENRY CONSTABLE

Needs must I leave, and yet needs must I love;
  In vain my wit doth tell in verse my woe;
  Despair in me, disdain in thee, doth show
How by my wit I do my folly prove.
All this my heart from love can never move.
  Love is not in my heart. No, Lady, no,
  My heart is love itself. Till I forego
My heart I never can my love remove.
How then can I leave love? I do intend
  Not to crave grace, but yet to wish it still;
Not to praise thee, but beauty to commend;
  And so, by beauty's praise, praise thee I will,
    For as my heart is love, love not in me,
    So beauty thou, beauty is not in thee.

Constable's style of balanced phrases, pushed further in this sonnet, leads to two peaks of expression: "Love is not in my heart. No, Lady, no, / My heart is love itself"; and "So beauty thou, beauty is not in thee." The two hyperboles gain force and conviction by being close to denial, as white shines in contrast with black.

141. *I would thou wert not fair, or I were wise*

NICHOLAS BRETON

I would thou wert not fair, or I were wise;
I would thou hadst no face, or I no eyes;
I would thou wert not wise, or I not fond;
Or thou not free, or I not so in bond.

But thou art fair, and I can not be wise:
Thy sun-like face hath blinded both mine eyes;
Thou canst not but be wise, nor I but fond;
Nor thou but free, nor I but still in bond.

Yet am I wise to think that thou art fair;
Mine eyes their pureness in thy face repair;
Nor am I fond, that do thy wisdom see;
Nor yet in bond, because that thou art free.

Then in thy beauty only make me wise;
And in thy face the graces guide mine eyes;
And in thy wisdom only see me fond;
And in thy freedom keep me still in bond.

So shalt thou still be fair, and I be wise;
Thy face shine still upon my clearèd eyes;
Thy wisdom only see how I am fond,
Thy freedom only keep me still in bond.

So would I thou wert fair, and I were wise;
So would thou hadst thy face, and I mine eyes;
So would I thou wert wise, and I were fond,
And thou wert free and I were still in bond.

Like Edmund Bolton's "A palinode" (poem 95) appearing in the same year, 1600, Breton's poem makes its key words, "fair," "wise," "face," "eyes," "fond," "free," "bond," rotate first slowly, then spinningly as their meanings shift to bring the poem beautifully full circle.

142. *No love, to love of man and wife*

RICHARD EEDES

No love, to love of man and wife;
No hope, to hope of constant heart;
No joy, to joy in wedded life;
No faith, to faith in either part:
  Flesh is of flesh, and bone of bone
  When deeds and words and thoughts are one.

No hate, to hate of man and wife;
No fear, to fear of double heart;
No death, to discontented life;
No grief, to grief when friends depart:
  They tear the flesh and break the bone
  That are in word or thought alone.

Thy friend an other friend may be,
But other self is not the same:
Thy wife the self-same is with thee,
In body, mind, in goods and name:
  No thine, no mine, may other call,
  Now all is one, and one is all.

Few Elizabethan poems recommend—and by the same token warn of—married love so cordially as this. It develops an emotional syllogism in terms of thesis, antithesis, and synthesis.

143. *To know just how he suffered would be dear*

EMILY DICKINSON

To know just how he suffered would be dear;
To know if any human eyes were near
To whom he could intrust his wavering gaze,
Until it settled firm on Paradise.

To know if he was patient, part content,
Was dying as he thought, or different;
Was it a pleasant day to die,
And did the sunshine face his way?

What was his furthest mind, of home, or God,
Or what the distant say
At news that he ceased human nature
On such a day?

And wishes, had he any?
Just his sigh, accented,
Had been legible to me.
And was he confident until
Ill fluttered out in everlasting well?

And if he spoke, what name was best,
What first,
What one broke off with
At the drowsiest?

Was he afraid, or tranquil?
Might he know
How conscious consciousness could grow,
Till love that was, and love too blest to be,
Meet—and the junction be Eternity?

The astonishing first line at once places death at the calm center of a love poem. This is not sorrow; it is almost joy.

Various theories are put forward to account for the increasingly discovered number of these apparent self-revelations. Is she in love with a married man? with several? with none? The facts will perhaps remain a mystery; Emily Dickinson is reticent in everything but her poems.

"Love that was, and love too blest to be" surely suggests a remaining true until "death do us unite." Or is it what Browning calls the "majority" of his poems, "Dramatic in principle, and so many utterances of so many imaginary persons, not mine"?

144. *Hurrahing in harvest*

GERARD MANLEY HOPKINS

Summer ends now; now, barbarous in beauty, the stooks arise
  Around; up above, what wind-walks! what lovely behaviour
  Of silk-sack clouds! has wilder, wilful-wavier
Meal-drift moulded ever and melted across skies?

I walk, I lift up, I lift up heart, eyes,
  Down all that glory in the heavens to glean our Saviour;
  And, éyes, heárt, what looks, what lips yet gave you a
Rapturous love's greeting of realer, of rounder replies?

And the azurous hung hills are his world-wielding shoulder
  Majestic—as a stallion stalwart, very-violet-sweet!—
These things, these things were here and but the beholder
  Wanting; which two when they once meet,
The heart rears wings bold and bolder
  And hurls for him, O half hurls earth for him off under his feet.

Hopkins' love affair with the universe is celebrated in nearly all his poems. It springs from and is surrounded by his love of God. But for Hopkins, creator and creation are all but synonymous.

In other poems he recognizes the world's imperfection. That does not enter here, at least obviously, except perhaps in the phrase "barbarous in beauty," and once again, by implication, in the last line. But the hills have to be worthy to bear, like a strong and delicate horse, their weight of godhead.

All is pure love, including its first shyness: "I walk, I lift up, I lift up heart, eyes." Emotion precedes vision, hardly daring to look, the anticipated beauty is so unbelievable. And then the surpassing realization: "These things, these things were here . . ."

The poem ends in *almost* complete ecstasy. "The heart . . . hurls for him, O half hurls earth for him off under his feet." Only the ecstasy of heaven can wholly do this. But Hopkins has to stop to remind himself.

The emotion of love, as expressed in poetry, is as various as any other and can include all shades of emotion. Laughter often enters into it; sorrow; anger; even intellect.

At the heart of all poetry, with its many and diverse means of expression and degrees of intensity, is the wish for identification; an intermingling with its subject, whether a girl, a flight of birds, an idea, a scoundrel or the universe. In this sense every poem is a love poem.

PART NINE

"And always use so large a fan"

The transition from love to laughter is not abrupt. They can often be mutually inclusive, as well as exclusive.

Perhaps there are as many forms of laughter as there are of love; it might be said to run on a scale between love and anger. We laugh with delight or derision.

It runs a scale, too, between the interior smile and the loud laugh. Whether the latter "bespeaks the vacant mind," it usually comes from the suddenly filled-up mind, suddenness and unexpectedness being properties of a joke.

Like poems, jokes are hard to explain because they belong as much to the listener as to the perpetrator. Whether we laugh or not depends on what we are prepared for. But there are slow laughs, too, and quietly built-up amusement.

In this inclusive sense, the poetry of laughter would take in, of the poems that have gone before, Keats' "The Mermaid Tavern" for high gaiety; Skelton's "With hey, lullay, lullay" for sarcasm; Waller's "The story of Phoebus and Daphne applied, etc." for wit; Mother Goose for gentle humor; Cowper's "John Gilpin" for mock heroic; Swift's "The progress of poetry" for scorn; Davenant's "O thou that sleep'st like pig in straw" for tender ridicule; "Oh what a plague is love!" for self-made foolishness; "Little Musgrave and Lady Barnard" for tragicomedy; Rowland's "Sir Eglamour" for travesty; "In Good King Charles's golden days" for satire; Tennyson's "The sisters" for—possibly—unintentional humor; Lear's "By way of preface" for intended self-clowning; Carew's "Ingrateful beauty threatened" for quip; James Stephens' "The rivals" for lyric brag. And not all the rest are humorless.

Laughter need not imply that a poem is not "serious." The distinction between poetry and "light verse" is too frail for me to grasp with any assurance. Some poems are lighter than others. This doesn't necessarily make them better or worse than poems that are "heavier."

145. *Pied Beauty*

GERARD MANLEY HOPKINS

Glory be to God for dappled things—
  For skies of couple-colour as a brinded cow;
    For rose-moles all in stipple upon trout that swim;
Fresh-firecoal chestnut-falls; finches' wings;
  Landscape plotted and pieced—fold, fallow, and plough;
    And áll trádes, their gear and tackle and trim.

All things counter, original, spare, strange;
  Whatever is fickle, freckled (who knows how?)
    With swift, slow; sweet, sour; adazzle, dim;
He fathers-forth whose beauty is past change:
          Praise him.

This is humorous in a very special way. What is apt to strike us first about it is its prevailing tone; its access of delight and joy. Everything in it—skies, cows, fish, chestnuts or coals, wings, landscape—is sensed as if for the first time.

It is framed in devotion, beginning "Glory be to God" and ending "Praise him." Especially when read aloud there is something strange about the rhythm of the first line. The impulse is strong to lilt it, with the affectionate negligence of an Irish colloquialism.

This impulse seems at first intrusive; surely "Glory be to God" is meant with all its original force and conviction. I think that both intentions are present. The light rhythm and the heavy rhythm, the easy meaning and the deeper meaning coalesce or counterpoint each other, rocking back and forth. (I'm not using "counterpoint" in Hopkins' own technical sense.) It's as if, saying "Bless you!" to a sneeze, we were suddenly to experience, in the reflex phrase, its full pristine power of benediction.

This emotional double take, or sacred witticism, is what I believe sets the key and is the clue to the poem. Everywhere there is a play between high and low, the exalted and the familiar: "Skies of couple-colour as a brinded cow." The sky, remote and mysterious, is brought as close as a creature. At the same time the creature is endowed with mystery. Instead of the familiar "brindled," the archaic "brinded" is used, suggesting a remote origin.

The couplings in the poem are usually of things or qualities that have suggestions of opposition: "couple-colour" itself—that is, clearness and cloud; skies and cows; roses and fish; fresh firecoals (leaping) and falling chestnuts or their flame-colored leaves; inanimate and animate; natural and man-made; "counter, original, spare, strange," and yet "fickle, freckled"; "With swift, slow; sweet, sour; adazzle, dim."

All of these opposites meet in a series of visual puns. Isn't every comparison a kind of pun: to see the sky in a cow, a cow in the sky? This is more than a verbal flicker, yet it is emphasized by a play on language that runs through the poem. Why is everything dappled, coupled, stippled, fickle, freckled? Why is all beauty, in the word of the title, "pied"?

The frequent *le* endings, carried through in other words like "tackle" and "adazzle," convey a sense of endearing belittlement. They are not all diminutives, but a latent feeling of smallness is everywhere suggested.

This is, I feel, part of the poem's happy irony. Its religious humor lies in its deliberate choice of a particular sequence of qualifications, each one of which, taken by itself, evokes a sense of the beautiful. Yet in all of them there is a buried suggestion of defect: "dappled"—that is, mottled or blotted; "brinded" or streaked (see the witches' chant from *Macbeth*, poem 183); "stippled" with "moles" or blemishes; "fickle" or inconstant; "freckled," covered with spots. Beauty is "pied" like the magpie; it is flawed; it flies away. Possibly, too, since Hopkins speaks of trades, he is thinking of printer's type. Natural beauty is "pied" or scrambled.

The poem is in praise of imperfection. When we think of devotional writing, we are apt to think of it as largely a turning away from earthly beauty, in order to contemplate the eternal. The visible world and its appeal to the senses are to be thought of as distractions, as in T. S. Eliot's "Ash-Wednesday" and parts of *Four Quartets*.

This is not always so, but seldom has a religious poem so thoroughly reversed it. Viewed through the frame of devotion, the flaws of the natural world are transformed. They are symbols, almost pieces, of the perfect, unchanging beauty that has created them. They may be contradictory and baffling; at once almost aggressively themselves: "counter, original, spare, strange" (how close to Whitman that sounds) and at the same time "fickle" and "freckled"—and who knows how that came about?

Yet for all this, as Hopkins says in "God's grandeur" (poem 96), "nature is never spent." Although the world is temporal and transitory, as viewed from the aspect of eternity, this poem's unique, joyously witty reversal says, "God be praised for imperfect beauty." It is only through imperfection that we can arrive at any notion of perfection.

Perhaps in sly corroboration Hopkins has written this poem in the form of what he calls a "Curtal"—that is, curtailed—sonnet.

146. *So sweet a kiss the golden sun gives not*

WILLIAM SHAKESPEARE

So sweet a kiss the golden sun gives not
  To those fresh morning drops upon the rose,
As thy eye-beams, when their fresh rays have smote
  The night of dew that on my cheeks down flows:
Nor shines the silver moon one half so bright
  Through the transparent bosom of the deep,
As doth thy face through tears of mine give light:
  Thou shinest in every tear that I do weep;
No drop but as a coach doth carry thee,
  So ridest thou triumphing in my woe:
Do but behold the tears that swell in me,
  And they thy glory through my grief will show:
But do not love thyself; then thou wilt keep
My tears for glasses, and still make me weep.
O Queen of queens! how far dost thou excel,
No thought can think, nor tongue of mortal tell.

This calls for a different kind of double take. The opening lines seem so lovely that it may not be until tears begin driving off as coaches that we come to realize a simile is being fetched rather far.

Possibly audiences first seeing *Love's Labour's Lost* could recognize which of Shakespeare's colleagues is being ribbed. Or his butt may be the very proclivity of all poets, including himself, to be carried away by their own devices.

So carried away by his own eloquence is the amateur versifier in the play—Ferdinand, King of Navarre—that at the end of his laboriously constructed sonnet he can't stop. The added couplet is not only irrelevant to the "thought" of the preceding fourteen lines. It denies thought itself.

147. *This winter's weather it waxeth cold*

ANONYMOUS

This winter's weather it waxeth cold,
  And frost it freezeth on every hill,
And Boreas blows his blasts so bold,
  That all our cattle are like to spill.
Bell, my wife, she loves no strife;
  She said unto me quietly,
Rise up, and save cow Crumbock's life!
  Man, put thine old cloak about thee!

HE: O Bell, my wife, why dost thou flyte?
  Thou kens my cloak is very thin,
It is so sore and ever wore,
  A crickë thereon cannot rin.
Then I'll no longer borrow or lend;
  For once I'll new apparelled be;
Tomorrow I'll to town and spend;
  For I'll have a new cloak about me.

SHE: Cow Crumbock is a very good cow;
  She has been always good to the pail;
She has helped us to butter and cheese I trow,
  And other things she will not fail.
I would be loath to see her pine.
  Good husband, counsel take of me;
It is not for us to go so fine.
  Man, take thine old cloak about thee!

HE: My cloak it was a very good cloak,
  It hath been always good to the wear;
It hath cost me many a groat;
  I have had it this four and forty year.
Sometime it was of the cloth in grain,
  It is now but a sigh clout, as you may see;
It will neither hold out wind nor rain;
  And I'll have a new cloak about me.

SHE: It is four and forty years ago
  Sine the one of us the other did ken;
And we have had, betwixt us two,
  Children either nine or ten;
We have brought them up to women and men;
  In the fear of God I trow they be.
And why wilt thou thyself misken?
  Man, take thine old cloak about thee!

HE: O Bell, my wife, why dost thou flyte?
  Now is now, and then was then.
Seek all the world now throughout,
  Thou kens not clowns from gentlemen;
They are clad in black, green, yellow, and blue,
  So far above their own degree;
Once in my life I'll take a view,
  For I'll have a new cloak about me.

SHE: King Stephen was a worthy peer;
  His breeches cost him but a crown;
He held them sixpence all too dear;
  Therefore he called the tailor lown.
He was a wight of high renown,
  And thou's but of a low degree.
It's pride that puts this country down:
  Man, put thy old cloak about thee!

HE: O Bell my wife, why dost thou flyte?
  Now is now, and then was then.
We will now live obedient life,
  Thou the woman and I the man.

It's not for a man with a woman to threap,
   Unless he first give o'er the play.
As we began, so we will keep;
   And I'll have mine old cloak about me.

spill: perish; *flyte:* scold; *kens:* knowest; *crickë:* cricket; *rin:* run; *cloth in grain:* scarlet cloth; *sigh clout:* rag for straining; *trow:* trust; *lown:* lout; *threap:* argue

The attempt of the male to revolt against a predominantly matriarchal society, postulated by Robert Graves in *The Greek Myths* as forming much of the content of early mythology, survives into the sixteenth century in this dialogue between Bell and her nameless husband. It carries the rhythms of family contention.

148. *"Thyrsis, sleep'st thou?"*

ANONYMOUS

"Thyrsis, sleep'st thou? Holla! Let not sorrow stay us.
Hold up thy head man," said the gentle Meliboeus.
"See summer comes again, the country's pride adorning,
Hark how the cuckoo singeth this fair April morning."
"O!" said the shepherd, and sighed as one all undone.
"Let me alone, alas, and drive him back to London."

Another perennial contest, this time between city and country man, is suggested in this sixteenth-century equivalent of a burlesque skit. If not quite so broad as the Old Howard, the last line is a true "black-out."

149. *Only Joy! now here you are*

SIR PHILIP SIDNEY

   Only Joy! now here you are,
   Fit to hear and ease my care,
   Let my whispering voice obtain
   Sweet reward for sharpest pain:
Take me to thee, and thee to me.
No, no, no, no, my dear, let be.

Night hath closed all in her cloak,
Twinkling stars love-thoughts provoke,
Danger hence good care doth keep,
Jealousy itself doth sleep:
Take me to thee, and thee to me.
No, no, no, no, my dear, let be.

Better place no wit can find,
Cupid's knot to loose or bind;
These sweet flowers on fine bed too,
Us in their best language woo:
Take me to thee, and thee to me.
No, no, no, no, my dear, let be.

That you heard was but a mouse,
Dumb sleep holdeth all the house:
Yet asleep, methinks they say,
"Young folks, take time while you may":
Take me to thee, and thee to me.
No, no, no, no, my dear, let be.

Niggard Time threats, if we miss
This large offer of our bliss,
Long stay, ere he grant the same:
Sweet, then, while each thing doth frame,
Take me to thee, and thee to me.
No, no, no, no, my dear, let be.

Your fair mother is a-bed,
Candles out and curtains spread;
She thinks you do letters write;
Write, but first let me indite:
Take me to thee, and thee to me.
No, no, no, no, my dear, let be.

Sweet, alas, why strive you thus?
Concord better fitteth us;
Leave to Mars the force of hands,
Your power in your beauty stands:

Take me to thee, and thee to me.
No, no, no, no, my dear, let be.

Woe to me! and do you swear
Me to hate, but I forbear?
Cursèd be my destines all,
That brought me so high to fall!
Soon with my death I will please thee.
No, no, no, no, my dear, let be.

but I forbear: except I forbear; *destines:* destinies

An equally ancient tug of war is going on here. Perhaps in a pre-masculine era the rôles are reversed; see Shakespeare's "Venus and Adonis" for a possible survival of this aspect of the myth. Here the lady's one and constant refrain proves to be—we hope—her undoing.

150. *Sweet, let me go!*
ANONYMOUS

Sweet, let me go! Sweet, let me go!
What do you mean to vex me so?
Cease, cease, cease your pleading force!
Do you think thus to extort remorse?
Now, now! no more! alas, you overbear me;
And I would cry, but some would hear, I fear me.

They capitulate more quickly in the seventeenth century.

151. *No platonic love*
WILLIAM CARTWRIGHT

Tell me no more of minds embracing minds,
And hearts exchanged for hearts;
That spirits spirits meet, as winds do winds,
And mix their subtlest parts;

That two unbodied essences may kiss,
And then like angels, twist and feel one bliss.

I was that silly thing that once was wrought
  To practise this thin love;
I climbed from sex to soul, from soul to thought;
  But thinking there to move,
Headlong I rolled from thought to soul, and then
From soul I lighted at the sex again.

As some strict down-looked men pretend to fast,
  Who yet in closets eat;
So lovers who profess they spirits taste,
  Feed yet on grosser meat;
I know they boast they souls to souls convey,
Howe'er they meet, the body is the way.

Come, I will undeceive thee, they that tread
  Those vain aërial ways,
Are like young heirs and alchemists misled
  To waste their wealth and days,
For searching thus to be forever rich,
They only find a medicine for the itch.

Cartwright's theme may have been suggested to him by two lines in John Donne's "The extasy":

Love's mysteries in souls do grow,
But yet the body is his book.

152. *Kind lovers, love on*
JOHN CROWNE

Kind lovers, love on,
Lest the world be undone,
And mankind be lost by degrees:

For if all from their loves
Should go wander in groves,
There soon would be nothing but trees.

This precursor of the limerick occurs in the Restoration play *Calisto.*

153. *A man may live thrice Nestor's life*
THOMAS NORTON

A man may live thrice Nestor's life,
Thrice wander out Ulysses' race,
Yet never find Ulysses' wife:
Such change hath chancèd in this case.

Less age will serve than Paris had,
Small pain—if none be small enough—
To find good store of Helen's trade:
Such sap, the root doth yield the bough.

For one good wife Ulysses slew
A worthy knot of gentle blood;
For one ill wife Greece overthrew
The town of Troy. Sith bad and good
Work mischief, Lord, let be thy will
To keep me free from either ill!

Irrefutable logic characterizes this moral drawn from the classics by a sixteenth-century poet, collaborator with Thomas Sackville, Earl of Dorset, on the first English tragedy, *Ferrex and Porrex*, afterward called *Gorboduc.*

154. *A catch*
HENRY ALDRICH

If all be true that I do think
There are five reasons we should drink:

Good wine, a friend, or being dry,
Or lest we should be by and by;
Or any other reason why.

This catch is translated from Aldrich's own Latin:

Si bene quid memini, causae sunt quinque bibendi;
Hospitis adventus, praesans sitis atque futura,
Aut vini bonitas, aut quaelibet altera causa.

Inveterate smoker and author of *Artis Logicae Compendium* (1691), a standard text for over a century, Henry Aldrich is now best remembered for his hymns, his design for the Peckwater Quadrangle of Christ Church, Oxford, of which he was dean, and these lines.

155. *On a favorite cat drowned in a tub of goldfishes*

THOMAS GRAY

'Twas on a lofty vase's side,
Where China's gayest art had dyed
  The azure flowers that blow;
Demurest of the tabby kind,
The pensive Selima, reclined,
  Gazed on the lake below.

Her conscious tail her joy declared;
The fair round face, the snowy beard,
  The velvet of her paws,
Her coat that with the tortoise vies,
Her ears of jet, and emerald eyes
  She saw, and purred applause.

Still had she gazed, but 'midst the tide
Two angel forms were seen to glide,
  The Genii of the stream:
Their scaly armor's Tyrian hue
Through richest purple to the view
  Betrayed a golden gleam.

The hapless nymph with wonder saw:
A whisker first, and then a claw
   With many an ardent wish
She stretched, in vain, to reach the prize.
What female heart can gold despise?
   What cat's averse to fish?

Presumptuous maid! with looks intent
Again she stretched, again she bent,
   Nor knew the gulf between.
Malignant Fate sat by, and smiled.
The slippery verge her feet beguiled,
   She tumbled headlong in.

Eight times emerging from the flood
She mewed to every watery God
   Some speedy aid to send.
No dolphin came, no Nereid stirred:
Nor cruel Tom, nor Susan heard.
   A favorite has no friend!

From hence, ye beauties, undeceived,
Know one false step is ne'er retrieved,
   And be with caution bold.
Not all that tempts your wandering eyes
And heedless hearts, is lawful prize;
   Nor all that glisters, gold.

The eighteenth century is as full as any other of a number of styles, among them Alexander Pope's great shoals of wit. He is seldom witty for very short, unless you take him in excerpts. "The rape of the lock" is delicious mock heroics, almost as much so as Byron's later and longer "Don Juan," although Pope *seems* longer because of his penchant for heroic couplets. At length, they are like a bludgeoning with rapiers.

The grandiloquent style, the well-turned phrase, and the resounding moral pronouncement are to be found here, in similar if warmer fashion.

156. *Fools, they are the only nation*

BEN JONSON

Fools, they are the only nation
Worth men's envy or admiration;
Free from care or sorrow-taking,
Selves and others merry making:
All they speak or do is sterling.
Your fool he is your great man's dearling,
And your lady's sport and pleasure;
Tongue and babble are his treasure.
E'en his face begetteth laughter,
And he speaks truth free from slaughter;
He's the grace of every feast,
And sometimes the chiefest guest;
Hath his trencher and his stool,
When wit waits upon the fool.
  Oh, who would not be
    He, he, he?

The Fool, a lovable fixture of Elizabethan drama, celebrates himself in this song from *Volpone*. Jonson winds up thoroughly immersing himself in the part.

157. *Fain would I have a pretty thing*

ANONYMOUS

Fain would I have a pretty thing
  To give unto my lady:
I name no thing, nor I mean no thing,
  But as pretty a thing as may be.

Twenty journeys would I make,
  And twenty ways would hie me,
To make adventure for her sake
  To set some matter by me.
    But I would fain have a pretty thing, . . .

Some do long for pretty knacks,
  And some for strange devices:
God send me that my lady lacks,
  I care not what the price is.
    Thus fain would I have a pretty thing, . . .

Some go here and some go there
  Where gazes be not geason;
And I go gaping everywhere,
  But still come out of season.
    Yet fain would I have a pretty thing, . . .

I walk the town and tread the street,
  In every corner seeking:
The pretty thing I cannot meet
  That's for a lady's liking.
    Fain would I have a pretty thing, . . .

The mercers pull me going by,
  The silk-wives say, "What lack ye?"
"The thing you have not," then say I,
  "Ye foolish folk, go pack ye!"
    But fain would I have a pretty thing, . . .

It is not all the silk in Cheape,
  Nor all the golden treasure,
Nor twenty bushels on a heap,
  Can do my lady pleasure.
    But fain would I have a pretty thing, . . .

The gravers of the golden shows
  With jewels do beset me,
The shemsters in the shops, that sews,
  They do nothing but let me.
    But fain would I have a pretty thing, . . .

But were it in the wit of man
  By any means to make it,
I could for money buy it than,
  And say, "Fair lady, take it!"
    Thus fain would I have a pretty thing, . . .

O lady, what a luck is this—
  That my good willing misseth
To find what pretty thing it is
  That my good lady wisheth!
    Thus fain would I have had this pretty thing
      To give unto my lady:
    I said no harm, nor I meant no harm,
      But as pretty a thing as may be.

geason: uncommon; *shemsters:* sempstresses; *let:* hinder; *than:* then

It seems curious that this popular ballad of the fifteen-sixties is not attributed to the Scots.

158. *I'll tell thee everything I can*

LEWIS CARROLL

I'll tell thee everything I can;
  There's little to relate.
I saw an agèd agèd man,
  A-sitting on a gate.
"Who are you, agèd man?" I said,
  "And how is it you live?"
His answer trickled through my head
  Like water through a sieve.

He said, "I look for butterflies
  That sleep among the wheat:
I make them into mutton-pies,
  And sell them in the street.
I sell them unto men," he said,
  "Who sail on stormy seas;
And that's the way I get my bread—
  A trifle, if you please."

But I was thinking of a plan
  To dye one's whiskers green,
And always use so large a fan
  That they could not be seen.
So, having no reply to give
  To what the old man said,
I cried, "Come, tell me how you live!"
  And thumped him on the head.

His accents mild took up the tale;
  He said, "I go my ways
And when I find a mountain-rill
  I set it in a blaze;
And thence they make a stuff they call
  Rowland's Macassar Oil—
Yet twopence-halfpenny is all
  They give me for my toil."

But I was thinking of a way
  To feed oneself on batter,
And so go on from day to day
  Getting a little fatter.
I shook him well from side to side,
  Until his face was blue;
"Come, tell me how you live," I cried,
  "And what it is you do!"

He said, "I hunt for haddock's eyes
  Among the heather bright,
And work them into waistcoat-buttons
  In the silent night.
And these I do not sell for gold
  Or coin of silvery shine,
But for a copper halfpenny
  And that will purchase nine.

"I sometimes dig for buttered rolls,
  Or set limed twigs for crabs;
I sometimes search the grassy knolls
  For wheels of Hansom cabs.
And that's the way" (he gave a wink)
  "By which I get my wealth—
And very gladly will I drink
  Your Honor's noble health."

I heard him then, for I had just
  Completed my design
To keep the Menai Bridge from rust
  By boiling it in wine.
I thanked him much for telling me
  The way he got his wealth,
But chiefly for his wish that he
  Might drink my noble health.

And now if e'er by chance I put
  My finger into glue,
Or madly squeeze a right-hand foot
  Into a left-hand shoe,
Or if I drop upon my toe
  A very heavy weight,
I weep, for it reminds me so
Of that old man I used to know—
Whose look was mild, whose speech was slow,
Whose hair was whiter than the snow,
Whose face was very like a crow,
With eyes, like cinders, all aglow,
Who seemed distracted with his woe,
Who rocked his body to and fro,
And muttered mumblingly, and low,
As if his mouth were full of dough,
Who snorted like a buffalo—
That summer evening, long ago,
  A-sitting on a gate.

I doubt if she knows it, but the White Knight's recital to Alice in *Through the Looking-Glass* bears striking resemblances to William Wordsworth's encounter in "Resolution and independence" with an old leech-gatherer.

Wordsworth, too, after asking the venerable old man, whom he meets on a moor, "What occupation do you there pursue?" goes mooning off and has to repeat, "How is it that you live, and what is it you do?" His thoughts, though woolly enough, are not quite so sublimely futile.

159. *Sonnet found in a deserted madhouse*

ANONYMOUS

Oh that my soul a marrow-bone might seize!
For the old egg of my desire is broken,
Spilled is the pearly white and spilled the yolk, and
As the mild melancholy contents grease
My path the shorn lamb baas like bumblebees.
Time's trashy purse is as a taken token
Or like a thrilling recitation, spoken
By mournful mouths filled full of mirth and cheese.

And yet, why should I clasp the earthful urn?
Or find the frittered fig that felt the fast?
Or choose to chase the cheese around the churn?
Or swallow any pill from out the past?
Ah, no Love, not while your hot kisses burn
Like a potato riding on the blast.

No especial poet seems to be the butt of this nineteenth-century dithyramb. Rather, as in Shakespeare's "So sweet a kiss the golden sun gives not" (poem 146), the natural proclivity of *all* poetry toward intensification is carried just a little too far.

160. *A song about myself*

JOHN KEATS

There was a naughty boy,
  A naughty boy was he,
He would not stop at home,
  He could not quiet be—
    He took
    In his knapsack
    A book
    Full of vowels
    And a shirt
    With some towels—
    A slight cap
    For night cap—
    A hair brush,
    Comb ditto,
    New stockings
    For old ones
    Would split O!
    This knapsack
    Tight at's back
    He rivetted close
  And followed his nose
    To the north,
    To the north,
  And followed his nose to the north.

There was a naughty boy
  And a naughty boy was he,
For nothing would he do
  But scribble poetry—
    He took
    An ink stand
    In his hand
    And a pen
    Big as ten
    In the other

And away
In a pother
He ran
To the mountains
And fountains
And ghostes
And postes
And witches
And ditches
And wrote
In his coat
When the weather
Was cool,
Fear of gout,
And without
When the weather
Was warm—
Och the charm
When we choose
To follow one's nose
To the north,
To the north,
To follow one's nose to the north!

There was a naughty boy
And a naughty boy was he,
He kept little fishes
In washing tubs three
In spite
Of the might
Of the maid
Nor afraid
Of his Granny-good
He often would
Hurly burly
Get up early
And go

By hook or crook
To the brook
And bring home
Miller's thumb,
Tittlebat
Not over fat,
Minnows small
As the stall
Of a glove,
Not above
The size
Of a nice
Little baby's
Little fingers—
O he made
'Twas his trade
Of fish a pretty kettle
A kettle
A kettle
Of fish a pretty kettle
A kettle!

There was a naughty boy
And a naughty boy was he,
He ran away to Scotland
The people for to see—
Then he found
That the ground
Was as hard,
That a yard
Was as long,
That a song
Was as merry,
That a cherry
Was as red,
That lead
Was as weighty,

That fourscore
Was as eighty,
That a door
Was as wooden
As in England—
So he stood in
His shoes and he wondered,
He wondered,
He stood in
His shoes and he wondered.

In many of his poems Keats is testing the reality of illusion. This, sent in a letter to his sister Fanny during a walking tour of Scotland in 1818, ambles along in a rhythm sometimes known as doggerel—because of its short feet?—toward an ultimate illusion of reality.

161. *Treason never prospers*

JAMES HARRINGTON

Treason never prospers. What's the reason?
For if it prospers, none dare call it treason.

There is more than one confirmation in modern times of this epigram by the seventeenth-century political writer.

162. *There was an old man in a tree*

EDWARD LEAR

There was an old man in a tree
Who was horribly bored by a bee;
When they said, "Does it buzz?"
He replied, "Yes, it does!
It's a regular brute of a bee!"

Lear disclaims inventing the limerick, which may or may not have any real connection with the town for which it is named. So far as I know, literary detection has not as yet solved this mystery, except to suggest that there are songs about Limerick that bear no resemblance to the five-line stanza.

This one is in the classic form, repeating one of the rhyme-words of the first couplet in the final line. This suits Lear's temperament and type of surprise which, distinguished from the American wisecrack, might be called the non-surprise or English joke; an epigram without a point.

163. *There was an old man of St. Bees*

W. S. GILBERT

There was an old man of St. Bees,
Who was stung in the arm by a wasp;
    When they asked, "Does it hurt?"
    He replied, "No, it doesn't,
But I thought all the while 'twas a hornet!"

It might seem impossible to parody a parody, but Sir William Schwenck Gilbert does just that, carrying non-surprise one step farther back.

164. *As a beauty I am not a star*

ANTHONY EUWER

As a beauty I am not a star,
There are others more handsome by far.
    But my face I don't mind it,
    For I am behind it.
It's the people in front get the jar.

Especially as it crosses the ocean, the limerick tends to develop in the direction of the gag-line. Euwer's limerick is said to have been a favorite of President Woodrow Wilson.

165. *I wish that my room had a floor*
GELETT BURGESS

I wish that my room had a floor.
I don't so much care for a door;
  But this walking around
  Without touching the ground
Is getting to be quite a bore.

Chiefly famous for his lines about a purple cow, the late Gelett Burgess' request here seems as reasonable as Charlie Chaplin's concern in *Shoulder Arms* over entering by the doorway.

166. *There was a young lady of Niger*
ANONYMOUS

There was a young lady of Niger
Who smiled as she rode on a tiger.
  They came back from the ride
  With the lady inside
And the smile on the face of the tiger.

The hazards of trying to improve on poets, even anonymous poets like the author of this late-nineteenth-century epic, are illustrated by a comparatively recent version—brought out, I might add, in an English publication.

The "young lady of Niger" belongs to that voluminous class of limericks that derive inspiration from place names. Recognizing that "Niger" should be pronounced with a soft g, the annoying and anonymous purist tries to clean up the limerick by substituting "Riga." It just won't do. "Riga" should be pronounced "Reega."

So intent is this Bowdler on correcting a minor slip that he perpetrates a major blunder. He neglects to place a smile on the face of the lady. This reduces the tiger's expression, on returning, to a perfunctory grimace, or archaic smile.

Other developments of the limerick are available only by word-of-mouth or in privately printed collections.

167. *On my joyful departure from the city of Cologne*

SAMUEL TAYLOR COLERIDGE

As I am a rhymer,
And now at least a merry one,
Mr. Mumm's Rudesheimer
And the church of St. Geryon
Are the two things alone
That deserve to be known
In the body-and-soul stinking town of Cologne.

According to psychiatry, a good deal of humor is a disguise for hostility. What does *this* mask?

168. *Here Jack and Tom are paired with Moll and Meg*

GEORGE MEREDITH

Here Jack and Tom are paired with Moll and Meg.
Curved open to the river-reach is seen
A country merry-making on the green;
Fair space for signal shakings of the leg.
That little screwy fiddler from his booth,
Whence flows one nut-brown stream, commands the joints
Of all who caper here at various points.
I have known rustic revels in my youth:
The May-fly pleasures of a mind at ease.
An early goddess was a country lass:
A charmed Amphion-oak she tripped the grass.
What life was that I lived? The life of these?

Heaven keep them happy! Nature they seem near.
They must, I think, be wiser than I am;
They have the secret of the bull and lamb.
'Tis true that when we trace its source, 'tis beer.

Meredith's nineteenth-century *Modern Love*, while not quite a novel in verse, follows a story line more closely than most sonnet sequences. But its individual sonnets are mainly separate, if linked, units.

This one, the eighteenth, is an interlude in the action. It belongs to the malicious-bucolic school, like Arnold Bennett's remark in *The Old Wives' Tale* that country people get up at three in the morning "and muddle through the day."

169. *Goodnight to the season!*

WINTHROP MACKWORTH PRAED

Goodnight to the season! 'tis over!
  Gay dwellings no longer are gay;
The courtier, the gambler, the lover,
  Are scattered like swallows away;
There's nobody left to invite one,
  Except my good uncle and spouse;
My mistress is bathing at Brighton,
  My patron is sailing at Cowes;
For want of a better employment,
  Till Ponto and Don can get out,
I'll cultivate rural enjoyment,
  And angle immensely for trout.

Goodnight to the season! the lobbies,
  Their changes, and rumors of change,
Which startled the rural Sir Bobbies,
  And made all the bishops look strange;
The breaches and battles and blunders
  Performed by the Commons and Peers;
The Marquis's eloquence thunders,
  The Baronet's eloquent ears;

Denouncing of Papists and treasons,
  Of foreign dominion, and oats;
Misrepresentation of reasons,
  And misunderstanding of notes.

Goodnight to the season! the buildings
  Enough to make Inigo sick;
The paintings, and plasterings, and gildings
  Of stucco, and marble, and brick;
The orders deliciously blended,
  From love of effect, into one;
The club-houses only intended,
  The palaces only begun;
The hell, where the fiend in his glory,
  Sits staring at putty and stones,
And scrambles from story to story,
  To rattle at midnight his bones.

Goodnight to the season! the dances,
  The fillings of hot little rooms,
The glancings of rapturous glances,
  The fancyings of fancy costumes;
The pleasures which fashion makes duties,
  The praisings of fiddles and flutes,
The luxury of looking at beauties,
  The tedium of talking to mutes;
The female diplomatists, planners
  Of matches for Laura and Jane,
The ice of her Ladyship's manners,
  The ice of his Lordship's champagne.

Goodnight to the season! the rages
  Led off by the chiefs of the throng,
The Lady Matilda's new pages,
  The Lady Eliza's new song,

Miss Fennel's macaw, which at Boodle's
  Was held to have something to say;
Miss Splenetic's musical poodles,
  Which bark "Batti—Batti!" all day;
The pony Sir Araby sported,
  As hot and as black as a coal,
And the lion his mother imported,
  In bearskins and grease, from the Pole.

Goodnight to the season! the Toso,
  So very majestic and tall;
Miss Ayton, whose singing was so-so,
  And Pasta, divinest of all;
The labor in vain of the ballet,
  So sadly deficient in stars;
The foreigners thronging the Alley,
  Exhaling the breath of cigars;
The loge, where some heiress, how killing,
  Environed with exquisites, sits,
The lovely one out of her drilling,
  The silly ones out of their wits.

Goodnight to the season! the splendor
  That beamed in the Spanish bazaar,
Where I purchased—my heart was so tender—
  A card-case,—a pasteboard guitar,—
A bottle of perfume,—a girdle,—
  A lithographed Riego, full-grown,
Whom bigotry drew on a hurdle,
  That artists might draw him on stone,—
A small panorama of Seville,—
  A trap for demolishing flies,—
A caricature of the devil,—
  And a look from Miss Sheridan's eyes.

Goodnight to the season! the flowers
  Of the grand horticultural fête,
When boudoirs were quitted for bowers,
  And the fashion was, not to be late;
When all who had money and leisure
  Grew rural o'er ices and wines,
All pleasantly toiling for pleasure,
  All hungrily pining for pines,
And making of beautiful speeches,
  And marring of beautiful shows,
And feeding on delicate peaches,
  And treading on delicate toes.

Goodnight to the season! another
  Will come with its trifles and toys,
And hurry away, like its brother,
  In sunshine, and odor, and noise.
Will it come with a rose, or a brier?
  Will it come with a blessing, or curse?
Will its bonnets be lower, or higher?
  Will its morals be better, or worse?
Will it find me grown thinner, or fatter,
  Or fonder of wrong or of right,
Or married, or buried?—no matter,—
  Goodnight to the season!—Goodnight!

This lively piece of boredom is about a hundred years older than Noel Coward's "Marvelous party," which Beatrice Lillie sings so *divinely*. If not quite so madcap and bizarre, it has its rococo moments.

170. *To a louse, on seeing one on a lady's bonnet, at church*

ROBERT BURNS

Ha! whare ye gaun, ye crowlin ferlie!
Your impudence protects you sairly:
I canna say but ye strunt rarely,
        Owre gauze and lace;
Tho' faith, I fear ye dine but sparely
        On sic a place.

Ye ugly, creepin, blastit wonner,
Detested, shunn'd by saunt an' sinner,
How dare ye set your fit upon her,
        Sae fine a lady!
Gae somewhere else, and seek your dinner
        On some poor body.

Swith, in some beggar's haffet squattle;
There ye may creep, and sprawl, and sprattle
Wi' ither kindred, jumping cattle,
        In shoals and nations;
Where horn nor bane ne'er dare unsettle
        Your thick plantations.

Now haud ye there, ye're out o' sight,
Below the fatt'rels, snug an' tight;
No, faith ye yet! ye'll no be right
        Till ye've got on it,
The vera tapmost, tow'ring height
        O' Miss's bonnet.

My sooth! right bauld ye set your nose out,
As plump and gray as onie grozet;
O for some rank, mercurial rozet,
        Or fell, red smeddum,
I'd gie you sic a hearty doze o't,
        Wad dress your droddum!

I wad na been surpris'd to spy
You on an auld wife's flainen toy;
Or aiblins some bit duddie boy,
On's wyliecoat;
But Miss's fine Lunardi! fie,
How daur ye do't?

O, Jenny, dinna toss your head,
An' set your beauties a' abread!
Ye little ken what cursèd speed
The blastie's makin!
Thae winks and finger-ends, I dread,
Are notice takin!

O wad some Pow'r the giftie gie us
To see oursels as others see us!
It wad frae monie a blunder free us
And foolish notion:
What airs in dress an' gait wad lea'e us,
And ev'n Devotion!

ferlie: fearful sight; *strunt*: strut; *wonner*: wonder; *fit*: foot; *swith*: swift; *haffet*: lock of hair; *squattle*: sprawl; *sprattle*: struggle; *bane*: bone; *fatt'rels*: ribbon ends; *grozet*: gooseberry; *rozet*: rosin; *smeddum*: powder; *sic*: such; *droddum*: breech, buttocks; *flainen* (*flannen?*) *toy*: old-fashioned flannel headdress; *aiblins*: perhaps; *duddie*: ragged; *wyliecoat*: flannel vest; *Lunardi*: bonnet named for Vincenzo Lunardi, who in 1784 made the first balloon ascent in England

This is a little farther along toward anger, though a good deal of it is mock. A louse taxes even Burns' affections, notably strong toward a field mouse turned up while plowing, a daisy plowed down, a wounded hare, scared waterfowl, Mailie the sheep tangled in her own tether, the old mare Maggie.

Yet he addresses the overbold creature with considerably less repugnance than he displays for the "Unco Guid," Holy Willie, or the toothache. It's rather the same feeling of uneasy camaraderie reserved for the devil. If a bit standoffish, he can at least speak plainly, as man to man. A spade's a spade "for a' that." Or, as he is supposed, in "The toadeater," to have silenced a man at dinner "talking mightily of dukes":

What of earls with whom you have supped,
And of dukes that you dined with yestreen?
Lord! a louse, sir, is still but a louse,
Though it crawl on the curls of a queen.

171. *Edmund Burke*

OLIVER GOLDSMITH

Here lies our good Edmund, whose genius was such,
We scarcely can praise it or blame it too much;
Who, born for the universe, narrowed his mind,
And to party gave up what was meant for mankind.
Though fraught with all learning, yet straining his throat
To persuade Tommy Townsend to lend him a vote;
Who, too deep for his hearers, still went on refining,
And thought of convincing while they thought of dining;
Though equal to all things, for all things unfit,
Too nice for a statesman, too proud for a wit;
For a patriot too cool; for a drudge, disobedient,
And too fond of the right to pursue the expedient.
In short, 'twas his fate, unemployed or in play, sir,
To eat mutton cold, and cut blocks with a razor.

Whether just or not, the balanced irony, so equally divided between scorn and admiration, is convincing. A full-length biography would be hard put to it to erase this impression.

Though it is cast as an epitaph, Burke survives Goldsmith by twenty-three years.

172. *Sing lullaby, as women do*

GEORGE GASCOIGNE

Sing lullaby, as women do,
Wherewith they bring their babies to rest;
And lullaby can I sing too,
As womanly as can the best.

With lullaby they still the child;
And, if I be not much beguiled,
Full many wanton babes have I,
Which must be stilled with lullaby.

First, lullaby my youthful years,
  It is now time to go to bed;
For crooked age and hoary hairs
  Have won the haven within my head.
With lullaby, then, youth, be still!
With lullaby content thy will!
Since courage quails and comes behind,
Go sleep, and so beguile thy mind!

Next, lullaby my gazing eyes,
  Which wonted were to glance apace;
For every glass may now suffice
  To show the furrows in my face.
With lullaby, then, wink awhile!
With lullaby your looks beguile!
Let no fair face, nor beauty bright,
Entice you eft with vain delight.

And lullaby my wanton will;
  Let reason's rule now reign thy thought,
Since all too late I find by skill
  How dear I have thy fancies bought.
With lullaby now take thine ease!
With lullaby thy doubts appease!
For trust to this, if thou be still,
My body shall obey thy will.

Eke lullaby my loving boy;
  My little Robin, take thy rest!
Since age is cold and nothing coy,
  Keep close thy coin, for so is best.

With lullaby be thou content!
With lullaby thy lusts relent!
Let others pay which have mo pence,
Thou art too poor for such expense.

Thus, lullaby my youth, mine eyes,
   My will, my ware, and all that was:
I can no mo delays devise;
   But welcome pain, let pleasure pass.
With lullaby now take your leave!
With lullaby your dreams deceive!
And when you rise with waking eye,
Remember then this lullaby!

eft: again; *mo:* more

Laughter can be sorrowful too. Some printings of this poem omit the most touching good night of all, to "little Robin." Others substitute "coign" for "coin." Both meanings seem clearly intended.

Not all shades of humor are represented here. Poetry rather seldom includes the explosive guffaw. But there is the delicious patter-song invented by Gilbert and Sullivan, where words and music are almost inextricable. The tradition comes down to us, modified, in the topical songs in musical comedy, in the witty lyrics of Noel Coward, Cole Porter and others.

Patter without music has been developed to a fine art by Ogden Nash. His face is familiar enough to need no introduction.

Of parodies, besides Lewis Carroll's playful dig at Wordsworth (poem 158), there are two I should especially have liked to include: C. S. Calverley's "The cock and the bull" and Henry Reed's "Chard Whitlow." To do them justice, sections at least of Robert Browning's *The Ring and the Book* and T. S. Eliot's *Four Quartets* would also have had to be included.

I must refer the reader to the source for another masterpiece of—among many other things—laughter: *Finnegans Wake.*

PART TEN

"Then give them all the lie"

As laughter may conceal anger, so anger is not necessarily devoid of humor. Humor implies a sense of proportion. But the ratio is seldom constant. "Tom o'Bedlam's song" (poem 52), for all its wry and eerie laughter, its lyric flights of wild fancy, contains moments of uncontrollable rage:

On the lordly lofts of Bedlam,
With stubble soft and dainty,
Bare bracelets strong, sweet whips, ding-dong,
With wholesome hunger plenty.

This is "funny" in the sense of saying the opposite of what it means; its rage for all that seems deeper than when it says straight out, "The palsy plagues my pulses" or "I repose at Powles with waking souls."

It all depends on the degree—shall we say the proportion?—of proportion. The sense of this, as of all qualities, varies not only from reader to reader but from time to time. When James Thomson—not of *The Seasons* but of *The City of Dreadful Night*—says:

Who is most wretched in this dolorous place?
I think myself. Yet I would rather be
My miserable self than He, than He
Who formed such creatures to his own disgrace . . .

we may, particularly if it is persuasively read, be carried away by the thunder of its resounding phrases. On repetition it is apt to become less and less thunderous and more and more funny; it overreaches itself.

When Burns says, in his epigram, "On hearing that there was falsehood in the Rev. Dr. B——'s very looks":

That there is falsehood in his looks
I must and will deny;
They say their master is a knave—
And sure they do not lie.

our sense of humor has been engaged; we are less apt to laugh *at* it.

Irony, or that kind of rage that includes laughter—no matter how bitter—would seem safer. Yet there are poems, I think, that lash out quite directly and savagely and continue to make the stings felt. There are all kinds.

173. *With how sad steps, O Moon, thou climb'st the skies!*

SIR PHILIP SIDNEY

With how sad steps, O Moon, thou climb'st the skies!
How silently, and with how wan a face!
What, may it be that even in heavenly place
That busy archer his sharp arrows tries?
Sure, if that long-with-love-acquainted eyes
Can judge of love, thou feel'st a lover's case—
I read it in thy looks; thy languished grace,
To me, that feel the like, thy state descries.
Then, even of fellowship, O Moon, tell me,
Is constant love deemed there but want of wit?
Are beauties there as proud as here they be?
Do they, above, love to be loved, and yet
  Those lovers scorn whom that love doth possess?
  Do they call virtue, there, ungratefulness?

This sonnet may not seem angry at all. It begins sweetly and sadly, like one more Elizabethan reading of the skies for a reflection of the "lover's case."

It slips into its anger casually, as if accidentally. His complaint is not that his lady is coy of her favors but that she thinks him a fool for seeking them; not that she is virtuous, but ungrateful.

The languorous beginning, I think, is bait to ensure her reading it. It promises to be yet another helpless tribute to her fascination.

174. *On the setting up Mr. Butler's monument in Westminster Abbey*

SAMUEL WESLEY

While Butler, needy wretch! was yet alive,
No generous patron would a dinner give:
See him, when starved to death and turned to dust,
Presented with a monumental bust!
The poet's fate is here in emblem shown;
He asked for bread, and he received a stone.

Sidney's sonnet (poem 173) is ostensibly a love poem in which anger is concealed by sorrow. Wesley's epigrammatic epitaph reveals its anger through its wit.

Samuel Butler, author of *Hudibras*, died in 1680; according to some, in extreme poverty. The bust referred to is one installed in 1721. Publication of the poem did not deter the erection of two later memorials.

It is quite appropriate for Samuel Wesley to turn a line from the Bible into an epigram. He is the eldest brother of John—fifteenth of nineteen children and the founder of Methodism—and Charles—eighteenth and copious hymn writer. Samuel did not become a Methodist.

175. *Well pleaseth me the sweet time of Easter*

EZRA POUND (after BERTRANS DE BORN)

Well pleaseth me the sweet time of Easter
That maketh the leaf and the flower come out.
And it pleaseth me when I hear the clamor
Of the birds, their song through the wood;
And it pleaseth me when I see through the meadows
The tents and pavilions set up, and great joy have I
When I see o'er the campagna knights armed and horses arrayed.

And it pleaseth me when the scouts set in flight the folk with their goods;
And it pleaseth me when I see coming after them an host of armed men.
And it pleaseth me to the heart when I see strong castles besieged,

And barriers broken and riven, and I see the host on the shore all about
shut in with ditches,
And closed in with lisses of strong piles.

Thus that lord pleaseth me when he is first to attack, fearless, on his armed charger; and thus he emboldens his folk with valiant vassalage, and then when stour is mingled, each wight should be yare, and follow him exulting; for no man is worth a damn till he has taken and given many a blow.

We shall see battle axes and swords, a-battering colored haumes and a-hacking through shields at entering melee; and many vassals smiting together, whence there run free the horses of the dead and wrecked. And when each man of prowess shall be come into the fray he thinks no more of (merely) breaking heads and arms, for a dead man is worth more than one taken alive.

I tell you that I find no such savor in eating butter and sleeping, as when I hear cried "On them!" and from both sides hear horses neighing through their head-guards, and hear shouted "To aid! To aid!" and see the dead with lance truncheons, the pennants still on them, piercing their sides.

Barons! put in pawn castles, and towns and cities before anyone makes war on us.

Papiol, be glad to go speedily to "Yea and Nay," and tell him there's too much peace about.

"Yea and Nay": Richard I, *Coeur de Lion*

The subject of "Well pleaseth me the sweet time of Easter" is Bertrans de Born, twelfth-century Provençal poet and author of the poem. I have no way of comparing Pound's translation with the original *langue d'oc*. More than a translation, it is an act of identification.

As he does with many other poets, Pound throws himself into being Bertrans de Born while remaining very definitely Ezra Pound. By a species of transference he is possessed of the rage and joy of battle: "I find no such savor in eating butter and sleeping."

Pound's impatience to come to grips with the poem, so that he moves from loosely cadenced stanzas to a run-together paragraph-stanza, adds to its urgency.

The kind of battle described is chivalric, between groups of men dedicated to fighting. It is perhaps more bloodthirsty but no less sporting and observant of the rules of combat than bullfights, prize fights and football games.

As Pound says in a footnote to this poem in *The Spirit of Romance:* "This kind of thing was much more impressive before 1914 than it has been since 1920. The pageantry can still be found in the paintings of Simone Martini and of Paolo Ucello."

176. *The war-song of Dinas Vawr*

THOMAS LOVE PEACOCK

The mountain sheep are sweeter,
But the valley sheep are fatter;
Therefore we thought it meeter
To carry off the latter.
We made an expedition;
We met a host, and quelled it;
We forced a strong position,
And killed the men who held it.

On Dyfed's richest valley,
Where herds of kine were browsing,
We made a mighty sally,
To furnish our carousing.
Fierce warriors rushed to meet us;
We met them, and o'erthrew them:
They struggled hard to beat us;
But we conquered them, and slew them.

As we drove our prize at leisure,
The king marched forth to catch us;
His rage surpassed all measure,
But his people could not match us.

He fled to his hall-pillars;
And, ere our force we led off,
Some sacked his house and cellars,
While others cut his head off.

We there, in strife bewildering,
Spilt blood enough to swim in:
We orphaned many children,
And widowed many women.
The eagles and the ravens
We glutted with our foemen;
The heroes and the cravens,
The spearmen and the bowmen.

We brought away from battle,
And much their land bemoaned them,
Two thousand head of cattle,
And the head of him who owned them:
Ednyfed, King of Dyfed,
His head was borne before us;
His wine and beasts supplied our feasts,
And his overthrow, our chorus.

A different complexion is put on a foray into Dyfed, an ancient region in southwest Wales. As the gaiety of the song mounts, the sympathy wanes. There is not a word of editorializing, although the curious "novel" from which it is taken, *The Misfortunes of Elphin*, is rather heavily sarcastic.

Laid in the Arthurian era, its intention is not altogether romantic. The passage leading up to the war song describes a carouse in the castle of Dinas Vawr, on the Towy. King Melvas has "marched with a great force out of his own kingdom, on the western shores of the Severn, to levy contributions in the county to the westward . . ."

He has taken the castle by storm, "cut the throats of the former occupants, thrown their bodies into the Towy, and caused a mass to be sung for the good of their souls . . ." He and his "magnanimous heroes" are "celebrating their own exploits in sundry chorusses, especially in that which follows, which is here put upon record as being the quintessence of all the war-songs that ever were written, and the sum and substance of all the appetencies, tendencies and consequences of military glory."

177. *Dulce et decorum est*

WILFRED OWEN

Bent double, like old beggars under sacks,
Knock-kneed, coughing like hags, we cursed through sludge,
Till on the haunting flares we turned our backs,
And towards our distant rest began to trudge.
Men marched asleep. Many had lost their boots,
But limped on, blood-shod. All went lame, all blind;
Drunk with fatigue; deaf even to the hoots
Of gas-shells dropping softly behind.

Gas! GAS! Quick, boys!—An ecstasy of fumbling,
Fitting the clumsy helmets just in time,
But someone still was yelling out and stumbling
And floundering like a man in fire or lime—
Dim through the misty panes and thick green light,
As under a green sea, I saw him drowning.

In all my dreams before my helpless sight
He plunges at me, guttering, choking, drowning.

If in some smothering dreams, you too could pace
Behind the wagon that we flung him in,
And watch the white eyes writhing in his face,
His hanging face, like a devil's sick of sin;
If you could hear, at every jolt, the blood
Come gargling from the froth-corrupted lungs,
Bitter as the cud
Of vile, incurable sores on innocent tongues,—
My friend, you would not tell with such high zest
To children ardent for some desperate glory,
The old Lie: Dulce et decorum est
Pro patria mori.

Dulce et decorum . . . : Sweet and fitting is it to die for one's country.

Pound's footnote to Bertrans de Born's poem (175) is given precise documentation here and in other poems of undisguised and compassionate indignation by Wilfred Owen, the English poet killed in action, at twenty-five, seven days before the end of the first of the world wars.

178. *The bonfire*

ROBERT FROST

'Oh, let's go up the hill and scare ourselves,
As reckless as the best of them tonight,
By setting fire to all the brush we piled
With pitchy hands to wait for rain or snow.
Oh, let's not wait for rain to make it safe.
The pile is ours: we dragged it bough on bough
Down dark converging paths between the pines.
Let's not care what we do with it tonight.
Divide it? No! But burn it as one pile
The way we piled it. And let's be the talk
Of people brought to windows by a light
Thrown from somewhere against their wallpaper.
Rouse them all, both the free and not so free
With saying what they'd like to do to us
For what they'd better wait till we have done.
Let's all but bring to life this old volcano,
If that is what the mountain ever was—
And scare ourselves. Let wild fire loose we will . . .'

'And scare you too?' the children said together.

'Why wouldn't it scare me to have a fire
Begin in smudge with ropy smoke and know
That still, if I repent, I may recall it,
But in a moment not: a little spurt
Of burning fatness, and then nothing but
The fire itself can put it out, and that
By burning out, and before it burns out

It will have roared first and mixed sparks with stars,
And sweeping round it with a flaming sword,
Made the dim trees stand back in wider circle—
Done so much and I know not how much more
I mean it shall not do if I can bind it.
Well if it doesn't with its draft bring on
A wind to blow in earnest from some quarter,
As once it did with me upon an April.
The breezes were so spent with winter blowing
They seemed to fail the bluebirds under them
Short of the perch their languid flight was toward
And my flame made a pinnacle to heaven
As I walked once around it in possession.
But the wind out of doors—you know the saying.
There came a gust. You used to think the trees
Made wind by fanning since you never knew
It blow but that you saw the trees in motion.
Something or someone watching made that gust.
It put the flame tip-down and dabbed the grass
Of over-winter with the least tip-touch
Your tongue gives salt or sugar in your hand.
The place it reached to blackened instantly.
The black was almost all there was by daylight,
That and the merest curl of cigarette smoke—
And a flame slender as the hepaticas,
Blood-root, and violets so soon to be now.
But the black spread like black death on the ground,
And I think the sky darkened with a cloud
Like winter and evening coming on together.
There were enough things to be thought of then.
Where the field stretches toward the north
And setting sun to Hyla brook, I gave it
To flames without twice thinking, where it verges
Upon the road, to flames too, though in fear
They might find fuel there, in withered brake,
Grass its full length, old silver goldenrod,
And alder and grape vine entanglement,

To leap the dusty deadline. For my own
I took what front there was beside. I knelt
And thrust hands in and held my face away.
Fight such a fire by rubbing not by beating.
A board is the best weapon if you have it.
I had my coat. And oh, I knew, I knew,
And said out loud, I couldn't bide the smother
And heat so close in; but the thought of all
The woods and town on fire by me, and all
The town turned out to fight for me—that held me.
I trusted the brook barrier, but feared
The road would fail; and on that side the fire
Died not without a noise of crackling wood—
Of something more than tinder-grass and weed—
That brought me to my feet to hold it back
By leaning back myself, as if the reins
Were round my neck and I was at the plow.
I won! But I'm sure no one ever spread
Another color over a tenth the space
That I spread coal-black over in the time
It took me. Neighbors coming home from town
Couldn't believe that so much black had come there
While they had backs turned, that it hadn't been there
When they had passed an hour or so before
Going the other way and they not seen it.
They looked about for someone to have done it.
But there was no one. I was somewhere wondering
Where all my weariness had gone and why
I walked so light on air in heavy shoes
In spite of a scorched Fourth-of-July feeling.
Why wouldn't I be scared remembering that?'

'If it scares you, what will it do to us?'

'Scare you. But if you shrink from being scared,
What would you say to war if it should come?
That's what for reasons I should like to know—
If you can comfort me by any answer.'

'Oh, but war's not for children—it's for men.'

'Now we are digging almost down to China.
My dears, my dears, you thought that—we all thought it.
So your mistake was ours. Haven't you heard, though,
About the ships where war has found them out
At sea, about the towns where war has come
Through opening clouds at night with droning speed
Further o'erhead than all but stars and angels,—
And children in the ships and in the towns?
Haven't you heard what we have lived to learn?
Nothing so new—something we had forgotten:
War is for everyone, for children too.
I wasn't going to tell you and I mustn't.
The best way is to come up hill with me
And have our fire and laugh and be afraid.'

It may seem strange to call Robert Frost laconic. He can be as garrulous as any terse New Englander comes and he cannot be said to withhold his words here. Yet something, I feel, is withheld, as in so many of his poems.

"The bonfire" lies in a region between Frost's lyric and narrative poetry. There's not such a world of difference between them. His narrative method is uniquely his; that is, to tell only so much of a story as will serve his poetic point. And both in his narratives and his more purely lyric poems, though he often seems to be making a point—many points, in fact—the crucial point is usually reserved for the reader.

It is seldom susceptible of being "put into so many words" without shrinking the poem. What is the point of "The road not taken" (*Complete Poems*, page 131)? It has made "all the difference"; he doesn't say what. And what is the angry comment in "The bonfire"? "You might as well *teach* children to play with fire"?

It suggests this. But the poem, laconically, doesn't say.

179. *A short song of congratulation*
SAMUEL JOHNSON

Long-expected one-and-twenty,
Lingering year, at last is flown;
Pomp and pleasure, pride and plenty,
Great Sir John, are all your own.

Loosened from the minor's tether,
Free to mortgage or to sell,
Wild as wind, and light as feather,
Bid the slaves of thrift farewell.

Call the Bettys, Kates, and Jennys,
Every name that laughs at care,
Lavish of your grandsire's guineas,
Show the spirit of an heir.

All that prey on vice and folly
Joy to see their quarry fly,
Here the gamester light and jolly,
There the lender, grave and sly.

Wealth, Sir John, was made to wander,
Let it wander as it will:
See the jockey, see the pander,
Bid them come, and take their fill.

When the bonny blade carouses,
Pockets full, and spirits high,
What are acres? What are houses?
Only dirt, or wet or dry.

If the guardian or the mother
Tell the woes of wilful waste,
Scorn their counsel and their pother,
You can hang or drown at last.

This is explicit in its satiric, moral dressing down of a young eighteenth-century rakehell. Its lilting, devil-may-care rhythm pungently underlines the "devil-take-you" conclusion.

180. *The bully*

JOHN WILMOT, EARL OF ROCHESTER, or THOMAS D'URFEY

Room, room for a blade of the town
  That takes delight in roaring,
And daily rambles up and down,
  And at night in the street lies snoring:
That for the noble name of Spark
  Dares his companions rally;
Commits an outrage in the dark,
  Then slinks into an alley.

To every female that he meets
  He swears he bears affection,
Defies all laws, arrests, and 'cheats,
  By the help of a kind protection.
Then he, intending further wrongs,
  By some resenting cully
Is decently run through the lungs,
  And there's an end of bully.

Another town character of a century earlier is given his comeuppance in "The bully," either by John Wilmot, Earl of Rochester, or by the dramatist Thomas d'Urfey. If the former, it might almost be a self-portrait. For a fancied slight, he is said to have had Dryden set upon by a gang of ruffians.

181. *I am: yet what I am who cares or knows?*
JOHN CLARE

I am: yet what I am who cares or knows?
  My friends forsake me like a memory lost.
I am the self-consumer of my woes;
  They rise and vanish, an oblivious host,
Shadows of life, whose very soul is lost,
And yet I am, I live, though I am tossed

Into the nothingness of scorn and noise,
  Into the living sea of waking dream
Where there is neither sense of life, nor joys,
  But the huge shipwreck of my own esteem
And all that's dear. Even those I love the best
Are strange; nay, they are stranger than the rest.

I long for scenes where man has never trod;
  For scenes where woman never smiled or wept;
There to abide with my creator, God,
  And sleep as I in childhood sweetly slept,
Full of high thoughts, unborn. So let me lie,
The grass below; above, the vaulted sky.

The rage that tears a man apart underlies this poem. Written in a spell of lucidity in the asylum to which Clare was confined for the latter part of his life, it anticipates in a startling way some of the emphases of present-day psychiatry.

More than a protest—although this is implied—against the terrifying conditions of being shut away from the world and from his friends, it expresses the most tragic loneliness of all; that of being shut away from himself, the "shipwreck of my own esteem." And his anguished longing to get completely out of himself is not unrelated to deep-sleep therapy, hypnotism, and other modern techniques.

There has always been uneasy awareness of connections between so-called madness and genius. Often it has taken on a protective coloring of scorn for the latter, as being outside the comfortable "normal" range of experience. As faith in the comforts of "normality" wanes, derangement comes to be less of a touchstone of ridicule. It is no accident that some of the more profound psychological insights have been gained from studies of the "abnormal."

182. *Oh, let us howl some heavy note*

JOHN WEBSTER

Oh, let us howl some heavy note,
  Some deadly doggèd howl,
Sounding as from the threatening throat
  Of beasts and fatal fowl!
As ravens, screech-owls, bulls and bears,
  We'll bell and bawl our parts,
Till irksome noise have cloyed your ears
  And còrrosived your hearts.
At last, when as our choir wants breath,
  Our bodies being blest,
We'll sing like swans to welcome death
  And die in love and rest.

The Elizabethan stage tradition often provides for the presence of fools or madmen, ostensibly as comic relief. The fools are seldom completely foolish, or the madmen merely funny. Shakespeare customarily introduces insanity with pity and respect, and I have known an "incurable," supposedly removed from human contact, at once console herself and comment on her condition in Ophelia's line, "Like sweet bells jangled, out of tune and harsh."

The song of the madmen, from Webster's *The Duchess of Malfi*, is closer to a blood-and-thunder convention. Like other songs in this and in *The White Devil*, it seems to be an escape hatch for feelings of rage not fully released even by the murderous and macabre transactions of the plot. Yet there is more than sheer bombast in the suggested relationship between depth and height, curse and blessing, "doggèd howl" and "sing like swans."

In *The Waste Land*, T. S. Eliot, by substituting "Dog" for "wolf" and "friend" for "foe," has translated two lines from *The White Devil*—"But keep the wolf far thence, that's foe to man, / For with his nails he'll dig them up again"—into a symbol for conscience. That this is not far from Webster's own intention seems plain from his use of the same image in *The Duchess of Malfi*, when Ferdinand, asked who will reveal the murder of his twin sister—ordered by himself—replies:

Oh I'll tell thee:
The wolf shall find her grave, and scrape it up:
Not to devour the corpse, but to discover
The horrid murther.

183. *Thrice the brinded cat hath mewed*

WILLIAM SHAKESPEARE

FIRST WITCH: Thrice the brinded cat hath mewed.
SECOND: Thrice and once the hedgepig whined.
THIRD: Harpier cries 'Tis time, 'tis time.
FIRST: Round about the cauldron go:
In the poisoned entrails throw.
Toad, that under cold stone
Days and nights has thirty-one,
Sweltered venom sleeping got,
Boil thou first i' the charmèd pot!
ALL: Double, double toil and trouble;
Fire burn, and cauldron bubble.

SECOND: Fillet of a fenny snake,
In the cauldron boil and bake;
Eye of newt and toe of frog,
Wool of bat and tongue of dog,
Adder's fork and blind-worm's sting,
Lizard's leg and owlet's wing,
For a charm of powerful trouble,
Like a hell-broth boil and bubble.
ALL: Double, double, toil and trouble;
Fire burn, and cauldron bubble.

THIRD: Scale of dragon, tooth of wolf,
Witch's mummy, maw and gulf
Of the ravined salt-sea shark,
Root of hemlock digged i' the dark,
Liver of blaspheming Jew,
Gall of goat, and slips of yew
Slivered in the moon's eclipse,
Nose of Turk and Tartar's lips,
Finger of birth-strangled babe
Ditch-delivered by a drab,
Make the gruel thick and slab:
Add thereto a tiger's chaudron,
For the ingredients of our cau'dron.

ALL: Double, double, toil and trouble;
Fire burn, and cauldron bubble.

SECOND: Cool it with a baboon's blood,
Then the charm is firm and good.

Are the witches in *Macbeth*, stirring their hell-broth of hate, intended by Shakespeare as creatures of the underworld or projections of Macbeth's disordered mind?

Like the ghosts in *Hamlet* and *Julius Caesar*, it seems possible to take them either way, "fancied" or "actual." Very likely German Shakespearean scholarship has marshaled all the arguments pro and con. So the imagination, doubling on itself, can "tease us out of thought."

184. *Squats on a toad-stool under a tree*

THOMAS LOVELL BEDDOES

Squats on a toad-stool under a tree
  A bodiless childfull of life in the gloom,
Crying with frog voice, "What shall I be?
Poor unborn ghost, for my mother killed me
  Scarcely alive in her wicked womb.

What shall I be? shall I creep to the egg
  That's cracking asunder yonder by Nile,
    And with eighteen toes,
    And a snuff-taking nose,
  Make an Egyptian crocodile
Sing, 'Catch a mummy by the leg
   And crunch him with an upper jaw,
   Wagging tail and clenching claw;
   Take a bill-full from my craw,
   Neighbor raven, caw, O caw,
   Grunt, my crocky, pretty maw!
    And give a paw.'

"Swine, shall I be you? Thou'rt a dear dog;
  But for a smile, and kiss, and pout,
  I much prefer your black-lipped snout,
   Little, gruntless, fairy hog,
   Godson of the hawthorn hedge.
  For, when Ringwood snuffs me out,
   And 'gins my tender paunch to grapple,
   Sing, ' 'Twixt your ankles' visage wedge,
    And roll up like an apple.'

"Serpent Lucifer, how do you do?
Of your worms and your snakes I'd be one or two:
  For in this dear planet of wool and of leather
'Tis pleasant to need neither shirt, sleeve, nor shoe,
  And have arm, leg, and belly together.
  Then aches your head, or are you lazy?
  Sing, 'Round your neck your belly wrap,
  Tail-a-top, and make your cap
    Any bee and daisy.'

"I'll not be a fool, like the nightingale,
Who sits up all midnight without any ale,
   Making a noise with his nose;
Nor a camel, although 'tis a beautiful back;
Nor a duck, notwithstanding the music of quack,
   And the webby, mud-patting toes.

I'll be a new bird with the head of an ass,
    Two pigs' feet, two men's feet, and two of a hen;
Devil-winged; dragon-bellied; grave-jawed, because grass
  Is a beard that's soon shaved, and grows seldom again
    Before it is summer; so cow all the rest;
    The new Dodo is finished. O! come to my nest."

"Here's what I made one night, while picking poisons / To make the rats a salad," says Isbrand, the Court-Fool of Beddoes' *Death's Jest-Book*. Then he launches into this quasi-ballade. Like the plot of the play, it teeters between sinister and ludicrous, yet with a ghoulish laughter all its own. Dylan Thomas used to read it to his audiences with the greatest relish.

Early in the nineteenth century Beddoes, the son of a distinguished physician, "disappeared" into German medical schools, where he made intensive studies of anatomy and physiology, apparently in the hope of gaining further insight into character to aid him in writing plays. A complicated theory of bone-symbolism figures in *Death's Jest-Book*.

After Beddoes' death, a box of his poems remained unopened for years in the possession of Robert Browning, who had professed admiration for his work. Edmund Gosse, then a young man, finally prevailed upon Browning to open the box.

Browning died before writing a promised opinion of the poems. Gosse died shortly after writing his.

185. *A memory of the players in a mirror at midnight*

JAMES JOYCE

They mouth love's language. Gnash
The thirteen teeth
Your lean jaws grin with. Lash
Your itch and quailing, nude greed of the flesh.
Love's breath in you is stale, worded or sung,
As sour as cat's breath,
Harsh of tongue.

This grey that stares
Lies not, stark skin and bone.
Leave greasy lips their kissing. None
Will choose her what you see to mouth upon.
Dire hunger holds his hour.
Pluck forth your heart, saltblood, a fruit of tears.
Pluck and devour!

Joyce's expression of loathing is like a grimace on the page.

186. *The prodigal*

ELIZABETH BISHOP

The brown enormous odor he lived by
was too close, with its breathing and thick hair,
for him to judge. The floor was rotten; the sty
was plastered halfway up with glass-smooth dung.
Light-lashed, self-righteous, above moving snouts,
the pigs' eyes followed him, a cheerful stare—
even to the sow that always ate her young—
till, sickening, he leaned to scratch her head.
But sometimes mornings after drinking bouts
(he hid the pints behind a two-by-four),
the sunrise glazed the barnyard mud with red;
the burning puddles seemed to reassure.
And then he thought he almost might endure
his exile yet another year or more.

But evenings the first star came to warn.
The farmer whom he worked for came at dark
to shut the cows and horses in the barn
beneath their overhanging clouds of hay,
with pitchforks, faint forked lightnings, catching light,
safe and companionable as in the Ark.

The pigs stuck out their little feet and snored.
The lantern—like the sun, going away—
laid on the mud a pacing aureole.
Carrying a bucket along a slimy board,
he felt the bats' uncertain staggering flight,
his shuddering insights, beyond his control,
touching him. But it took him a long time
finally to make his mind up to go home.

This double sonnet probes an emotional experience very similar to what religious writers call "the dark night of the soul." The symbol of the pigsty, described in its day-to-day detail, seems to strike a balance between repulsion and—almost—attraction.

Gradually but inexorably, this very sense of duration, of getting used to the situation, comes to be recognized as the essential horror. The poem is a model of subtle directness.

187. *'Tis better to be vile than vile esteemed*

WILLIAM SHAKESPEARE

'Tis better to be vile than vile esteemed,
When not to be receives reproach of being,
And the just pleasure lost, which is so deemed
Not by our feeling, but by others' seeing.
For why should others' false adulterate eyes
Give salutation to my sportive blood?
Or on my frailties why are frailer spies,
Which, in their wills, count bad what I think good?
No! I am that I am; and they that level
At my abuses, reckon up their own:

I may be straight, though they themselves be bevel;
By their rank thoughts my deeds must not be shown;
  Unless this general evil they maintain,—
  All men are bad, and in their badness reign.

Shakespeare's temper is not often aroused in the sonnets, but in CXXI he lashes out at an unspecified slander.

The opening line has sometimes been taken to condone evil-doing so long as it is not found out. This is a misreading of the line, not only in its context but in its tone. It is angry clean through, and putting its anger in the strongest possible terms. To be falsely judged is so repugnant to him that he would almost prefer having given cause for it.

188. *So shall I live, supposing thou art true*

WILLIAM SHAKESPEARE

So shall I live, supposing thou art true,
Like a deceivèd husband; so love's face
May still seem love to me, though altered-new;
Thy looks with me, thy heart in other place:
For there can live no hatred in thine eye;
Therefore in that I cannot know thy change.
In many's looks the false heart's history
Is writ, in moods, and frowns, and wrinkles strange;
But heaven in thy creation did decree,
That in thy face sweet love should ever dwell;
Whate'er thy thoughts or thy heart's workings be,
Thy looks should nothing thence but sweetness tell.
  How like Eve's apple doth thy beauty grow,
  If thy sweet virtue answer not thy show!

Sonnet XCIII seems full of latent rage. On the surface it is all sweetness and seeming praise. But the image of Eve's apple conjures up the suspicion of a serpent, which casts its venom back on the preceding lines.

189. *Farewell! thou art too dear for my possessing*

WILLIAM SHAKESPEARE

Farewell! thou art too dear for my possessing,
And like enough thou know'st thy estimate:
The charter of thy worth gives thee releasing;
My bonds in thee are all determinate.
For how do I hold thee but by thy granting?
And for that riches where is my deserving?
The cause of this fair gift in me is wanting,
And so my patent back again is swerving.
Thyself thou gav'st, thy own worth then not knowing,
Or me, to whom thou gav'st it, else mistaking;
So thy great gift, upon misprision growing,
Comes home again, on better judgment making.
  Thus have I had thee as a dream doth flatter,
  In sleep, a king; but waking, no such matter.

Sonnet LXXXVII would seem later than the preceding, if its air of finality is more than a passing mood and if it is addressed to the same person. There is nothing but conjecture for the facts behind any of the sonnets, or the order in which they are written.

In itself, though it might seem all-sorrowful resignation, the tone alters considerably if "dear" is thought of not only as endearment but as literally "costly." The repeated emphasis on business transactions whets this edge of scorn.

190. *The lie*

SIR WALTER RALEIGH

Go, soul, the body's guest,
  Upon a thankless arrant:
Fear not to touch the best;
  The truth shall be thy warrant.
    Go, since I needs must die,
    And give the world the lie.

Say to the court, it glows
  And shines like rotten wood;
Say to the church, it shows
  What's good, and doth no good:
    If church and court reply,
    Then give them both the lie.

Tell potentates, they live
  Acting by others' action,
Not loved unless they give,
  Not strong but by their faction:
    If potentates reply,
    Give potentates the lie.

Tell men of high condition
  That manage the estate,
Their purpose is ambition,
  Their practice only hate:
    And if they once reply
    Then give them all the lie.

Tell them that brave it most,
  They beg for more by spending,
Who, in their greatest cost,
  Seek nothing but commending:
    And if they make reply,
    Then give them all the lie.

Tell zeal it wants devotion;
  Tell love it is but lust;
Tell time it is but motion;
  Tell flesh it is but dust:
    And wish them not reply,
    For thou must give the lie.

Tell age it daily wasteth;
  Tell honor how it alters;
Tell beauty how she blasteth;
  Tell favor how it falters:
    And as they shall reply,
    Give every one the lie.

Tell wit how much it wrangles
  In tickle points of niceness;
Tell wisdom she entangles
  Herself in over-wiseness:
    And when they do reply,
    Straight give them both the lie.

Tell physic of her boldness;
  Tell skill it is prevention;
Tell charity of coldness;
  Tell law it is contention:
    And as they do reply,
    So give them still the lie.

Tell fortune of her blindness;
  Tell nature of decay;
Tell friendship of unkindness;
  Tell justice of delay:
    And if they will reply,
    Then give them all the lie.

Tell arts they have no soundness,
  But vary by esteeming;
Tell schools they want profoundness,
  And stand too much on seeming:
    If arts and schools reply,
    Give arts and schools the lie.

Tell faith it's fled the city;
  Tell how the country erreth;
Tell, manhood shakes off pity;
  Tell, virtue least preferreth:
    And if they do reply,
    Spare not to give the lie.

So when thou hast, as I
  Commanded thee, done blabbing,
Although to give the lie
  Deserves no less than stabbing,
    Stab at thee he that will,
    No stab the soul can kill.

Raleigh's wholesale denunciation is sometimes thought to have been written in the Tower of London while he was under sentence of death. Other scholars place it earlier, when he was imprisoned on the relatively minor charge of seducing Lady Throgmorton, maid-of-honor to Queen Elizabeth. In either case, the freebooter and intermittent court favorite, once alleged to have spread his cloak in the mud for royalty to walk upon, here yanks it out from under everything.

Poems of rage can be laughing, sorrowful, even loving. There is no doubting the love in Shakespeare's sonnets, even the angriest. It is his love that gives point to the anger.

The rage that lashes out at pretension in Raleigh's "The lie" finds its modern counterpart in E. E. Cummings. Just as an anthology could be made of his love poems, so an equally fat one could be made of his "hate" poems. They range from the early, relatively gentle satire of "the Cambridge ladies who live in furnished souls" (*Poems: 1923–1954*, page 58) to the Swiftian savagery of "ygUDuh" (page 393). For Cummings, too, hatred is the other face of love.

PART ELEVEN

"The eternal note of sadness"

Like sensations, emotions are activities; states of mind—sometimes *under* the mind—where we may rest for a time or pass more or less rapidly from one to another.

Their expression in poems is not apt to be so fluctuating. Poems are partly objects; if more malleable than stone, less vaporous than air. From the printed poem we collect spoken sounds. From the sounds we draw or deduce an emotion.

There can be no question of exactly reproducing the original intention. Even a consensus of critics, while possibly valuable, can never be precise. The areas of agreement are limited and never constant. In a very real sense, every poem is for each reader, sometimes for each reading, a somewhat different poem.

Poems are seldom all "love," all "laughter," all "hate," or all "sorrow." Melancholy poems, too, may be loving, angry, even laughing. The variety of poems in this cluster may be extended to include, of those that have gone before, Hopkins' anguished sonnet "To R.B." with its as if inadvertent triumph; Shelley's "To a skylark" for all its exultation; Edward Lear's "By way of preface," and not just because it mentions weeping; Keats' "La belle Dame sans merci"; for all its cleverness, Betjeman's "The arrest of Oscar Wilde"; "Tom O'Bedlam's song" with its rage and soaring fantasy; and many others, not excluding George Gascoigne's "Sing lullaby, as women do."

191. *Chorus sacerdotum*

FULKE GREVILLE, LORD BROOKE

Oh wearisome condition of humanity!
Born under one law, to another bound:
Vainly begot, and yet forbidden vanity;
Created sick, commanded to be sound:
What meaneth nature by these diverse laws?
Passion and reason, self-division cause.

Is it the mark or majesty of power
To make offences that it may forgive?
Nature herself doth her own self deflower,
To hate those errors she herself doth give.
For how should man think that, he may not do
If nature did not fail, and punish too?

Tyrant to others, to herself unjust,
Only commands things difficult and hard;
Forbids us all things which it knows is lust,
Makes easy pains, unpossible rewards.
If nature did not take delight in blood,
She would have made more easy ways to good.

We that are bound by vows, and by promotion,
With pomp of holy sacrifice and rites,
To teach belief in good and still devotion,
To preach of heaven's wonders, and delights:
Yet when each of us in his own heart looks,
He finds the God there, far unlike his books.

still: instill(?)

There is plenty of spleen in Greville's chorus from the unplayable and not-intended-to-be-played "tragedy" *Mustapha.* That it is recited by priests seems to add to its religious quality of skepticism. The complaint voiced against "nature" appears to take in nature's creator: if there is mercy, it too is tainted:

Is it the mark or majesty of power
To make offences that it may forgive?

This is the sorrowful question for which "the books" provide no answer. The poem is one of religious grief.

192. *The exequy*
HENRY KING

Accept, thou shrine of my dead saint,
Instead of dirges this complaint;

And for sweet flowers to crown thy hearse,
Receive a straw of weeping verse
From thy grieved friend, whom thou might'st see
Quite melted into tears for thee.

Dear loss! since thy untimely fate
My task has been to meditate
On thee, on thee: thou art the book,
The library whereon I look
Though almost blind. For thee (loved clay)
I languish out, not live, the day,
Using no other exercise
But what I practise with mine eyes:
By which wet glasses I found out
How lazily time creeps about
The one that mourns; this, only this
My exercise and business is:
So I compute the weary hours
With sighs dissolvèd into showers.

Nor wonder if my time go thus
Backward and most preposterous;
Thou hast benighted me, thy set
This eve of blackness did beget,
Who wast my day, though overcast
Before thou hadst thy noon-tide past;
And I remember must in tears,
Thou scarce hadst seen so many years
As day tells hours. By thy clear sun
My life and fortune first did run;
But thou wilt never more appear
Folded within my hemisphere,
Since both thy light and motïon
Like a fled star is fallen and gone,
And 'twixt me and my soul's dear wish
An earth now interposèd is,
Which such a strange eclipse doth make
As ne'er was read in almanake.

I could allow thee for a time
To darken me and my sad clime,
Were it a month, a year, or ten,
I would thy exile live till then;
And all that space my mirth adjourn,
So thou wouldst promise to return;
And putting off thy ashy shroud
At length disperse this sorrow's cloud.

But woe is me! the longest date
Too narrow is to calculate
These empty hopes: never shall I
Be so much blest as to descry
A glimpse of thee, till that day come
Which shall the earth to cinders doom,
And a fierce fever must calcine
The body of this world like thine,
My Little World! That fit of fire
Once off, our bodies shall aspire
To our soul's bliss: then we shall rise,
And view our selves with clearer eyes
In that calm region, where no night
Can hide us from each other's sight.

Meantime, thou hast her, earth: much good
May my harm do thee. Since it stood
With heaven's will I might not call
Her longer mine, I give thee all
My short-lived right and interest
In her, whom living I loved best:
With a most free and bounteous grief,
I give thee what I could not keep.
Be kind to her, and prithee look
Thou write into thy Doom's-day Book
Each parcel of this rarity
Which in thy casket shrined doth lie:
And yield her back again by weight;
See that thou make thy reckoning straight,

For thou must audit on thy trust
Each grain and atom of this dust,
As thou wilt answer Him that lent,
Not gave thee, my dear monument.

So close the ground, and 'bout her shade
Black curtains draw, my bride is laid.

Sleep on, my Love, in thy cold bed
Never to be disquietèd!
My last good night! Thou wilt not wake,
Till I thy fate shall overtake:
Till age, or grief, or sickness must
Marry my body to that dust
It so much loves; and fill the room
My heart keeps empty in thy tomb.
Stay for me there; I will not fail
To meet thee in that hollow vale.
And think not much of my delay;
I am already on the way,
And follow thee with all the speed
Desire can make, or sorrows breed.
Each minute is a short degree,
And every hour a step towards thee.
At night when I betake to rest,
Next morn I rise nearer my west
Of life, almost by eight hours' sail,
Than when sleep breathed his drowsy gale.

Thus from the sun my bottom steers,
And my day's compass downward bears:
Nor labor I to stem the tide
Through which to thee I swiftly glide.

'Tis true, with shame and grief I yield,
Thou like the van first took the field,
In thus adventuring to die
Before me, whose more years might crave
A just precedence in the grave.

But hark! My pulse like a soft drum
Beats my approach, tells thee I come;
And slow however my marches be,
I shall at last sit down by thee.

The thought of this bids me go on,
And wait my dissolutïon
With hope and comfort, dear (forgive
The crime) I am content to live
Divided, with but half a heart,
Till we shall meet and never part.

Bishop King's poem on his wife is remarkable for its sustained tone of cheerful grief. Like Emily Dickinson, he is confident of reunion; so much so that he can afford to jest with the earth that covers her:

See that thou make thy reckoning straight
And yield her back again by weight.

Sorrow can laugh too. This is worthy of his friend and fellow churchman, John Donne, whose literary executor he was.

193. *A slumber did my spirit seal*

WILLIAM WORDSWORTH

A slumber did my spirit seal;
   I had no human fears;
She seemed a thing that could not feel
   The touch of earthly years.

No motion has she now, no force;
   She neither hears nor sees;
Rolled round in earth's diurnal course,
   With rocks, and stones, and trees.

Simply and directly, this conveys the numbed, stunned feeling of grief. No hope is expressed.

194. *Requiescat*
MATTHEW ARNOLD

Strew on her roses, roses,
  And never a spray of yew!
In quiet she reposes;
  Ah, would that I did too!

Her mirth the world required;
  She bathed it in smiles of glee.
But her heart was tired, tired,
  And now they let her be.

Her life was turning, turning,
  In mazes of heat and sound.
But for peace her soul was yearning,
  And now peace laps her round.

Her cabined, ample spirit,
  It fluttered and failed for breath.
Tonight it doth inherit
  The vasty hall of death.

Without the consolation of specific immortality, Arnold's "Requiescat" accepts cessation as a form of peace. The emotional contrast is between confinement and release. Life, for all its activity—"turning, turning / In mazes of heat and sound"—is not spacious enough for the "ample spirit."

195. *Requiescat*
OSCAR WILDE

Tread lightly, she is near
  Under the snow.
Speak gently, she can hear
  The daisies grow.

All her bright golden hair
  Tarnished with rust,
She that was young and fair
  Fallen to dust.

Lily-like, white as snow,
  She hardly knew
She was a woman, so
  Sweetly she grew.

Coffin-board, heavy stone,
  Lie on her breast;
I vex my heart alone,
  She is at rest.

Peace, peace; she cannot hear
  Lyre or sonnet;
All my life's buried here.
  Heap earth upon it.

"Every man's death diminishes me," says John Donne in a sermon. This contagion of death, as an active force, is present in Arnold's poem: "Ah, would that I did too!" It enters even more strongly, I feel, into the conclusion of Oscar Wilde's "Requiescat."

196. *For a dead lady*

EDWIN ARLINGTON ROBINSON

No more with overflowing light
Shall fill the eyes that now are faded,
Nor shall another's fringe with night
Their woman-hidden world as they did.
No more shall quiver down the days
The flowing wonder of her ways,
Whereof no language may requite
The shifting and the many-shaded.

The grace, divine, definitive,
Clings only as a faint forestalling;
The laugh that love could not forgive
Is hushed, and answers to no calling;
The forehead and the little ears
Have gone where Saturn keeps the years;
The breast where roses could not live
Has done with rising and with falling.

The beauty, shattered by the laws
That have creation in their keeping,
No longer trembles at applause,
Or over children that are sleeping;
And we who delve in beauty's lore
Know all that we have known before
Of what inexorable cause
Makes Time so vicious in his reaping.

This combines tenderness, anger, and, perhaps more than any of the preceding poems, a sense of inscrutability. Personal loss, conveyed by the intimacy of "The forehead and the little ears," is placed against abstraction—"where Saturn keeps the years"—and the ironic conclusions of "philosophy."

197. *Here lies a lady*

JOHN CROWE RANSOM

Here lies a lady of beauty and high degree.
Of chills and fever she died, of fever and chills,
The delight of her husband, her aunt, an infant of three,
And of medicos marveling sweetly on her ills.

For either she burned, and her confident eyes would blaze,
And her fingers fly in a manner to puzzle their heads—
What was she making? Why, nothing; she sat in a maze
Of old scraps of laces, snipped into curious shreds—

Or this would pass, and the light of her fire decline
Till she lay discouraged and cold, like a stalk white and blown,
And would not open her eyes, to kisses, to wine;
The sixth of these states was her last; the cold settled down.

Sweet ladies, long may ye bloom, and toughly I hope ye may thole,
But was she not lucky? In flowers and lace and mourning,
In love and great honor we bade God rest her soul
After six little spaces of chill, and six of burning.

These gay rhythms shock us into vivid awareness of death. The poem itself carries out Arnold's image of life, "turning, turning / In mazes of heat and sound." It celebrates vivacity at its high point, the moment when it stops.

This *seeming* gaiety is unique among poems about death. Unique except among Ransom's; in "Bells for John Whiteside's daughter" (*Selected Poems*, page 8) he seems to be scolding the dead child.

198. The holy innocents

ROBERT LOWELL

Listen, the hay-bells tinkle as the cart
Wavers on rubber tires along the tar
And cindered ice below the burlap mill
And ale-wife run. The oxen drool and start
In wonder at the fenders of a car,
And blunder hugely up St. Peter's hill.
These are the undefiled by woman—their
Sorrow is not the sorrow of this world:
King Herod shrieking vengeance at the curled
Up knees of Jesus choking in the air,

A king of speechless clods and infants. Still
The world out-Herods Herod; and the year,
The nineteen-hundred forty-fifth of grace,
Lumbers with losses up the clinkered hill
Of our purgation; and the oxen near
The worn foundations of their resting-place,

The holy manger where their bed is corn
And holly torn for Christmas. If they die,
As Jesus, in the harness, who will mourn?
Lamb of the shepherds, Child, how still you lie.

The religious sorrow here is not unmixed with rage: "and the year, / The nineteen-hundred forty-fifth of grace." The mild and powerful oxen, symbols like Christ of purity and sorrow, are obsolete in a world of fenders and war.

The poem's anguish lies, I feel, in the deep doubt of its religious questioning. Does the world truly "out-Herod Herod"? Is the Christ child, as a symbol of spiritual rebirth, included among its "speechless clods and infants"? The question goes unanswered.

199. *Piano*

D. H. LAWRENCE

Softly, in the dusk, a woman is singing to me;
Taking me back down the vista of years, till I see
A child sitting under the piano, in the boom of the tingling strings
And pressing the small, poised feet of a mother who smiles as she sings.

In spite of myself, the insidious mastery of song
Betrays me back, till the heart of me weeps to belong
To the old Sunday evenings at home, with winter outside
And hymns in the cozy parlor, the tinkling piano our guide.

So now it is vain for the singer to burst into clamor
With the great black piano appassionato. The glamour
Of childish days is upon me, my manhood is cast
Down in the flood of remembrance, I weep like a child for the past.

This is very close in its nostalgic sadness to Tennyson's "Tears, idle tears, I know not what they mean" (poem 88). Tennyson starts with the general emotion and lets it include him; its music seems to carry him like a swimmer in its current.

Typically, Lawrence begins with himself and a specific occasion.

The music of the poem with its pianistic, gliding notes takes us with him into his own past. He allows us, rather than relies upon us, to share it.

This is not a qualitative comparison. Each poem expresses, besides an emotion, the temperament of its maker.

200. *The retreat*

HENRY VAUGHAN

Happy those early days, when I
Shined in my angel-infancy!
Before I understood this place
Appointed for my second race,
Or taught my soul to fancy aught
But a white, celestial thought;
When yet I had not walked above
A mile or two from my first Love,
And looking back, at that short space
Could see a glimpse of His bright face;
When on some gilded cloud or flower
My gazing soul would dwell an hour,
And in those weaker glories spy
Some shadows of eternity;
Before I taught my tongue to wound
My conscience with a sinful sound,
Or had the black art to dispense
A several sin to every sense,
But felt through all this fleshly dress
Bright shoots of everlastingness.
   Oh how I long to travel back,
And tread again that ancient track!
That I might once more reach that plain,
Where first I left my glorious train;
From whence the enlightened spirit sees
That shady city of palm trees!
But ah! my soul with too much stay
Is drunk, and staggers in the way:—

Some men a forward motion love,
But I by backward steps would move;
And when this dust falls to the urn,
In that state I came, return.

A different route to childhood is followed here. The way is closer to that of Wordsworth's in his "Ode" (poem 94), said to be inspired by "The retreat."

Wordsworth's is the more philosophic, Vaughan's the more religious contemplation of that pre-existing state of innocence in which both believe. Seventeenth-century physician and, as he says, convert of George Herbert, Vaughan seems more confident in his reaching back behind consciousness. His sorrow is that of temporary separation.

The attempt of consciousness to go beyond time has an interesting parallel in Henry Vaughan's twin brother Thomas' desire, as an alchemist, to reach back through matter and discover "the universal solvent."

201. *That time of year thou may'st in me behold*

WILLIAM SHAKESPEARE

That time of year thou may'st in me behold
When yellow leaves, or none, or few, do hang
Upon those boughs which shake against the cold,
Bare ruined choirs, where late the sweet birds sang.
In me thou see'st the twilight of each day
As after sunset fadeth in the west;
Which by and by black night doth take away,
Death's second self, that seals up all the rest.
In me thou see'st the glowing of such fire,
That on the ashes of his youth doth lie,
As the death-bed whereon it must expire,
Consumed with that which it was nourished by.
  This thou perceiv'st, which makes thy love more strong,
  To love that well which thou must leave are long.

Shakespeare's regret in Sonnet LXXIII is very judiciously sustained on a note that will not make his aging seem too unattractive. How artfully the line "Bare ruined choirs, where late the sweet birds sang" gives itself the lie.

202. *Death, be not proud*
JOHN DONNE

Death, be not proud, though some have callèd thee
Mighty and dreadful, for thou art not so:
For those, whom thou think'st thou dost overthrow,
Die not, poor Death, nor yet canst thou kill me.
From rest and sleep, which but thy pictures be,
Much pleasure, then from thee much more must flow;
And soonest our best men with thee do go,
Rest of their bones, and souls' delivery.
Thou art slave to fate, chance, kings, and desperate men,
And doth with poison, war, and sickness dwell;
And poppy or charms can make us sleep as well
And better than thy stroke, why swell'st thou then?
One short sleep past, we wake eternally,
And death shall be no more: Death, thou shalt die.

The triumph here is over sorrow, as that of Donne's love poems is over disappointment and cynicism. The same hyperbole and gusto go into both.

Other "Holy Sonnets" spar with his God, as with a beloved adversary. "Thou hast made me, and shall thy work decay?" he asks in one; and in another:

Batter my heart, three-personed God; for, you
As yet but knock, breathe, shine, and seek to mend . . .

The tone is not unlike that in some of the late sonnets of Hopkins:

Thou art indeed just, Lord, if I contend
With thee; but, sir, so what I plead is just.

Hopkins' despair does not always seem resolved by his faith. But Donne's confidence and power come from no easily won serenity. They are not the sign of a prevailingly optimistic temperament; rather an active and continuous conquest of doubts and of his recurrent states of ill-health.

203. *Dover Beach*
MATTHEW ARNOLD

The sea is calm tonight.
The tide is full, the moon lies fair
Upon the straits:—on the French coast the light
Gleams and is gone; the cliffs of England stand,
Glimmering and vast, out in the tranquil bay.
Come to the window, sweet is the night air!
Only, from the long line of spray
Where the sea meets the moon-blanched land,
Listen! you hear the grating roar
Of pebbles which the waves draw back, and fling,
At their return, up the high strand,
Begin, and cease, and then again begin,
With tremulous cadence slow, and bring
The eternal note of sadness in.

Sophocles long ago
Heard it on the Aegean, and it brought
Into his mind the turbid ebb and flow
Of human misery; we
Find also in the sound a thought,
Hearing it by this distant northern sea.

The sea of faith
Was once, too, at the full, and round earth's shore
Lay like the folds of a bright girdle furled.
But now I only hear
Its melancholy, long, withdrawing roar,
Retreating, to the breath
Of the night-wind, down the vast edges drear
And naked shingles of the world.

Ah, love, let us be true
To one another! for the world, which seems
To lie before us like a land of dreams,
So various, so beautiful, so new,
Hath really neither joy, nor love, nor light,
Nor certitude, nor peace, nor help for pain;
And we are here as on a darkling plain
Swept with confused alarms of struggle and flight,
Where ignorant armies clash by night.

Perhaps because of his stature as critic Arnold is sometimes disparaged as a poet. It may be that he is *expected* to be, in a limiting sense, intellectual.

There is no doubt that "Dover Beach" is a thinking poem. But what unaffected thought, what a personal tone. "Come to the window, sweet is the night air!"

Direct address is often used in poetry; seldom, it seems to me, with quite this warmth of invitation. We find ourselves in the room of the poem. With Arnold, we look out from it and hear—in seemingly easy, incredibly subtle rhythms; in disappearing, echoing, and returning rhymes—the ocean's ebb and flow.

This is a rhetoric of familiar speech, such as Wordsworth aspires to and rather infrequently perfects. It is apparently as natural as a man talking. Yet it never becomes, for all its plainness, prose.

It is a modern tone. Not that nothing before it, or everything since, is like it. But in speech and attitude, in point of view, in large despair and single hope, its universe is ours.

The emotions can, of course, be classified in different and more intricate ways than the four rather broad divisions: love, laughter, anger, and sorrow. But these are unrestrictive enough, I think, to allow the poems within them to find their own levels, often to overflow their boundaries.

Like the primary colors, emotions mix with each other in diverse, sometimes unpredictable ways. As with images, the spectrum is inexhaustible. Poetry continues to reflect these spectra; perhaps to add new colors of its own.

PART TWELVE

"Ripe apples drop about my head"

Arnold's poem (203) addresses itself to the mind as well as sensations and emotions. To a degree, this is true of all poetry, but the wave lengths vary. What we think of as ideas are often subordinate. But it would be as hard to think of a "thoughtless" poem as it is to think of one completely without emotion.

A poem that concerns itself chiefly with ideas is W. H. Auden's "New Year letter," in his *Collected Poetry* and also published separately, with notes, as *The Double Man*. This is a brilliant analysis of the predicament of our time, tracing it to the doubleness—a war of half-truths—in our world and in ourselves. Like much of Dryden and Pope, it approaches the essay; it is a didactic or teaching poem. Yet its ideas are routed through the sensibilities; they achieve an intensity seldom reached by the special excellences of the prose essay.

Many of Wallace Stevens' poems are philosophic speculations on the relationships between reality and the imagination. The two perform dances together, joining, separating, weaving, and reuniting. Such poems remind us that the intellect need not be devoid of emotion, nor sensation of thought. In their acrobatic beauty they sometimes recall that masterpiece of the late sixteenth century, Sir John Davies' *Orchestra, or a Poem of Dancing.*

Excerpts cannot do it justice, it is so amazingly sustained, dancing throughout in stanzas like:

This is true Love, by that true Cupid got,
Which danceth galliards in your amorous eyes,
But to your frozen heart approacheth not;
Only your heart he dares not enterprize;
And yet through every other part he flies,
  And everywhere he nimbly danceth now,
  That in yourself, yourself perceive not how.

Besides didactic or "idea" poems—usually, though by no means necessarily, long—there are those, including many in the preceding groups, that so fuse sensation, emotion and thought as to become symbols of the whole man.

204. Are they shadows that we see?
SAMUEL DANIEL

Are they shadows that we see?
And can shadows pleasures give?
Pleasures only shadows be,
Cast by bodies we conceive,
And we make the things we deem
In those figures which they seem.

But these pleasures vanish fast
Which by shadows are expressed,
Pleasures are not, if they last;
In their passing is their best:
Glory is most bright and gay
In a flash, and so away.

Feed apace then, greedy eyes,
On the wonder you behold:
Take it sudden as it flies,
Though you take it not to hold:
When your eyes have done their part,
Thought must length it in the heart.

Daniel's poem should help dispose of the notion that a poem of idea need be heavy. In eighteen lines light as bubbles, it whirls together three motifs usually thought of quite separately.

The first is the evanescence of physical sensation. This is a sentiment that leads more commonly to renunciatory advice: shun the ephemeral; seek the eternal. But instead of crying out "Vanity of vanities!" the poem proceeds to its second motif: therefore seize it quickly. Herrick's "Gather ye rosebuds while ye may" is the most frequently quoted expression of this philosophy.

Where Herrick stops short, Daniel continues. What happens when the rose blows? "Thought must length it in the heart." For Daniel, thinking is not a turning away from vanishing delight, but its culmination.

205. *The glories of our blood and state*

JAMES SHIRLEY

The glories of our blood and state
  Are shadows, not substantial things;
There is no armor against fate;
  Death lays his icy hand on kings:
    Sceptre and crown
    Must tumble down
And in the dust be equal made
With the poor crooked scythe and spade.

Some men with swords may reap the field,
  And plant fresh laurels where they kill:
But their strong nerves at last must yield;
  They tame but one another still:
    Early or late
    They stoop to fate,
And must give up their murmuring breath
When they, pale captives, creep to death.

The garlands wither on your brow;
  Then boast no more your mighty deeds;
Upon Death's purple altar now
  See where the victor-victim bleeds:
    Your heads must come
    To the cold tomb;
Only the actions of the just
Smell sweet, and blossom in their dust.

This is more in the nature of moral precept. The "shadows" of this somewhat later seventeenth-century poem refer more specifically to vain-glorious action and the results of conquest. Three hundred years later, the "victor-victims" "tame but one another still."

206. *Laid in my quiet bed, in study as I were*

HENRY HOWARD, EARL OF SURREY

Laid in my quiet bed, in study as I were,
I saw within my troubled head a heap of thoughts appear.
And every thought did show as lively in mine eyes,
That now I sighed, and then I smiled, as cause of thought did rise.
I saw the little boy in thought how oft that he
Did wish of God to scape the rod, a tall young man to be.
The young man, eke, that feels his bones with pains opprest,
How he would be a rich old man, to live and lie at rest.
The rich old man that sees his end draw on so sore,
How he would be a boy again, to live so much the more.
Whereat full oft I smiled, to see how all these three,
From boy to man, from man to boy, would chop and change degree.
And, musing thus, I think, the case is very strange
That man from wealth, to live in woe, doth ever seek to change.

Thus thoughtful as I lay, I saw my withered skin,
How it doth show my dented chews, the flesh was worn so thin.
And eke my toothless chaps, the gates of my right way,
That opes and shuts as I do speak, do thus unto me say:
"Thy white and hoarish hairs, the messengers of age,
That show, like lines of true belief, that this life doth assuage,
Bid thee lay hand, and feel them hanging on thy chin;
The which do write two ages past, the third now coming in.
Hang up therefore the bit of thy young wanton time:
And thou that therein beaten art, the happiest life define."
Whereat I sighed, and said: "Farewell, my wonted joy!
Truss up thy pack, and trudge from me to every little boy,
And tell them thus from me; their time most happy is,
If, to their time, they reason had to know the truth of this."

chews: jowls

Although not usually printed as such, this would seem to be a double sonnet. Its paired rhymes and alternation of six and seven-foot lines, used later by Fulke Greville, are not usual to sonnets, but the action of the thought is.

In them Surrey turns a thought around in his mind in verses that turn with the thought. Like the motions of musing, they lengthen out and return, question, come to a conclusion, reach beyond it and return, add them together, and spiral toward a new conclusion.

207. *Ode to solitude*

ALEXANDER POPE

Happy the man, whose wish and care
  A few paternal acres bound,
Content to breathe his native air
    In his own ground.

Whose herds with milk, whose fields with bread,
  Whose flocks supply him with attire;
Whose trees in summer yield him shade;
    In winter, fire.

Blest, who can unconcernedly find
  Hours, days, and years slide soft away
In health of body, peace of mind;
    Quiet by day,

Sound sleep by night; study and ease
  Together mixed; sweet recreation,
And innocence, which most does please
    With meditation.

Thus let me live, unseen, unknown;
  Thus unlamented let me die;
Steal from the world, and not a stone
    Tell where I lie.

The last line of Surrey's poem has an odd bearing on Pope's ode. Its ripe philosophy might seem that of a man who has tasted all life has to offer and is renouncing activity for contemplation. In fact, it is the poem, written about 1700, of a twelve-year-old boy.

208. *Sailing to Byzantium*

W. B. YEATS

That is no country for old men. The young
In one another's arms, birds in the trees
—Those dying generations—at their song,
The salmon-falls, the mackerel-crowded seas,
Fish, flesh, or fowl, commend all summer long
Whatever is begotten, born, and dies.
Caught in that sensual music all neglect
Monuments of unageing intellect.

II

An aged man is but a paltry thing,
A tattered cloak upon a stick, unless
Soul clap its hands and sing, and louder sing
For every tatter in its mortal dress,
Nor is there singing school but studying
Monuments of its own magnificence;
And therefore I have sailed the seas and come
To the holy city of Byzantium.

III

O sages standing in God's holy fire
As in the gold mosaic of a wall,
Come from the holy fire, perne in a gyre,
And be the singing-masters of my soul.
Consume my heart away; sick with desire
And fastened to a dying animal
It knows not what it is; and gather me
Into the artifice of eternity.

IV

Once out of nature I shall never take
My bodily form from any natural thing,
But such a form as Grecian goldsmiths make
Of hammered gold and gold enamelling
To keep a drowsy Emperor awake;
Or set upon a golden bough to sing
To lords and ladies of Byzantium
Of what is past, or passing, or to come.

Yeats' poem bears resemblance to elements of Eastern religions whose founders, after active, sometimes quite sensual careers, retire into deity.

"That country" is unspecified. It might be any young country, as America has seemed to Europeans. It is a land of youth and abundance, the domain of "sensual music."

"Perne in a gyre"—the hawk or honey buzzard in spiraling flight?—perhaps relates the poem to Yeats's spiral conception of personality and destiny, as described in his book *A Vision*. In another spelling, "pirn" means a bobbin.

At sixty or thereabouts, Yeats feels he is reaching a new plane of existence. More appropriate to this than the "birds in the trees" is the golden bird of eternity suggested by Byzantine art.

Youth, if it is being renounced, is not lightly left behind, as the cadences of the opening stanza tell us. Nor is the sought-for "magnificence" symbolized in a way that traduces the senses. It is tangible permanence; an immortality not of ideas but of ideas incorporated in things. He looks forward to an eternal youth "out of nature."

A further development of this theme, "Byzantium" (*Collected Poems*, page 243) is said to have been sent in answer to a complaint that his symbol for eternity, the golden bird, is man-made. Curiously, the image that stands, like "perne in a gyre," for communication with the supernatural is "Hades' bobbin."

209. *The salutation*

THOMAS TRAHERNE

These little limbs,
These eyes and hands which here I find,
This panting heart wherewith my life begins,
Where have ye been? Behind
What curtain were ye from me hid so long?
Where was, in what abyss, my new-made tongue?

When silent I
So many thousand thousand years
Beneath the dust did a chaos lie,
How could I, smiles or tears,
Or lips or hands or eyes or ears, perceive?
Welcome ye treasures which I now receive.

I that so long
Was nothing from eternity,
Did little think such joys as ear or tongue
To celebrate or see:
Such sounds to hear, such hands to feel, such feet,
Such eyes and objects, on the ground to meet.

New burnished joys
Which finest gold and pearl excel!
Such sacred treasures are the limbs of boys,
In which a soul doth dwell;
Their organizèd joints and azure veins
More wealth include than the dead world contains.

From dust I rise,
And out of nothing now awake;
These brighter regions which salute mine eyes,
A gift from God I take.
The earth, the seas, the light, the lofty skies,
The suns and stars are mine; if these I prize.

A stranger here
Strange things doth meet, strange glory see;
Strange treasures lodged in this fair world appear,
Strange all and new to me;
But that they mine should be, who nothing was,
That strangest is of all, yet brought to pass.

Where Yeats looks forward to eternity, Traherne, in the seventeenth century, looks back to it. The poem has resemblances to Vaughan's "The retreat" (poem 200). But Traherne, rather than going behind consciousness, celebrates its strangest sensation: that of having been formed out of nothing. It is a kind of thinking beyond the bounds of thought.

210. *The garden*

ANDREW MARVELL

How vainly men themselves amaze
To win the palm, the oak, or bays,
And their uncessant labors see
Crowned from some single herb or tree,
Whose short and narrow-vergèd shade
Does prudently their toils upbraid,
While all flowers and all trees do close
To weave the garlands of repose!

Fair Quiet, have I found thee here,
And Innocence, thy sister dear?
Mistaken long, I sought you then
In busy companies of men.
Your sacred plants, if here below,
Only among the plants will grow;
Society is all but rude
To this delicious solitude.

No white nor red was ever seen
So amorous as this lovely green.
Fond lovers, cruel as their flame,
Cut in these trees their mistress' name.
Little, alas! they know or heed,
How far these beauties hers exceed!
Fair trees! wheres'e'er your bark I wound,
No name shall but your own be found.

When we have run our passion's heat,
Love hither makes his best retreat.
The gods, that mortal beauty chase,
Still in a tree did end their race;
Apollo hunted Daphne so,
Only that she might laurel grow;
And Pan did after Syrinx speed,
Not as a nymph, but for a reed.

What wondrous life is this I lead!
Ripe apples drop about my head;
The luscious clusters of the vine
Upon my mouth do crush their wine;
The nectarine, and curious peach,
Into my hands themselves do reach;
Stumbling on melons, as I pass,
Insnared with flowers, I fall on grass.

Meanwhile the mind, from pleasure less,
Withdraws into its happiness;—
The mind, that ocean where each kind
Does straight its own resemblance find;
Yet it creates, transcending these,
Far other worlds, and other seas,
Annihilating all that's made
To a green thought in a green shade.

Here at the fountain's sliding foot,
Or at some fruit-tree's mossy root,
Casting the body's vest aside,
My soul into the boughs does glide:
There, like a bird, it sits and sings,
Then whets and combs its silver wings,
And, till prepared for longer flight,
Waves in its plumes the various light.

Such was that happy garden-state,
While man there walked without a mate:
After a place so pure and sweet,
What other help could yet be meet!
But 'twas beyond a mortal's share
To wander solitary there:
Two paradises 'twere in one,
To live in paradise alone.

How well the skillful gardener drew
Of flowers, and herbs, this dial new;
Where, from above, the milder sun
Does through a fragrant zodiac run,
And, as it works, the industrious bee
Computes its time as well as we!
How could such sweet and wholesome hours
Be reckoned but with herbs and flowers?

Here Marvell lets his mind rove in and out of nature. As the light, easy tone suggests, he does not take himself in deadly earnest. This is not the poem of a recluse. It will not preclude him from taking a very active part in the world, including the turbulent politics of the seventeenth century.

It is rather the poem of a man who returns to nature as to a center of repose:

Annihilating all that's made
To a green thought in a green shade.

For all its leafiness, the important word is, after all, "thought." How close it is to James Stephens' "Something I can never find" at the conclusion of "The goat paths."

Unobtrusively "The garden" comes to symbolize the maturing mind, its thoughts not forced or "specialized" but dropping like "ripe apples . . . about my head." And as airily as he seems to put love from him in this poem, he will return to it in others.

211. MARIANNE MOORE

The mind is an enchanting thing

is an enchanted thing
like the glaze on a
katydid-wing
subdivided by sun
till the nettings are legion.
Like Gieseking playing Scarlatti;

like the apteryx-awl
as a beak, or the
kiwi's rain-shawl
of haired feathers, the mind
feeling its way as though blind,
walks along with its eyes on the ground.

It has memory's ear
that can hear without
having to hear.
Like the gyroscope's fall,
truly unequivocal
because trued by regnant certainty,

it is a power of
strong enchantment. It
is like the dove-
neck animated by
sun; it is memory's eye;
it's conscientious inconsistency.

It tears off the veil; tears
   the temptation, the
mist the heart wears,
      from its eyes,—if the heart
      has a face; it takes apart
dejection. It's fire in the dove-neck's

iridescence; in the
   inconsistencies
of Scarlatti.
      Unconfusion submits
      its confusion to proof; it's
not a Herod's oath that cannot change.

It is often Marianne Moore's practice, as here, to begin her poem in the title, which serves as both title and first line, an integral part of the poem.

Thoughts turning into fruits, fruits into emotions, characterize her poems. They may have all the cogency and wealth of information that are to be found in the most learned essays.

For all that, and for all her expert use and subjugation of prose rhythms, they are never prose masquerading as verse. Her ideas have the intensity of sensations; the sensations, minutely and with hairbreadth accuracy described, the clarity of ideas. In "Nevertheless" (*Collected Poems*, page 127), "fortitude" can be seen entering the stem "to make the cherry red."

"The mind is an enchanting thing" is truly, in Wallace Stevens' phrase, a "poem of the act of the mind." It dissects and animates in the same breath: "like the glaze on a / katydid-wing / subdivided by sun / till the nettings are legion." This flashing, spreading action of insight, illuminating and transforming experience, recurs twice, in "the dove- / neck animated by / sun" and in "fire in the dove-neck's / iridescence."

Between them lies the spadework of the mind: its interpretive powers like Gieseking, its close observations "with its eyes on the ground," its use of past experience and correction of past error, its liberating imagination and emotion.

The triple scintillations describe increasingly active involvements with the "sun," the source of intelligence. The first more or less passively receives and spreads light. The second is "animated" by it. In the third, the sun's light has entered it and becomes the "fire" of its "iridescence."

This autobiography of Marianne Moore's mind ends, as all honest personal history must, on a note of change. No insight is final. The unconfused mind—and "mind" has come to mean the whole person, described, analyzed, and synthesized in one continuous action—is that which is most aware of the possibility of confusion. It is therefore capable, unlike Herod, of transcending its own "oath."

212. *The thought*

EDWARD HERBERT, LORD OF CHERBURY

If you do love as well as I,
Then every minute from your heart
   A thought doth part;
And wingèd with desire doth fly
Till it hath met, in a straight line,
   A thought of mine
So like to yours, we cannot know
Whether of both doth come, or go,
   Till we define
Which of us two, that thought doth owe.

I say then, that your thoughts which pass,
Are not so much the thoughts you meant,
   As those I sent:
For as my image in a glass
Belongs not to the glass you see,
   But unto me;
So when your fancy is so clear
That you would think you saw me there,
   It needs must be
That it was I did first appear.

Likewise, when I send forth a thought,
My reason tells me, 'tis the same
  Which from you came,
And which your beauteous image wrought.
Thus while our thoughts by turns do lead,
  None can precede;
And thus, while in each other's mind
Such interchangèd forms we find,
  Our loves may plead
To be of more than vulgar kind.

May you then often think on me,
And by that thinking know 'tis true
  I thought on you;
I in the same belief will be:
While, by this mutual address,
  We will possess
A love must live, when we do die,
Which rare and secret property
  You will confess,
If you do love as well as I.

Like Marianne Moore, George Herbert's elder brother treats a thought as though it were an object. Paradoxically the more tangible it seems, the more elusive it becomes. It corresponds to the sensation of a kiss. Who can tell, when a kiss is shared, to which mouth it belongs?

So the poem ties mutual thoughts into an intellectual love knot. Thinking is seen to be, not a separate action from sensation and emotion, but their prolongation. Whether deliberately or not, this is an extension of Samuel Daniel's concluding line in poem 204: "Thought must length it in the heart."

213. *Two loves I have of comfort and despair*
WILLIAM SHAKESPEARE

Two loves I have of comfort and despair
Which like two spirits do suggest me still;
The better angel is a man right fair,
The worser spirit a woman, colored ill.

To win me soon to hell, my female evil
Tempteth my better angel from my side,
And would corrupt my saint to be a devil,
Wooing his purity with her foul pride.
And whether that my angel be turned fiend,
Suspect I may, yet not directly tell;
But being both from me; both to each friend,
I guess one angel in another's hell.
  Yet this shall I ne'er know, but live in doubt,
  Till my bad angel fire my good one out.

A woman's face, with nature's own hand painted,
Hast thou, the master-mistress of my passion;
A woman's gentle heart, but not acquainted
With shifting change, as is false women's fashion;
An eye more bright than theirs, less false in rolling,
Gilding the object whereupon it gazeth;
A man in hue, all hues in his controlling;
Which steals men's eyes, and women's souls amazeth.
And for a woman wert thou first created;
Till nature, as she wrought thee, fell a-doting,
And by addition me of thee defeated,
By adding one thing, to my purpose nothing.
  But since she pricked thee out for women's pleasure,
  Mine be thy love, and thy love's use their treasure.

My mistress' eyes are nothing like the sun;
Coral is far more red than her lips' red;
If snow be white, why then her breasts are dun;
If hairs be wires, black wires grow on her head.
I have seen roses damasked, red and white,
But no such roses see I in her cheeks;
And in some perfumes is there more delight
Than in the breath that from my mistress reeks.
I love to hear her speak, yet well I know
That music hath a far more pleasing sound;
I grant I never saw a goddess go,—
My mistress, when she walks, treads on the ground;

And yet, by Heaven, I think my love as rare
As any she belied with false compare.

Take all my loves, my love, yea, take them all;
What hast thou then more than thou hadst before?
No love, my love, that thou may'st true love call;
All mine was thine, before thou hadst this more.
Then if for my love thou my love receivest,
I cannot blame thee, for my love thou usest;
But yet be blamed, if thou thyself deceivest
By willful taste of what thyself refusest.
I do forgive thy robbery, gentle thief,
Although thou steal thee all my poverty;
And yet love knows, it is a greater grief
To bear love's wrong, than hate's known injury.
Lascivious grace, in whom all ill well shows,
Kill me with spite; yet we must not be foes.

Beshrew that heart that makes my heart to groan
For that deep wound it gives my friend and me!
Is't not enough to torture me alone,
But slave to slavery my sweetest friend must be?
Me from myself thy cruel eye hath taken,
And my next self thou harder hast engrossed;
Of him, myself, and thee, I am forsaken;
A torment thrice three-fold thus to be crossed.
Prison my heart in thy steel-bosom's ward,
But then my friend's heart let my poor heart bail;
Whoe'er keeps me, let my heart be his guard;
Thou canst not then use rigor in my gaol:
And yet thou wilt; for I, being pent in thee,
Perforce am thine, and all that is in me.

Those petty wrongs that liberty commits
When I am sometime absent from thy heart,
Thy beauty and thy years full well befits;
For still temptation follows where thou art.
Gentle thou art, and therefore to be won,
Beauteous thou art, therefore to be assailed;

And when a woman woos, what woman's son
Will sourly leave her till she have prevailed?
Ah me! but yet thou might'st my seat forbear,
And chide thy beauty and thy straying youth,
Who lead thee in their riot even there
Where thou art forced to break a two-fold truth:
  Hers, by thy beauty tempting her to thee,
  Thine, by thy beauty being false to me.

So now I have confessed that he is thine,
And I myself am mortgaged to thy will;
Myself I'll forfeit, so that other mine
Thou wilt restore, to be my comfort still.
But thou wilt not, nor he will not be free,
For thou art covetous, and he is kind.
He learned but, surety-like, to write for me,
Under that bond that him as fast doth bind.
The statute of thy beauty thou wilt take,
Thou usurer, that put'st forth all to use,
And sue a friend, came debtor for my sake;
So him I lose through my unkind abuse.
  Him have I lost; thou hast both him and me:
  He pays the whole, and yet I am not free.

That thou hast her, it is not all my grief,
And yet it may be said I loved her dearly;
That she hath thee, is of my wailing chief,
A loss in love that touches me more nearly.
Loving offenders, thus I will excuse ye:
Thou dost love her, because thou know'st I love her;
And for my sake even so doth she abuse me,
Suffering my friend for my sake to approve her.
If I lose thee, my loss is my love's gain,
And losing her, my friend hath found that loss;
Both find each other, and I lose both twain,
And both, for my sake, lay on me this cross:
  But here's the joy; my friend and I are one.
  Sweet flattery! then she loves but me alone.

A more complex relationship forms the basis of Shakespeare's sonnets: that between himself, his friend and his mistress. From the printer's inscription in the first edition (1609), "To the only begetter of these ensuing sonnets, Mr. W. H.," conjecture sometimes connects the friend with William Herbert, later Earl of Pembroke, son of the lady memorialized by William Browne (poem 5), nephew of Sir Philip Sidney and distantly related to Lord Herbert of Cherbury and George Herbert.

It is on this theory that Mary Fitton, Herbert's mistress in 1600 and sometimes described as brunette, is alleged to be the "dark lady" of the sonnets. There is little proof for or against any supposition; even the possibility of Herbert's being twelve years old when the sonnets urging Shakespeare's friend to beget a son are thought to have been written. Their dates, too, are highly inferential. Yet marriage is customarily thought of very early in Elizabethan circles, Herbert of Cherbury marrying at sixteen and Sir Philip Sidney betrothed, though the match was broken off, even earlier. Several of Shakespeare's heroes in the plays would be regarded today as adolescent.

I have brought together a group of the sonnets referring to this triple relationship. It begins with a late-numbered sonnet in the printed version, CXLIV: "Two loves I have of comfort and despair." Since this refers with doubt to a situation accepted as fact in some of the earlier-numbered sonnets, it seems likely to have been written before them.

Following this is Sonnet XX, describing the friend: "A woman's face with nature's own hand painted"; then Sonnet CXXX, describing the mistress: "My mistress' eyes are nothing like the sun." After these come three sonnets, XL, XLI, and XLII, to his friend, interspersed with two to his mistress, CXXXIII and CXXXIV; they are thought to have been written concurrently.

The alternation is arbitrary but seems suggestive: XL: "Take all my loves, my love, yea, take them all"; CXXXIII: "Beshrew that heart that makes my heart to groan"; XLI: "Those petty wrongs that liberty commits"; CXXXIV: "So now I have confessed that he is thine"; and XLII: "That thou hast her, it is not all my grief."

The sequence, as it concerns the specific situation between his friend and his mistress, is a triumph of love over jealousy. If we substitute "friendship" for "love" it does not diminish the force of Shakespeare's affection. For him, the two are identical.

In the first of these sonnets Shakespeare compares his friend and his mistress, to the disadvantage of the latter. This is not the idealization of a man as against a woman, but the comparison of a full relationship with a partial one. It is clear from other sonnets that the mistress has never been exclusively his. She is beloved but no friend.

Both friend and mistress come to symbolize, in this sonnet, a division in Shakespeare's own nature that has led him to make such incompatible choices. It is inevitable that they should have come together.

The sonnet describing his friend seems to be very early. For the friend is still "not acquainted / With shifting change." He is

A man in hue, all hues in his controlling;
Which steals men's eyes, and women's souls amazeth.

This would seem to mean that, although not yet a man in years, he is already so much so in bearing and behavior as to cause astonishment. There may be, too, some private reference in the word "hue," which from the preceding lines cannot mean "color." From Shakespeare's playfulness with words, there might be an allusion to "hew": he has the "cut" of a man; and to the "hue" in "hue and cry": he is a man "in full cry"; almost a man. And is he called "Hugh," a name that occurs in the Herbert family?

The sonnet is so frank that it has sometimes been misinterpreted. The fullness of affection is so strong that had the friend been a woman "love" and "love's use" might not have had to be separated. As it is, they are, clearly and unequivocally.

The sonnet to his "mistress' eyes" flouts both a popular conception of beauty and the approved fashion of celebrating it. The lady is not "fair," nor will he belie her "with false compare." There is little affection here. In effect, he is saying: "I'll match my taste with any man's."

A preoccupation with her being "colored ill" extends to several of the sonnets and seems to have an echo in *A Midsummer Night's Dream:* "The lover, all as frantic, / Sees Helen's beauty in a brow of Egypt." This leads by suggestion to *Antony and Cleopatra.* In that play, after being defeated at sea when his fleet follows Cleopatra's in flight, and suspecting her of currying favor with his conqueror, Antony turns on the Egyptian Queen:

I found you as a morsel cold upon
Dead Caesar's trencher. Nay, you were a fragment
Of Cneius Pompey; besides what hotter hours,
Unregistered in vulgar fame, you have
Luxuriously picked out . . .

This is strikingly similar to some of the reproaches Shakespeare heaps upon his mistress; as that, in Sonnet CXLII, she has "Robbed others' beds revenues of their rent."

The remaining five sonnets, as I have arranged them, alternate between gentle, all-but-withheld reproof of his friend and outright scoldings of his mistress. He can afford the latter; her loss would not affect him so deeply. Yet he is still, as if in spite of himself, drawn to her. It is his friend who has really hurt him, not by pursuing affairs with women —we gather from other sonnets that such is his proclivity—but by entangling himself with this particular woman.

Their friendship is threatened on another occasion, alluded to in Sonnet LXXXVI: "Was it the proud full sail of his great verse" (poem 30). In this there is jealousy in the thought that his friend has transferred his affections. It may be partly professional jealousy, though Shakespeare disclaims it. But there is no suggestion of betrayal; no reproof; rather a sorrow so great that it prevents him, for a time, from writing:

But when your countenance filled up his line,
Then lacked I matter; that enfeebled mine.

The two jealousies are clear and distinct. In the amorous situation, Shakespeare's love is great enough to grant his friend everything; even his own "poverty." It is the suspicion that this fullness of love is not reciprocated that rankles and that must be gradually, artfully and rather ruefully surmounted.

The sonnets reveal a temperament that sees and feels all sides of any situation. Shakespeare takes every attitude toward it, expected and unexpected; not from vacillation but in order fully to resolve it. His extraordinary conclusions are reached, not by blinking at the facts, nor by turning his back on ordinary, even petty, human motives and desires. Rather, giving each its full weight, he balances them together, a true dialectic of emotion.

We see how, in the plays, our sympathies may be engaged by each character in turn, including the so-called villains. They are never mouthpieces for ideas; they become living vehicles of emotion.

So, too, the "message" of the plays is seldom a pat or foreordained moral. It arises from, and is modified by, the characters as well as the situation. *Antony and Cleopatra* may contain the precept: "Sensual love is the undoing of a soldier." Yet in the manner of their deaths, Antony and Cleopatra triumph over their destiny and become symbols of undying love.

214. *Let me not to the marriage of true minds*

WILLIAM SHAKESPEARE

Let me not to the marriage of true minds
Admit impediments: love is not love
Which alters when it alteration finds,
Or bends with the remover to remove.
Oh, no! it is an ever-fixèd mark
That looks on tempests, and is never shaken;
It is the star to every wandering bark,
Whose worth's unknown, although his height be taken.
Love's not Time's fool, though rosy lips and cheeks
Within his bending sickle's compass come;
Love alters not with his brief hours and weeks,
But bears it out even to the edge of doom:
  If this be error, and upon me proved,
  I never writ, nor no man ever loved.

A full savoring of experience goes into Sonnet CXVI. This is not a romantic protestation. It is rather the complete expression of a total personality.

There is an unfounded legend that Shakespeare, as an actor, suffered from stammering and placed the difficult *m* sounds in "admit impediments" rather in the spirit of Demosthenes training out a speech difficulty with pebbles. This is not at all alien to the spirit of the sonnet.

The impediments are there: the "alteration," "the remover," the "tempests," the "wandering," the "bending sickle," the "brief hours," even the "edge of doom." They are all very real and ever-present.

Love, the "marriage of true minds," does not deny them. It will not "admit" them; a far different thing. It remains constant, as if stationary—"an ever-fixèd mark"—through its action; the continuous action of warding off everything that threatens it. This is the "mountain's heartbeat" reached through "jungles of despair."

If this love exists, Shakespeare wrote.

There are poems, like Marianne Moore's "The mind is an enchanting thing" (poem 211), like Cummings' "if everything happens that can't be done" (*Poems: 1923–1954*, page 422), like Matthew Arnold's "Shakespeare" (poem 29), that may be taken as explicit symbols of "the whole man." Others exhibit him, like Shakespeare's sonnets; like Whitman's *Leaves of Grass*.

I am not speaking here of greater or lesser works of art. There is a place for comparative criticism; this is not the book for it.

And by "the whole man" I do not mean "everything that can be known about him." The "whole man" is one who fulfills his potentialities as completely as possible. For each poet he is a different man.

There is a sense in which nearly all poetry symbolizes wholeness. It would be pretentious to push this too far; obviously there are poems —and good ones—too slight to bear such a weight. But in regarding poems in the light of sensations, emotions and ideas, it has been equally obvious that very few poems can lay claim to only one, or even two, of these. The emphasis may lie here or there, but poetry tends to draw them all together.

The particular way it has of drawing them together is the poet's style. Styles are as various as the personalities they express. There may, to be sure, be greater and lesser styles, according to whether they are more or less inclusive. But that is a later consideration, irrelevant here.

For no poet, however great—Shakespeare, Donne, Hopkins or Whitman—can invent a style for other poets to follow. Style is the expression of a temperament; it cannot be formulated in a set of rules.

When Shakespeare writes, in Sonnet LXIV,

Ruin hath taught me thus to ruminate—
That time will come and take my love away,

he achieves an irony that is uniquely his. The mocking quality of the first line, with its ponderous, deliberately pompous stress on "ruin" and "ruminate" ("I've made a deep study of this, I can tell you"), sets off the heartbreaking simplicity of the second. Its conclusion is all the more heartbreaking for being something that any fool might have told him. That is the point of Shakespeare's irony.

Part of the ironic effect is gained through alliteration. But there is no guarantee that such devices will work again. In other sonnets, especially when he is repeating an idea he has already expressed, Shakespeare can put down lines as perfunctory as these, concluding Sonnet XII:

And nothing 'gainst Time's scythe can make defence,
Save breed, to brave him when he takes thee hence.

If a technique can go slack, even in the hands of its master, it is no wonder that imitation falls flat. Shakespearean language, in plays other than Shakespeare's, sounds like so much blank verse. You can hear the words getting up on their toes, trying to exalt themselves by their bootstraps. The lines of *Hamlet*, when the actors know how to speak them, are living speech. Techniques wither, but the poem remains fresh.

So poetry comes full circle. It defines itself, yet like Marianne Moore's mind, it is "not a Herod's oath that cannot change." Its own definitions are not definitive. Not only do they vary from poem to poem; each poem changes with a different reading.

It is written by poets. Each poet is somewhat different from every other, and from himself in different poems.

It approaches, sometimes intimately, the arts of music, painting, sculpture, prose and the dance, cooking and architecture; all the various "makings" of man. Yet where it is closest, as often to music, it is most distinct. It is traditional and revolutionary; the epitome of spirit and earth; water and fire; air, angels and pins.

Perhaps its least and best description is to be found in Shakespeare's reeling conversation between Lepidus and Antony while they are wining aboard Pompey's galley "near Misenum":

LEPIDUS: *What manner of thing is your crocodile?*

ANTONY: *It is shaped, sir, like itself; and it is as broad as it hath breadth; it is just so high as it is, and moves with its own organs; it lives by that which nourisheth it; and, the elements once out of it, it transmigrates.*

LEPIDUS: *What color is it of?*

ANTONY: *Of its own color too.*

LEPIDUS: *'Tis a strange serpent.*

ANTONY: *'Tis so. And the tears of it are wet.*

Index of Authors and Titles

Index of First Lines